C000258613

IS THIS THE WINE
YOU ORDERED, SIR?

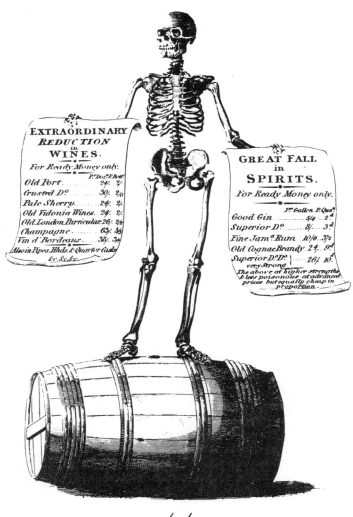

EXTRAORDINARY
REDUCTION
in
WINES.

For Ready Money only.

	P.^r Do.^z	Pr Bot.
Old Port	24/.	2/.
Crusted D.^o	30/.	2/6
Pale Sherry	24/.	2/.
Old Vidonia Wines	24/.	2/.
Old London Particular	26/.	2/4
Champagne	63/.	4/8
Vin d'Bordeaux	38/.	3/4

Also in Pipes, Hhds. & Quarter Casks
&c. &c. &c.

GREAT FALL
in
SPIRITS.

For Ready Money only.

	Pr Gallon	P. Qua.^r
Good Gin	5/4	2.^d
Superior D.^o	8/.	3.^d
Fine Jam.^a Rum	10/6	3/2
Old Cognac Brandy	24/.	9.^d
Superior D.^o D.^o very strong	26/.	10.

The above at higher strengths
& less poisonous at advanced
prices, but equally cheap in
proportion.

——————— *look on me,*

. Me who have touched and tasted ———

Milton.

IS THIS THE WINE YOU ORDERED, SIR?

—◆—

*The dark side of
the wine trade*

Christopher Fielden

CHRISTOPHER HELM
London

© 1989 Christopher Fielden

Christopher Helm (Publishers) Ltd, Imperial House,
21–25 North Street, Bromley BR1 1SD

ISBN 0-7470-1013-7

A CIP catalogue record for this book
is available from the British Library

Typeset by Florencetype Ltd, Kewstoke, Avon
Printed and bound in Great Britain by Billing and Sons Ltd, Worcester

Contents

To PEGGY
who, during her many years on the bench,
much to her disappointment never came across a case of wine-fraud

Foreword by John Arlott

This is essentially the book of a wine man, one who has devoted his life to the subject with enthusiasm, discrimination, and a quite unusual breadth of study. There are points in it where the reader is almost overwhelmed by the horror of some of the facts of wine-making—and the activities of growers, negociants, grocers, blenders, merchants, label-printers, manufacturers, dealers and even waiters—which last used at one time to sell used Champagne corks. Yet it is all completely factual.

Above all, it is an authoritative work by a man who has looked at it from all its angles. Christopher Fielden started at the bottom. He was a picker in a French vineyard almost as soon as he could get there. He went on to work in wine-making establishments, to become a travelling representative, dealing in spirits as well as wine, to be the only Englishman ever to be appointed to the board of one of the most prestigious French wine companies, to appointment as the British agent for a major Spanish wine firm, and to travel the wine countries of the world. He did so with his eyes wide and keenly open.

He also began to study the history of wine-making and to make an impressive collection of wine books—as the bibliography to this study shows. He has done all the odd jobs about vineyards, and wine shops, and studied his subject with an enthusiasm which has never waned. He has tasted countless wines with a sensitively enquiring palate and an astute mind. When he tells us that, until 1971, Germany sold wine under 30,000 different names, he is only, in a way, preparing us for the Teutonisation of wine within the Common Market. It is when he discusses such subjects that the reader appreciates the width and the depth of his study.

If he first grew up in his subject in France, that was fitting, for France is the most knowledgeable, varied and profoundly rich country in wine-growing, and it was there that he gained valuable years of experience. On the other hand, he has travelled the vineyards of the world watching the modern growth and development of his subject. If his collection of wine books goes back—as it does—to a seventeenth-century study in French, it also comes forward to the latest technical reports on wine-making in Spanish.

All this sounds very scholarly; and, at heart, it is; on the other hand, the reader will feel compelled again and again to say to anyone else in the room, 'listen to this'. Much of the content is quite sensational, from early laws about wine-making to the vast number of additives—both permitted and illegal—and techniques of recent years which have been reported with the headline 'Wine Sensation' or 'Amazing Wine Fraud'.

It is not, though, for a mere preface-writer to steal his author's thunder—and Mr Fielden's thunder is thunderous indeed. Suffice it to say that, having shown us the vast extent of wine fraudulence, falsity and, in some cases, sheer non-wine-wine throughout history, he himself continues to drink it with the utmost enthusiasm.

Introduction

I hope that the reader of this book will not look upon it as a bitter exposé of the hidden secrets of the wine-trade, for it is certainly not intended as such. I have made my living from wine for the last 30 years and I feel that, if I was ever asked for my entry for *Who's Who*, I would happily list it as a hobby. The drinking of wine is only a part of the whole pleasure. For me reading about it is another and the collection of old books on the subject yet another. It is through this last aspect that this book has been conceived. The more that one reads early writers on wine, the more one realises that much has changed, whilst much has stayed the same.

Today's international groundswell towards more healthy eating and drinking and more accurate labelling of products is no more than a reflection of what was being said, and written, in Victorian times. Malpractices in the wine-trade form only a minor part of the whole topic, but they have received considerable exposure, particularly with the Austrian 'anti-freeze' scandal. Such stories are nothing new; there has always been abuse, and there always will be. I hope that this book will put these abuses into some form of perspective.

On hearing about my project, some friends in the trade asked first of all whether I thought that it was wise to write such a book. Was there not a danger that the trade might be brought into disrepute? As soon as I explained in more detail what I hoped to achieve, they were all happy to contribute their little anecdote. One that I liked the most, and I will tell now, because it does not particularly fit into any other slot in the book, concerns a good friend who started in the trade, more than 30 years ago, with a 'fine' wine-merchant in Manchester. At that time they imported most of their wine requirements in cask and, as far as red wines were concerned, this consisted of just one wine. If you asked for Beaune or Beaujolais, you received it in a Burgundy bottle; if you asked for Saint Julien or Saint Emilion, you received it in a claret bottle. Occasionally, when they ran out of labels, they would have to suggest an alternative wine to the customer. In fact, it made no difference for it was the same wine. Apparently no one ever complained.

This lack of knowledge by the customer is not peculiar to Manchester, it can also happen at a much higher level. I have confused old Burgundies with old clarets, and vice versa. Owen Redman, the well-known Australian wine-maker, told me that he used to win prizes with the same wine in both the Burgundy and the Claret classes at Australian shows—it just depended on what bottles he could get from the manufacturer.

There is fraud in the wine-trade, but I am sure that there is fraud in every trade and profession. That there is possibly more apparent fraud with wine is, largely, because it is a very severely controlled trade. There are perhaps more regulations for the making and label-ling of wine than for any other consumer item. If one finds a better and cheaper way of making a mousetrap, one is fêted. If one finds a better and cheaper way of making Chambertin, it is forbidden.

Whilst this book is sub-titled 'An Anti-Social History of the Wine-Trade', it is written with affection and, to some extent, with tongue in cheek. As a history, it can only give a limited glimpse of certain aspects of what has gone on in the wine-trade, and what is going on. As a history, it must be incomplete, for it is open-ended. As I write, I can think of three wine 'scandals' which are gestating, for, whilst they have been exposed, the accused have not yet come to court — and may not. Indeed, this is one of the disturbing aspects of wine illegalities. Because wine has become for many countries an important source of revenue, the authorities often seek to cover up any scandals.

Let me give an example of this. At present, one of the largest merchants in the Muscadet stands accused of passing other wines off as Muscadet. Whilst his business has been closed down, his son has rented his father's premises and continues business just as in the past. Because the exports of Muscadet are increasing rapidly, particularly to Japan, there are many in the region who feel that it would be disastrous for the matter to reach court and receive the attention of the press.

My thanks are due to all those people who have made this book possible. First must come the thousands of people that I have met during my 30 years in the trade; the many straight and the few crooked. Second are all those writers who have come before; it is on their experiences that this book is firmly based. A colleague, who read this text, criticised it as being too full of quotations. I make no apology for that. I would have liked to have said that it is such quotations that give this book its authenticity, but for a large part, authenticity is not what it is about!

If I help some readers to recognise what might be a fraudulent wine, to enjoy wine more, towards a fuller understanding of the back-ground of wine, then I have achieved something worthwhile, and had much pleasure in doing so.

What is an 'honest wine'?

Something over a century ago, a writer in the *New Quarterly Magazine* said: 'Those interested in the trade are not fit persons to write a book to instruct the public.' He was quoted, and criticised, by a member of the wine-trade, Charles Tovey, in the introduction to his book *Wine and Wine Countries*, which attacked many of the doubtful practices that occurred in the world of wine in his day. I, too, would take issue with that anonymous writer, for it is by being in the wine-trade that one can put in perspective the malpractices that have taken place since wine was first known, in the earliest of historical times, until today. There is no point in trying to hide the fact that, in the wine-trade, as in any other, there are those who try to exploit the consumer by selling fraudulent wine.

At a seminar on controls in the British wine-trade, some years ago, a merchant sought to define the role of the wine importer. His answer was: 'To procure honest wines of consistent quality and to offer the best value for money in that sector of the market in which he operates.'

This book will focus its attention on just two words from that definition, 'honest wines', by trying to show what is dishonest. One might assume that a wine is one thing or another, either honest or dishonest, but this is not always totally the case. Nowadays it is easier to separate the sheep from the goats, for each country has a mass of legislation defining exactly what can be called wine and what can not. However, over the centuries there has been a much more liberal

1

interpretation of the matter, and, whilst even in classical Greek times sanctions were foreseen for breaches of the wine-laws, they must have been difficult to apply.

Whilst there is legislation for not only each country, but also each wine-producing region, these vary considerably. Thus, in Burgundy and Champagne, it is quite legal to chaptalise one's wine (that is, add sugar to the unfermented grape must to increase the alcoholic strength); in the south of France it is totally forbidden. Similarly, in California, a shortfall on rain can be made up for by spraying in the vineyards; in Europe, this is not permitted, though in Chablis, and elsewhere, there might be a sprinkler amongst the vines to prevent them from frost damage. Until recently a Riesling wine from California might, quite legally, have contained no more than 51 per cent of wine made from that grape, whilst the Riesling from Alsace, by law, must be a total thoroughbred. In each of these cases, it is not certain that the wine made under the more restrictive legislation is a better wine. However, in perhaps the fairest interpretation, it is an honest wine.

Early in the book, therefore, we come across a question that is often posed: 'Is it better to have a wine that is made totally honestly, but which might not taste so agreeable, or a wine which has been *arranged* to suit the palate of the consumer?' This is the classic defence of almost every *fraudeur* that we shall come across in this book. Sad to say, virtually no abuses in the wine-trade are exposed because of complaints by the consumer. In almost every occasion a disgruntled employee is at the basis of the exposure.

In the main there are four types of fraud. The first, and this might be considered the least important, is the technical fraud, whereby the letter of the law might be breached, but the quality of the wine does not suffer. As a classic example of this, from my own personal experience, I can quote the case of an aristocratic grower in the Minervois. As a trial, he planted in his vineyard a number of Cabernet Sauvignon vines and added the grapes that they produced to his Minervois. The resulting wine was excellent and, indeed, won the first prize in the local wine fair. Unfortunately, the authorities found out. As a result, he now makes a lower quality Minervois and vinifies the Cabernet Sauvignon grapes separately, making a *vin de pays*, theoretically a lower quality wine in the hierarchy, which he is able to sell at a higher price than his Minervois. All this came about because the Cabernet Sauvignon is not a variety traditionally used in making Minervois. Thus, it is forbidden.

A second type of fraud, and I suppose in many ways the worst, is the sale as 'wine' of a product that has nothing to do with grapes. In Europe, in this age of Common Market wine-lakes, there is little incentive to construct wines without using grapes, as the raw materials can be had for a lower price than the alternatives would cost. Surprisingly, one aspect of the recent Austrian wine scandal, that failed to hit the headlines, was the fact that a considerable amount of 'wine' was circulating in the country which was totally artificial. The attention of the world was drawn more to those wines artificially sweetened with diethylene-glycol.

Another case of artificial wine occurred in Italy in 1966, when the wine-company Ferrari was accused, with many others, of selling a product which they glorified with a number of well-known names like Chianti, Frascati and Lambrusco, but which they were able to produce in a matter of hours from a recipe which included the sludge from banana boats, ox-blood, tap water and sugar. One must recognise the merits of a wine-chemist whose researches led him into the holds of banana boats.

In the end the court case was never finished, although one of the accused admitted that: 'I might be the king of wine-fraud, but I am one amongst many and they are not all in this dock.' This, too, is a recurring statement from those caught out in wine malpractices.

More common is the wine which is made from grapes, but also a great deal else. Many things are permitted in the making of wine. Walter Taylor, the maverick New York State wine-maker, claimed that the local laws allowed him to add 57 different products to his grapes, but that he was quite capable of making a good wine without any of them. As we have already seen sugar is commonly added, sometimes with good intent, but more harmful additives are nothing new in the wine-trade. In *Henry IV* Part I, Falstaff says to the landlord of the Boar's Head Tavern, in Eastcheap, 'You rogue, here's lime in this Sack too; there is nothing but a roguery in villainous man; yet a coward is worse than a cup of Sack with lime in it.'

The fourth type of fraud is that of passing-off. This is the one that is most difficult to guard against and the one that is likely to become more common in the future. With the number of wine-drinkers increasing around the world, there must be increasing demand for those wines that have built up a wide reputation for themselves over the centuries. Whilst the area under vines in a region like Chablis has increased considerably over the past few years (in the lasty twenty-five, the production has increased ten-fold), it still has difficulty in keeping pace with demand. How much more so it must be in a smaller village appellation, like for example Pommard, or a single vineyard. This increasing demand can only lead to increased prices at the higher end of the wine hierarchy. This, in its turn, will tend to encourage the unscrupulous to try to satisfy the demand with wines which are not genuine.

It is a sad fact that the majority of wine-drinkers lack the know-ledge, or perhaps the confidence, to reject a wine about which they have doubts. This is scarcely surprising, for it is impossible for anyone to know all about wine. Each region, each village, each vineyard changes from year to year. It is even less surprising when one considers the official attitude. I have sat on a number of occasions on tasting panels in Burgundy to grant, or refuse, certificates of authenticity. From my experience, wines were never rejected because they were untypical of the appellation that the label bore, but only because they were bad as wines.

It must be said in some mitigation that the structure of the vineyards in Burgundy is so confused that the styles of a wine depend almost as much on the person who made it as on the village, or the vineyard from which it might come. If the professionals themselves have difficulty in describing the parameters for their wines, how much more difficult it must be for the layman to reject a bottle that is offered him. There are numerous examples which can be quoted of thousands of fraudulent bottles which have been consumed without a single complaint. The Austrian wine scandal is just one recent example of this. Sadly, it may be that the consumer does not expect too much from his wine.

For there to be a wine-fraud, there must be a wine-law or alternatively recognised wine-names. Whilst individual wines have been named from the earliest of times, there have been less restrictions as to how they should be made. In the Bible, for example, there are a number of mentions of wines by name, but the instructions as to how they should be made are few. This is especially strange when one considers how constricted by law the life of the Jews was. In Leviticus XIX it says: 'Thou shalt not glean thy vineyard, neither shalt thou gather every grape of thy vineyard; thou shalt leave them for the poor and the stranger.' Later instructions are given that the vines shall not be tended every seventh year, nor again every fiftieth year, but these seem to be the total of regulations on the subject.

In classical times, there were a number of wines which had managed to create outstanding reputations. Amongst the Greeks, those of Thasos and Lesbos were widely sought after, and in the Roman empire Falernian wines were the highest rated and even a number of individual *crus* within the appellation were recognised. Passing-off of lesser wines under greater names was considered to be a serious offence, often punished with severe flogging.

Drinking of wine then was a rather different matter than it is nowadays. Many of the wines were very sweet and concentrated. As a result, they were often mixed with three or four times as much water. In a comedy by a fourth-century BC playwright, Alexis, mention is made of a street wine-seller watering his wine down so, and one cannot tell whether it is with tongue in cheek or not, as to make it more healthy, rather than to increase the merchant's profit. Honey was also added to wine to make it more palatable and pitch and resin also appear to have been used. In the Greek islands salt water was also mixed with the wine. The criticism of the use of additives was as present in those days as it is nowadays. H. Warner Allen, in *A History of Wine*, quotes Pliny: 'So many poisons are needed to make it fit to drink and yet we are surprised that it gives us indigestion.'

It appears that another practice, common in later years, was not unknown to the Romans. Recipes abounded for making wines in the manner of the most famous. Even that model of classical puritanism Marcus Porcius Cato 'The Censor', does not hesitate to give in his book *On Agriculture*, a recipe for making Greek Coan wine from native Italian grapes. The other great Latin writer on agricultural matters, Columella, even talks of the addition of gypsum to wine, a habit that is still continued in the production of Sherry, and which was severely criticised in Victorian times.

Over the centuries, laws were enacted concerning the production of wine, though at the beginning there was little attempt to protect the names of the wines. At the beginning of the sixth century AD, the Burgundian king, Gondebaud, introduced an elaborate codex, the Gombetta law, which was to serve as a model for centuries to come. It covered all aspects of life, including the planting and control of vineyards. It gave owner's rights to whosoever might plant a vineyard on scrubland and forbade small animals to go into the vineyards. If they did so they could be shot. Even if the owner went into the vineyards after dark and was shot by mistake by the guardian, there was to be no punishment for the latter.

At the end of the eighth century, the Emperor Charlemagne brought out a series of laws, many of which dealt with the question of hygiene in wine-making. Indeed even the pressing of grapes by foot was forbidden. 'The wine-presses on our properties are to be constructed with the utmost care and our stewards must see that the grape crop is not crushed by foot, but that all work is carried out with the most meticulous cleanliness.' Even the state of the wine-casks had to be seen to: 'We wish that our stewards take care that our casks are always in good condition and held together with iron hoops so that they can be transported either to the army or to the Court. We also wish that leather wine vessels should no longer be made.'

By the beginning of the fourteenth century in England, there was detailed legislation to protect the wine consumer. This protection took two forms, first against adulteration and secondly against short measures. On 8 November 1327, Edward III decreed that weak and out of condition wine could not be mixed with any other. Every customer had the right to see his wine being drawn from the cask and it was forbidden to put a curtain over the doorway to the cellar, so that all might have a clear view. New and old wine could not be blended or even stored in the same inn. Obviously as a precaution against passing-off, wines from the Rhine could not be sold by someone who sold the wines of Gascony, La Rochelle and Spain. Also if the innkeeper chose to sell sweet wines, he was allowed to sell no other. In this age of discussion of the size of a wine-glass, it is interesting to note that wine could only be sold in a standard measure that bore the seal of the sheriffs and alderman, rather than by the cruskyn, or earthenware mug, which was the traditional vessel for drinking wine.

The application of these wine-laws came to be left to the members of the Mistery of Vintners, a trade-guild which received many of its privileges as a result of a banquet organised by Sir Henry Picard, a wine-merchant and later Lord Mayor of London, in 1363. Present were King Edward III of England, King David II of Scotland, King Hugh IV of Cyprus, King John the Good of France and King Waldemar of Denmark. However, these rights were often in dispute and there was some confusion as controls were also applied by the Mayor and Corporation of the City of London, and, as far as Rhine wines were concerned, by another trade-guild, the merchants of the Steelyard.

It is interesting to note that some 600 years later much of the control of wine legislation is still in the hands of the successors to the Mistery of Vintners, the Worshipful Company of Vintners, who control the Wine Standards Board, which oversees the wholesale end of the wine-trade.

Perhaps not coincidentally there were similar laws at about the same time in Alsace. In 1364, the town council of Colmar made it an offence for an innkeeper to sell more than one wine a day, and on this wine he had to pay a tax, the *Umgeld*. If he failed to pay the tax he was expelled from the town for a month, or had to pay a fine of five *livres*. Similarly, he was forbidden to adulterate his wine by adding water, brandy, sulphur, salt or any other ingredient. The fine for adding brandy was five *livres* again, with compulsory exile from the town for a year. Other interesting regulations forbade the harbouring in inns of women of evil reputation, and the serving of wine after the evening bell had sounded to others than those who were spending the night in the inn, or who came equipped with a lantern.

In conjunction with the controls on the quality of wine once it was made, and on its selling, efforts were also made from early times in France to see that quality wine was made. One of the earliest and widest quoted decrees is that of Philip the Bold in 1395. He was concerned about the quality of wine that was being made in his Burgundian dominions and he blamed the falling off in standards firmly on the Gamay grape. In the preamble he says that he has been petitioned by many of his citizens from the 'good town of Beaune, Dijon, Chalon and the surrounding countryside' who are worried that the quality of the wines of their region, 'the best and the most precious and fitting wines of the kingdom of France' as appreciated by 'the Pope, the King and several lords, both of the Church and the laity' was falling. The reason for this is that the vineyards have been planted with a 'very evil and disloyal plant, the Gamay, from which evil plant comes a great abundance of wine, and the exceptional quantity of these evil wines has laid bare and in ruin those good places from where come and grow good wine.' In addition bad manuring had led to the wines becoming 'yellow, fat, and in such condition that no human being can satisfactorily use them without risk to his being.'

The sentence was: 'We solemnly command those who have those vine-plants called Gamay, that they cut them down, or have them cut down, wherever they might be in our country, within a month, upon pain of a fine of sixty *sous tournois* for every *ouvrée* of such vines or plants.'

'Furthermore, we herewith forbid those who might be so bold as to take, or to have taken, carted, carried or brought by any means into their vines or those of others, such dung, droppings or manure, upon pain of their losing and our confiscating such beasts and carts used in carting such dung and droppings.'

However severe this edict might have seemed, its actual effect must have been limited, for during subsequent centuries, the Gamay came in for criticism in Burgundy as providing the growers with an easy way out; a way of making large quantities of inferior wine. The ban was renewed in 1444 and again in 1459, when Philip the Good again criticised the Gamay for 'when it is young, it can deceive foreigners by its sweetness'. Just 400 years later, Auguste Luchet could still write: 'I am ashamed to confess it; but, on the Côte d'Or, some fools have grubbed up the pinot and replaced it with the gamay; as one might say, they have replaced the cantaloup with the pumpkin. The gamay produces three times as much as the other; there, sadly, is the excuse.'

In Alsace, too, there has been a continual struggle between planting those varieties that give a large yield of mediocre wine, and those which produce smaller quantities of fine wine. As early as 1575, the Magistrate at Riquewihr issued a decree distinguishing between the noble and the lesser grape varieties. Unfortunately, because of the Thirty Years War, the laws were little respected and they were renewed in 1630 and 1644. 'It is publicly recognized' the decree began, 'not just in the immediate neighbourhood, but by all the peoples of the holy Empire that the best wine of Alsace, which exceeds in vigour and in spirit all the other wines of Germany and which is transported far and wide by sea and by land grows in the parish of Riquewihr.'

'Our ancestors, have, from the earliest times, maintained the principle of only planting noble grape varieties, knowing from experience that this village, by the nature of its soil, lends itself particularly to the vine and that, thanks to the favourable outlook of the vineyards, the grapes reach their ideal maturity. This ruling honoured our fore-fathers and assured their well-being. Nevertheless, in the course of time, out of a spirit of curiosity it happened that ordinary grape-varieties were planted . . . To fight against these bad habits, it is necessary to renew these laws and the Magistrate condemns the common varieties to a double fine; for each vine of a forbidden variety, a fine of 2 crowns 6 batz and a shilling. As a result, all forbidden vines must be grubbed up.' For those who were unaware that they had planted forbidden vines, the fine was remitted, but the grubbing up still took place.

Over the years the law was strictly enforced and amongst those having to pay fines was the village priest in 1589, the burgermaster, Jacques Stüb, in 1650, his successor, Michael Lorentz, and 15 other growers in 1662, and shortly afterwards, the Baron de Berckheim. The question of what varieties should, and should not, be planted is one that has continued in Alsace until the present day, The efforts of the local growers, since the Second World War, to increase the reputation of their wines has relied largely on strictly controlling the grapes that are planted.

Another perennial problem in the region has been where vines should be planted. In 1731, 1771 and 1790, there were decrees for-bidding the plantation of vines on the plain, where the soil is much richer. Whilst the controls on the varietals might have succeeded over the years, those about the Alsace plantings have been much less successful. Monsieur Doutrelant in his book *Les Bons Vins et Les Autres* repeats the criticisms of 250 years ago when he says that many of the places where vines are now growing in Alsace are much better suited to the production of cabbages than anything else.

Similarly at times, too, there were forceful efforts made to protect the integrity of the Jura wines of Arbois. As early as the year 1464, one finds the Magistrates giving instructions that vines that produced inferior quality wine should be grubbed up. In 1656, in order to prevent adulteration, any wines from vineyards outside the juris-diction of the town authorities were forbidden permission to enter within the town walls. In 1718, once again, there was a request to the Parliament for the prohibition of certain grape varieties—and also of vineyards planted on the plain. As in Burgundy, it was the Gamay, particularly, which came in for criticism, for as long ago as 1567, Philip II, King of Spain and Count of Burgundy, on the advice of his Parliament, sitting at Dole, restricted the land where vines might be planted, and 'forbade once again the planting and increase in the Gamay, the Melon and other wines of a similar type and nature.' Despite all the efforts to suppress the Gamay in the Jura vineyards, it must have been the most popular of varieties, for, once again, in January 1725, its destruction was commanded, and it was calculated that more than 2,000 hectares of vines would have to be grubbed up. Not all the growers accepted these decisions gracefully and the story has it that in about 1760, a grower called Courvoisier had three *ouvrées* of Gamay, in full production, in a vineyard called Ménegode, at Salins. When he heard that the authorities were coming to uproot all the Gamay vineyards, he covered his vines, which were laden with fruit, with soil. As a result, his vineyard was overlooked and, although there was a certain amount of damage, he was able to pick his abundant crop. As a contemporary writer says: 'When growers are so forthright with their obstinacy, they have every right to go unpunished.'

In Burgundy, there were particular problems with the naming of the wines. Generally speaking, from the Middle Ages onwards, the wines of northern Burgundy, what is now the Yonne *département*, were called Burgundy; those of the Côte d'Or, Beaune and those of Southern Burgundy, Mâcon. It is interesting to see in the original statute of the wine-brokers, in Beaune, dated 31 August 1607, what steps were taken to preserve the identity of the wines of the town itself. The brokers were not allowed to take potential buyers outside the town itself, without the express permission of the Mayor and they were also bound to report any sign of fraud or trickery that they might come across to the municipal authorities. The statute runs to 40 paragraphs, of which the final one is: 'If any broker contravenes any of the present articles of the statute, or any that might be enacted in the future, he shall immediately be relieved of his responsibilities.'

In the following year a number of brands in the form of the letter B were made, and given to the town magistrates that were responsible for the tasting of all the wines sold in the town. If the wine was approved, the cask was then marked with the official seal. It seems that the wines of Pommard and Volnay also came under the control of the Beaune officials, for in 1620 it was decided that: 'Henceforth, the town brand for marking wines will not be given to the brokers for taking to Pommard and Volnay, but will be carried to the said places by one of the magistrates who will taste the wine, for whom a horse will be found by the broker for this purpose.'

That the importance of maintaining the image of the wines of Beaune was considered before all else can be seen by an entry in the Minutes of the Guild of Wine Brokers of 12 October 1691. 'For the good and the benefit of the town, we have been accustomed all these years, as soon as possible after the vintage, and as soon as the wines are fit to travel, to taste the finest wines of Beaune, of Pommard and of Volnay, that the brokers, merchants and other interested parties dispatch to Paris and elsewhere, that are commonly known as the first convoy; with this in mind the Chamber has habitually appointed people capable of recognising the quality of the wines and seeing that they are the best of the vintage; and as it is of outstanding importance to the town that they select the first wines that are sent to Paris, so as to avoid any abuses or troubles that could occur if they slip up in this selection which was first created in the utmost wisdom, for if the finest wines were not sent with the first load, it would be capable of totally ruining our trade in wine.' This is the beginning of the recognition of the importance of continuing quality, if a village is to sell a wine under its own name.

That there were occasional attempts to avoid the controls can be seen from an entry of 10 December 1642. 'Sire Pierre Domino, broker, having brought into Beaune wines from the Maconnais in contravention of the regulations concerning brokers, the Chamber decides that he will be relieved of his office, the wine will be confiscated and Domino will be fined.' With Beaune the fashionable drink throughout all the courts in Europe, it was essential that standards were maintained.

In Spain, too, regulations were introduced over the years in the various wine-producing areas controlling the wine-trade. As early as 1530, an English merchant, Juan Esvique, fell foul of the authorities for contravening the restrictive practices in Jerez, where foreigners were forbidden to act as agents on behalf of customers overseas. Despite a lengthy plea, and a threat that he would go elsewhere to seek for wines for his customers, he was sentenced to a heavy fine and six months in prison.

The Sherry trade does not appear to have been totally controlled, however, until the establishment of a trade-guild, the Gremio de la Vinatería, whose statutes received royal approval in 1733. Amongst the responsibilities of the Gremio were the fixing of prices, control of wages, arranging of export quotas and the standardisation of cooperage. Amongst the early decrees that they issued was one banning the introduction of wines from other regions into Jerez, for the consumption of the local inhabitants. Perhaps, sadly, other wines were allowed in if they were destined for onward shipment, and it is certain that this permission subsequently led to a number of other wines being passed off as Sherry.

In Málaga, the city authorities, in 1552, drew up a series of ordinances to control the sale of wine in the local taverns. The innkeepers were not permitted to sell wine that had not been registered by the town clerk and they had to 'issue a signed and sworn guarantee declaring the quantity of wine sold and on what day and to what person.'

Whilst one can see that there had been local attempts from early times to protect the image and, in some way, guarantee quality of certain wines, it was generally accepted that the name that a wine might bear often had little to do with what was in the bottle. For the most part this did not worry the consumer until the nineteenth century when a number of writers, particularly in Britain, began to condemn aggressively what was in many of the bottles that were on sale. Books were widely available giving detailed instructions on how to make a whole host of artificial wines, from readily available materials. This was nothing new. From at least the eighteenth century many books openly gave 'recipes' for the production of artificial, or as they sometimes called them, 'bastard' wines. A small book, which was published in French in Turin in 1783 under the title of *L'Art de Faire, d'Ameliorer et de Conserver les Vins*, gives a number of recipes including one for making Rhine wine from white wine, Cognac, honey and brown sugar; bastard Spanish wine from white wine, Canary wine, syrup and spices; and Alicante from almost anything that you can lay your hands on. Perhaps in a spirit of revenge a Spanish book by Rodriguez, published in 1885, tells you how to make artificial Bordeaux from nothing more than 40 litres of red wine, 10 litres of white wine, 15 grammes of 'Essence of Médoc' (about which more in due course) and 100 grammes of tartaric acid. However, the Spanish author also has some national pride, for he also tells you how to make artificial dry Sherry, Pedro Ximenez, Málaga, as well as Champagne, Port, Madeira . . .

During the nineteenth century Hamburg and Sète were well-renowned centres for the production of more or less artificial wines, and their produce was widely distributed throughout Europe. Charles Tovey, writing in 1861, is at his best, or perhaps his most biting, on these centres. Of the former he says: 'The enterprising firms transfer their adulterations to Hamburg, at which place the most unblushing operations are carried on. Thousands of gallons of ports and sherries are imported every month into England, where they are re-manufactured, and by puffing advertisements, circulars and agents (generally grocers) are disposed of under claptrap titles, and specially low prices, to unsuspecting purchasers, who not only suffer in their pockets, but if they consume these compounds freely, prepare for themselves years of suffering and dyspepsia.' He quotes from a trade magazine the costings of the production of 'Elbe Sherry': 'Take forty proof gallons of fine potash spirit at 1s 4d per gallon on the spot £2 15s 6d; 56 gallons of pure Elbe water, cost *nil*; 4 gallons of Capillaire, £1; and to be liberal, allow that 10 gallons of luscious wine or grape juice are added at a cost of £2; then for cask, 12s; harbour and shipping charges, 10s; commission 2s 6d; discount for cash, 4s; total £7 2s. The mixture was shipped as Elbe Sherry, at £7 15s and £8 per butt of 108 gallons.'

Whilst Hamburg might have been a one or two product town, this certainly could not be said for Sète. Mr Tovey does not totally agree with a certain Mr Shaw, whom he quotes: 'Cette is a by-word for adulteration, but its bad name is not deserved. Adulteration means the admixture of foreign matter with the juice of the grape. This is practised in Cette as well as in many other places, but probably

11

comparatively little there, because there is such an ample choice of every description of grape juice for honest blending that some of the kinds are cheaper and more suitable for the imitations desired than anything else. It is alleged that if you tell a Cette merchant at 9 a.m. you wish to have 50 pipes of Port, 50 butts of Sherry, and 50 hogsheads of claret, he will promise to deliver them at 4 p.m. There is a good deal of (exaggerated) truth in this, but he can accomplish it, because he possesses an almost unlimited supply of a great variety of wines, with body and flavour that his experience has taught him how to use, so that by certain combinations he will produce a remarkably close resemblance to that of any other quality or country.' Tovey grudgingly admits that, because of its higher wine content, the produce of Sète is less obnoxious than that of Hamburg, but 'honest blending' appears a charitable description when you read some of the local recipes quoted by Bertall. It is fair to say there is a minimum of 86 per cent of wine in everything from Port, to Sherry, to Lacryma-Christi and Constantia. Nevertheless, other ingredients required in the kitchen include essence of tar (for Málaga) and walnut juice and high strength alcohol for just about everything.

The addition of alcohol to most wines sold on the British market seems to have been accepted as a generality, but it attracted the unfavourable comments of a number of writers including not only Charles Tovey, but also James Denman in his *Wine and its Counterfeits* and the anonymous *One of the Old School*, who in 1829 published his *Wine and Spirit Adulterators Unmasked*.

In France itself, there appears to have been little criticism of such practices and there were no movements to legislate on a national scale for honesty in wine production. Surprisingly enough, the phylloxera plague was one of the root causes of pressure on the authorities. The total collapse of the wine-trade led merchants to look for alternative products with which to satisfy their customers. Of these, the most important was 'wine' made from imported raisins from Greece. This rapidly became a major industry and it took the government some time to react and apply the taxes that would protect the renascent real wine industry from this cheap competitor.

Nevertheless, 1 August 1905 saw the introduction of the first legislation to guarantee the source of French wines. This law outlined certain geographical wine-producing regions; however, it neither mentioned permitted (or forbidden) grape-varieties, nor controlled the methods of making the wine. The main disadvantages of the law were that the regions that were outlined were based more on history than viticultural traditions. In addition, there was no control on the extensive planting of hybrid vines, which had come about as the first reaction to phylloxera.

The following years saw two major 'peasants' revolts as a result of lack of control in the wine industry. The first started in the Minervois in 1907. Whilst the local growers had replanted after phylloxera, they found, not unnaturally, that it was difficult to compete with the raisin wine. In addition, many of the local merchants had begun to import vast quantities of wine from Algeria at very low prices. As early as 1903, Marcellin Albert, a small-time grower and bar owner in the village of Argèles, had foreseen the difficulties that there would be. He formed a series of local trade defence committees and a newspaper, *Le Tocsin*, to attack the fraudulent happenings.

By 1907 the problems were coming to a head and the growers becoming restive. Marcellin Albert sent a telegram to Clemenceau and then went to Narbonne to present a petition to the Sous-Préfet. Neither move met with any reaction from the authorities. The snowball began to grow with a succession of Sunday public meetings; at the first at Argeliers, there were just 87 people present, at the second at Ouveillan, more than 1,000, 5,000 at Coursan, 95,000 at Capestang. On 5 May, a procession was led by Albert, Dr Ferroul, the mayor of Narbonne, a recent convert and a man carrying an effigy of a wine fraudster hanging from a lamp-post. The meeting of more than 150,000 people heard a speech from Albert calmly, but after there was some rioting and some people were injured. From Narbonne, the circus moved to Béziers and then a week later to Perpignan where a delegation was rebuffed by the Préfet, with the words: 'If you can't sell your wine, plant almond trees.' In the following riots, the troops were called out and one grower was killed.

In Carcassonne on 26 May, there were 250,000 people present; one week later at Nîmes, 300,000, with Albert having difficulty in calming the crowd. On Sunday 9 June, there were an estimated 800,000 people in the crowd at Montpellier. Amongst them were a number of *agents provocateurs*. It was obvious that there would soon be an explosion.

On 19, 20 and 21 June, there was fighting in the streets in Narbonne, Béziers, Montpellier and Perpignan. One army regiment mutinied, rather than obey the command to fire on the wine-growers, and was despatched in disgrace to Tunisia.

Albert went to see Clemenceau in Paris, but received no satisfaction and even had to borrow some money from him for the return train journey to the Midi. The whole movement collapsed, but if it had achieved little, it had at least drawn the government's and the consumers' attention to the vast quantitites of fraudulent wine that were being produced.

In comparison to the happenings in the Midi in 1907, those in Champagne four years later were on a much smaller scale. Again, faudulent trading was at the root of the problem. It became difficult for many of the growers to sell their wine to the Champagne houses, for some of the less scrupulous of the latter did not hesitate to buy in wine from Saumur, the Midi and even North Africa, which they sparkled and sold as Champagne. The situation, on this occasion, was aggravated by the fact that the growers were joined by a number of professional agitators and anarchists who were determined to cause trouble. Also there were the fun-seekers like the flamboyant Bolo-Pasha, son of a wealthy Marseilles family, who ultimately was shot for spying for the enemy during the First World War.

On 17 January 1911, the general discontent in Champagne burst into flames, when a mob dumped a load of wine from the Midi in the river Marne and rampaged through the cellars of one of the most notorious fraudsters in Damery. The red flag was soon flying over the town hall and the following day the trouble spread to Hautvillers. The army was called out and the Préfet promised to stop the trafficking in illegal wines.

On 10 February, the government voted new laws for the production of Champagne, which laid down that the wine had to be made in the area and from grapes and wine which came only from the area. Unfortunately, the area that was defined as Champagne included a number of parishes in the Aisne *département*, whilst totally excluding the vineyards of the Aube. In addition, the message came through from Paris that the government was proposing a Bill which would 'assure the repression of fraud, but not maintain the territorial restrictions which sow discord amongst all Frenchmen'. On 11 April, the growers attacked a number of cellars of supposed fraudsters in Damery, Dizy and Ay and on the following day, took place the battle of Ay. Whilst no one was killed, the confrontation between the rioters and a squadron of cavalry led to the sack of further cellars, including those of totally innocent merchants.

In the event the troubles sputtered to a halt, with satisfaction as far as the growers in the Marne were concerned, but rather less so for the growers in the Aube. Whilst they were allowed to sell their wine as Champagne, the label had to bear the derogatory addition of the words *Deuxième Zone*.

On a much smaller scale, though just as important in its own way, was a civil disobedience campaign carried out in Arbois in 1906. The previous year a new tax system had been introduced which effectively encouraged wine fraud and, as a result, many markets were lost to the local growers, including the important one of Switzerland. In protest, the local growers refused to pay any taxes and finally the authorities had to cave in and restore the fiscal *status quo ante*.

The next major move came after the Great War, with the Law of 6 May 1919, which was subsequently modified in July 1927. This finally constructed the framework for the French *Appellation Contrôlée* laws, as we know them today. Integrated into the laws were the concepts of tradition; in future, to benefit from the AC status, wines had to be made in the ways that they had been made traditionally, from the grape varieties and the vineyard areas that had long been recognised. No longer was the use of hybrid grape varieties tolerated and civil courts were granted the rights to make local decisions.

French wine law has, quite naturally, developed over the last 60 years, but it still remains within the same parameters. There are now basically four levels of wine. At the bottom are the ordinary table wines, the *vins de table*. These often come in plastic or returnable bottles, can be produced anywhere in France and, as long as it is mentioned on the label, can be blended with similar wines from elsewhere within the Common Market. When the supplier's address is mentioned, it must not lead one to believe that it comes from *appellation contrôlée* vineyards. Thus if the table wine is blended by a merchant in Burgundy, the supplier's name and address appears as 'Gaspard Teloutel, Négociant à 21200 France'.

The next level up is that of Vin de Pays. Officially, this is still a *vin de table*, but it is one attached to a geographical region, which might be as large as one or more *départements* or might on the other hand be quite small. There are limitations on the quantities that may be produced and broad choices as to the grapes that might be used. It has proved to be a very useful vehicle for the selling varietal wines. Thus, when the Burgundy company of Louis Latour decided to plant vineyards in the Ardèche with the Chardonnay grape, the resultant wine is sold as a Vin de Pays de L'Ardèche. Before gaining the *vin de pays* status, all wines have to be submitted to a tasting panel. Over recent years, the *vin de pays* have played a very important role in the rapid movement of the consumer towards drinking better wines.

The next step up the ladder is into the quality wine range, with the VDQS, or *Vin de Qualité Supérieure*. For the most part, these are regional wines that are in the process of bettering themselves. Many of them, especially in the South of France, consider themselves to be at a transitory level, as they hope ultimately to gain full *appellation contrôlée* status. Some, on the other hand, are regional, traditional wines, that have limited local distribution, but a long history. In the first group were such wines as Minervois, which has now arrived at the full AC level, and in the latter the Sauvignon de Saint Bris from the Chablis neighbourhood and the Côtes de Toul, of Lorraine. There are certain advantages in not progressing above this level, higher yields and less restrictive tax implications, for example, which have led some regions to stick where they are. The growers of Bugey, in Franche-Comté, have for long resisted the idea of any further promotion.

At the top of the ladder are the *appellation contrôlée* wines (AC), the *crème de la crème* of the world of wine, as one French government promotional booklet describes them. According to the National Institute that controls the application of AC, 'the classification signifies:

To the wine industry: a true recognition of and protection for the product. In accepting the rigorous restrictions to which the appellation is subject, the producer benefits from a price which reflects the quality of production and from protection against malpractice and the misuse of the designation.

To the consumer: an assurance of quality and origin guaranteed by the label.

Now, of the total production of wine in France, more than one bottle in four is sold with an *appellation contrôlée* label. Admittedly the 1982 vintage was one of exceptional size, but in that year almost 20 million hectolitres of AC wine was produced, or, to put it in more graphic terms, more than 2,500 million bottles. To control this, the Institute has a staff of 130 based in the office in Paris and 23 others around the provinces. In other words, each employee is responsible for 'guaranteeing' the quality and origin of approximately 20 million bottles of wine.

Here lies the real problem, the figures I have quoted have applied to France, but there are similar legislation and similar control problems in nearly every wine-producing country in the world. The situation is made even more complicated in that, at the higher levels, it is a very cosmopolitan product. Whilst French wines must naturally respect the wine-laws of France, they must also now respect those of the Common Market and, if they are to be sold in the United States, for instance, those of America. In an age of protectionism, it is easy enough to keep out another country's wines by, for example, demanding ingredient listing on the label. As wine-laws become more complicated, so do they become more difficult to apply.

During the course of the book, we will meet the wine-laws of other countries than France, and how they are applied. For the most part, my sympathies lie with the inspectors who are responsible for their application. Their task is formidable and thankless. One vat of wine looks much like another and one bottle in a bin without a label cannot be distinguished from another. The control of the wine-trade, certainly in the producing countries, has to be on paper and this book will show what magical properties paper can have in the hands of an unscrupulous conjuror.

2

Bordeaux mixture

La Bouillie Bordelaise is the term for copper sulphate solution, which for generations has been sprayed on plants, particularly vines, as a treatment against parasitic fungi. It is that which gives the leaves in so many vineyards their bluish tinge. *La Bouillie Bordelaise* is also the name of a book by Bernard Ginestet, who, 15 years ago, was the *enfant terrible* of the Bordeaux wine-trade.

Literally, *bouille* can be translated as gruel, or a boil-up, and thus gives a clear idea of what Monsieur Ginestet had in mind, when he wrote his exposé of the mentality of the Bordeaux wine-trade. For more than a century now, la *bouillie bordelaise* has been known to English-speaking horticulturalists as Bordeaux Mixture, which gives a slightly different visual impression to the French. However, for my purposes, I find it just as apt and whilst I apologise to Monsieur Ginestet for borrowing, or adapting his title, I have no conscience about it.

Of all the vineyard areas of the world, Bordeaux has always had the most patrician image. Whether this image is totally merited is a different matter, but the façade of the trade there is the elegant château of the Médoc, fronted by Counts and Marquesses, of refined meals in formal settings and merchants and growers who affect an Englishness that is truer than life. Of course, there is much to justify this; many of the names show their origins in the British Isles: the Bartons, the Lawtons and the Johnstons. The first connections were made when Aquitaine belonged to the English and the traces proudly remain. Indeed, there are some who still claim that the worst thing that ever happened to the region was when the English were driven out.

There is a formality about Bordeaux, that you find nowhere else in France, except possibly in Champagne. In Burgundy, I would not be surprised if I were invited to a meal in the family kitchen and I would enjoy it. In Bordeaux, it would probably be in a restaurant, or a châteaux with waitresses in white gloves. I would not like to suggest that the Bordelais is any less hospitable than the Burgundian, but that he has a very different character. What is more, the people of Bordeaux have always adopted a much higher profile, not just in the world of wine but in that of, for example, politics.

When the Bordeaux wine-scandal broke upon the world in 1974, there was a feeling of unhealthy pleasure in the minds of many. Here were those who had set themselves up as purists at last being brought to justice. The greatest names in the trade were found to have been associating with many less than savoury characters. There have been similar reactions in Britain, when Conservative politicians have been accused of consorting with prostitutes. The Winegate Scandal, as it came to be called, may have attracted the attention of the media around the world, but it was no more than the culmination of practices which, in one form or another, had been going on for centuries.

The strength, and the weakness, of Bordeaux since the beginning of time has been its geographical position, on the river Garonne, near to its confluence with the Dordogne, where jointly they take on the name of the Gironde. It was an important port in Roman days and since then has been ideally situated for the shipment not only of the wines from the immediate neighbourhood, the wines of Bordeaux, but of those from up-river, the High Country as it used to be called. Bordeaux was an important centre of learning, with a university founded as early as AD 286. From its beginning its students were held in high regard and there are records of their having travelled as far as Trier, Rome, Lerida and Constantinople. In addition, students were attracted from Normandy, Syracuse, Sicily and Athens. All this must have helped with spreading the reputation of the wines of the region.

The danger in Bordeaux's being a port on a major river system is that it has served as an entrepôt for all the wines that were being produced in the hinterland. Indeed, over the centuries, the importance of Bordeaux as a port grew to such an extent that it served as the shipping centre for wines from as far away as Languedoc. Thus temptation, from the earliest times, was placed in the hands of the local merchants. Bordeaux was not the sole port in the region; Libourne, on the river Dordogne, was also responsible for a substantial proportion of the export wine-trade.

Henri Enjalbert, in his *Histoire de la Vigne et du Vin*, quotes that the average shipments from Libourne and Bordeaux during the years 1305 and 1336 amounted to almost three-quarters of a million hecto-litres per year, with just over ten per cent passing through Libourne, and well over half being accounted for by wines from the High Country; Quercy, Périgord and Bergerac.

With so many 'foreign' wines passing through the port, there was a real danger that the wines of Bordeaux would have difficulty in finding a market even in the city itself. Protective measures were however taken and, as in many other towns, it was forbidden that any other than local wines should be sold in the inns. Here too it was forbidden to serve blasphemers, vagabonds and married men who leave their wife and children to go drinking. It seems as though fraud was not unknown, as, in May 1415, the town innkeepers were summoned to the town hall to be told that if there were any more cases discovered of the passing-off of other wines as those of Bordeaux, the offenders would be put in the pillory and banished from the town.

Also, in a bid to protect their own interests, at the end of the fifteenth century, no High Country wine was allowed to pass through the city until after Christmas, and then only if it was des-tined for export. Some 50 years later, the oath that the wine-brokers took each year forbade them to sell anything other than Bordeaux wines 'and not to take part in any fraudulent business'.

During the seventeenth century, the traffic in High Country wines declined, for many of them were now used for distillation, which took place on the spot. The Bordelais appear to have been successful in keeping out many of these foreign wines but Colbert, in the interests of gaining more business on export markets, decreed that other wines could be brought into the city for blending purposes, for eventual shipment onwards to Holland and England. Permission was only given on the understanding that the resultant blend should be of a style to appeal to the consumers in those two countries. Here is the seed of many future practices, not just in Bordeaux, but perhaps more particularly in Burgundy. It seems sad, just over three centuries ago, that the French government should have supported the concept that a fraudulent wine may be permitted as long as it is acceptable to an ignorant foreign consumer and brings in much-needed foreign currency.

There appears to have been some flexibility as to when wines from outside the region might be allowed into Bordeaux. Certainly in 1698, when there was a small vintage in the Médoc, the bringing in of wine from Languedoc to fill the gap was permitted. On the other hand, in December 1738, a Monsieur Malleret, the cellar-master of the Bor-deaux merchants Caussade, was arrested at Marmande, where he was buying 130 *tonneaux* of wine. He was ultimately fined 2,000 *livres*, which must have been a considerable sum of money in those days.

About the same time a report was drawn up by Monsieur Thibaut, on behalf of the municipal authorities, on the excessive number of warehouses for High Country wines springing up in the city. He seems to have been overwhelmed by some of the happenings, as he wrote: 'One would never finish if one went into all the frauds that are practised daily be several of these new brokers.' Legally these wines could only be stocked in Bordeaux from after Christmas until the following September, but in a statement in the city archives, it is recorded that in the period from December 1754 up to August 1755, there came into the city no less than 3,659 *tonneaux* of wines from the Languedoc, 6,330 from the High Country and 6,920 from Quercy and Cahors. In a note attached to these figures, an anonymous contemporary hand has written: 'One can add that a part of those wines that arrive in Bordeaux from Cahors, do so fraudulently and are used for blending with the wines from Bordeaux.' (More recently, the situation has somewhat changed. One of the better hidden wine-scandals of the past years has been in Cahors, where a well-known merchant was found to be selling rather more wine of that name than was being produced in total.)

Even though there were strict controls on the shipments of wines from Quercy, it is interesting to note that the figures increased almost fifteen-fold in the first half of the eighteenth century. The business must have been profitable to justify the vineyard planting that this must have implied. Even in those days, there was no shortage of merchants trying to evade the controls. Over the Christmas period in 1756, a merchant called La Place racked some Quercy wine into the official Bordeaux barrels, in an effort to ship them out of the country. He was arrested, the casks were broached and the wine poured into the river and he was fined a total of 10,000 *livres*.

The quasi-monopoly of trade, that Bordeaux had managed to maintain for its wines within the city, came to an end in 1789. This meant that the authorities ceased to show any interest in the wines that were being brought into the local cellars and this no doubt gave impulse to those who were happy, or perhaps determined, to make their living by fraud. There is little doubt that even the finest wines from the Médoc owed their reputations to careful blending with wines from elsewhere. The pioneer of wine-production in Australia, and later in New Zealand, James Busby, visited the wine company of Richard et Fils in Tain, in December 1832, and noted to his amazement that: 'The finest Clarets of Bordeaux are mixed with a portion of the finest red wine of Hermitage, and four-fifths of the quantity of the latter which is produced, are thus employed.'

That Hermitage was widely used in Bordeaux is apparent from other sources, but it is also apparent that it was only used for the best wines. In 1848 M.-A. Puvis, a retired artillery officer, produced a book on viticulture, which included a detailed survey on Hermitage and its wines. He writes: 'The value of the wines of Hermitage is very high in the good years; the Bordelais take the majority and mix them in varying proportions in their top qualities, to give them body, spirit and a good nose; these wines make an ideal marriage; Hermitage leaves Bordeaux its soft, full nose, whose character is enhanced without being weakened by that of the Hermitage. Over these past few years, the Bordelais have been in much less of a hurry to buy; this outlet increased the prices considerably in 1825, the wine was all sold at a thousand francs the hogshead. Since this outlet became less certain, prices have fallen by half. This export market which enriched the region for many years has also definitely damaged certain contacts; the great wines of Hermitage have no standing in the trade or with the consumer; the result is that, when the Bordelais do not buy them, they are obliged to wait and seek out customers, as they have no other regular outlets, conditions are in no way favourable for the producer.'

Cyril Ray quotes André Simon as having come across an invoice of an Edinburgh wine-merchant, dated in the 1830s, which talks of 'Lafite Hermitaged', without any derogatory feeling. For lesser wines a smaller proportion of Hermitage would be used and Spanish wines such as Alicante and Bernicarlo substituted.

That much was not right in Bordeaux is apparent from the foreword to a book (admittedly on the wines of Burgundy) which appeared in 1858. Written by a certain August Luchet, it launches into a vigorous diatribe against many of the merchants involved in the Bordeaux wine-trade. Whenever the growers announce that the vintage is a disaster, 'the Trade is there. When it wishes to be, the wine-trade is God, and part of its equipment is the miracle at Cana. Proprietors, growers, journalists, the Préfet announce dearth and plague; the merchants, never. It has reached the point that Bordeaux has expanded, just as its trade has done, and today all France is a part of it. Everywhere, East and South, wherever the grape grows, its juice is transformed into Médoc. Bordeaux buys everything and makes wine with everything. There are chemists who construct its scent and distill its bouquet. It's on public sale; *Sève de Médoc, one flask for four barrels*. You take a long narrow bottle, made from fine, clear glass; you pour in as much wine as you want, add a little iris, raspberry or violet, cork it with a long cork, seal it in red; and there you have it, a wine from Bordeaux.

'As for the doctors . . . they have recommended the wines of Bordeaux to their patients, imagining that they are all, like those that they have known, Margaux, Latour, Lafite, Haut-Brion, or at least a Larose or a Rauzan, having never imagined that in Bordeaux itself this divine nectar is worth eight to fifteen or even twenty francs a bottle.'

'This does not prevent the bars of Paris offering a large glass of

Bordeaux, to anyone who asks for it, at two sous a glass. As the trade sells it, so do they resell it. Some, perhaps, embellish it even more. I know famous shops where you can find as much *genuine* Château Margaux as you want at three or four francs. The customers go there in confidence and come away satisfied. "They want it at that price, so we must give it them at that price", say the merchants to the judges on the rare occasion that anyone complains. Last year, one of my friends at Bercy showed me a handsome man, well turned-out and booted, of whom he said this, "There you see one of our merchants. His role is to visit the vineyards, blend together to his taste a vat somewhere, on which he will make a good profit. As soon as he has the wine, he will dispatch it to his customers, with a stamp of a well-known vineyard on the cask, and on the bung and the spile a red wax seal with the picture of an imaginary château. As soon as this is done he draws sight drafts on his customers, for fear of any complaints when they receive the goods. Two things can happen: either the victim sees that he has been robbed, or he does not. If nothing happens, this gentleman has made fifty per cent profit; if there is a complaint, he is the first to propose a reduction of ten per cent. It is like the piquet player, who, to be sure of his game, gives himself fifty points start and, if his opponent is astonished at this, agrees to knock off ten."

'That is business. One does not respect this gentleman, one suffers him. Nobody, I am afraid has a clear enough conscience to throw the first stone. Bordeaux, more honest, borrows its wine from Hermitage, from Cahors, from Narbonne, from Benicarlo.'

Whilst Monsieur Luchet is obviously rather prejudiced against the wines of Bordeaux, or, at least, most of the wines of Bordeaux that were available at the time, there must have been considerable justification for what he wrote. Perhaps surprisingly, Charles Tovey, who wrote at about the same time, and rarely hesitated to expose fraud when he came across it, is full of praise for the wines of Bordeaux that he found on his travels. He does however criticise severely the claret that was available in English hotels at the time. One apparently was a hock from Ingleheim, though red and labelled as a claret with the shipper's address in Mainz.

The main lesson to be learnt from what Monsieur Luchet has to say is one that is, sadly, still applicable today. Few customers know much about wine and, if they have doubts about its quality, are too often unprepared to do anything about it. This fact is known to some unscrupulous members of the trade at all levels, and they will not hesitate to profit from the fact.

It seems likely that conditions in the Bordeaux region changed little over the ensuing years. A decree dated 1764 talks of the Dutch importers who 'note that the wines are being blended and falsified to such an extent that they can no longer rely upon their quality'. At the beginning of the twentieth century it was the smaller grower in Bordeaux who took up the complaint. Yet another source of wine suitable for blending had appeared upon the scene, Algeria. The wines were full-bodied and thus ideal for balancing out many of the thin lesser wines of Bordeaux; they were cheap; the foreign customers liked their taste; and, as well, it provided almost limitless supplies, of a standard quality every year. Whilst this was bad news for the growers of the Midi, it was another weapon in the hands of any merchant who was out to defraud.

Algeria remained a regular source of wine for the merchants of Bordeaux until it gained independence and until that time openly remained the basis of many of their table wine blends. Nicholas Faith in *The Winemasters* quotes Ian Maxwell Campbell as saying that his regular Bordeaux suppliers could not let him have 'cheap claret because we are not allowed to import any wine from Algeria'. This has, however, been taken out of context as the real suggestion was that the shipper had, of necessity, used his cheap claret for table wine on the home market, as he could not import any wine—or am I being too naïve?

The one group of people to suffer was the producers of the lesser wines of Bordeaux. This level of trade did not touch the owners of the great Châteaux, and the merchants and brokers were turning over considerable quantities of wine from a variety of sources. Matters came to a head in the year 1913 and the result was the notorious 'Bordeaux Agreement'. This meant that in future the merchants would sell no more wine under the name of Bordeaux than they had bought. The price that was paid for their tacit support was that there would be no enquiries as to what went on in the merchant's cellars. Thus bad Bordeaux could be bought cheaply from the growers; it could be 'improved' in the cellars and sold at a much higher price. The poor wine could be sold off in the basic blends of *vin de table*. The grower gained, because it guaranteed an outlet for his wines if they were produced within the Bordeaux region; the merchant gained, because he had official approval for doubtful practices that had been going on for centuries; the customer gained because whilst he still might not be getting a genuine wine as labelled, he was probably getting a better bottle of wine than he was used to.

When the *appellation contrôlée* laws were introduced in 1919, legal blessing was given to this system. In future all wines, and even grapes, would have to be accompanied by official documents. It was generally understood, however, that whilst the officials would have access to all the merchant's books and his cellars, if they were to make a visit, they would give due notice, so that any necessary 'tidying up' might be carried out. There was an interesting parallel to the 'Bordeaux Agreement' in Burgundy, where the 'Tunnel System' was devised.

It is with this doubtful background of centuries of trading in wines from other than just the local sources that the city of Bordeaux was the breeding ground for the Winegate Scandal. However, the trading situation of the early 1970s was the incubator for the addled egg that was about to hatch. The American market had begun to wake to wine-drinking and claret became a symbol of wine-knowledge on the far side of the Atlantic. Everybody wanted to be in on the act, with diversification into the wine-trade being the name of the game for every conglomerate. In the lead was the tobacco company, Liggett and Myers, whose subsidiary Austin Nichols, under the direction of Ab Simon and Gerald Asher, swiftly built up one of the biggest inventories ever seen in the wine world. On their say depended the future of many companies not only in Bordeaux, but throughout France. They had to expand to meet the demands of Austin Nichols, and their rivals, or opt out of the game.

In Bordeaux, there was another problem. Ever since the 1859 classification of the vineyards of the Médoc, Château Mouton Rothschild had resented its, unjustified, classification amongst the second growths. Its reputation and its price justified its claim to be a first growth. How was it to achieve this status? The plan decided upon by Baron Philippe de Rothschild was to increase his prices above those of the first growths, particularly that of Château Lafite, which belonged to his cousin and rival Baron Elie de Rothschild. As far as the trading situation was concerned, a better moment could not have been chosen, as the buyers were happy to follow the rapidly increasing prices, like sparks up a chimney. To complicate the situation, the leaders in this idiocy would announce opening prices, for only a small fraction of their crop, thus keeping most of their cards covered until their competitors showed their hands. Naturally, the other owners were prepared to follow where the great led and Bordeaux had never seen a price spiral on the same scale. Quality had nothing to do with the prices. Whilst the 1970 vintage was a great one, that of 1971 was small, though of good quality. The 1972 vintage, however, gave poor hard wines—yet was released at the highest prices yet.

Throughout the whole structure of the Bordeaux wine-trade there was an unprecedented demand for wine—wine, which for the most part, had not found an ultimate consumer. Investment in claret gave way to speculation. Even British governmental bodies, supposedly created to help with financing projects in the Commonwealth, spent millions of pounds on purchasing wine.

As in wild life, when there is a sick animal, there is always a wolf snapping at its heels, waiting for the flesh that it knows will come its way. In Bordeaux, the sick animal that we all came to hear about was the venerable merchant house of Cruse et Fils, Frères, and the wolf that attracted all the attention was the self-confessed, but amusing, rogue Pierre Bert. The house of Cruse was one of the most venerable in Bordeaux. The family came originally from the Danish, Schleswig-Holstein, and established itself in the wine-trade in Bordeaux in 1819. According to Edmund Penning-Rowsell, their fortune was made by 'daring speculation in the 1847 vintage'. By 1973, the company had expanded enormously and was under considerable pressure from its customers, especially in the United States, to find adequate quantities of red Bordeaux. The company also suffered an old reputation and a new generation of management. Like many of the Bordeaux houses, it existed in a rarified atmosphere of its own creation. The situation is reminiscent of John Collins Bossidy's poem of his home city:

> I come from the city of Boston,
> The home of the bean and the cod,
> Where the Cabots speak only to Lowells,
> And the Lowells speak only to God.

Such was the life in Bordeaux, as far as the cosmopolitan trading families, the Chartronnais, were concerned.

Pierre Bert, too, came from a wine-trade family. His grandfather Louis had built up considerable vineyard estates and specialised in supplying sweet white wines, many of which appeared in England under the all-embracing label of Sauternes. Pierre Bert was to inherit his family firm with vast financial problems and had to sell out, only to open up again a few years later.

His freewheeling approach to the wine-laws soon came to the attention of the authorities and he was fined on at least two occasions. The fevered atmosphere of the early 1970s was created for someone with the inventiveness of Pierre Bert. His mainstream operation depended on one simple fact. The official documents did not show the colour of a wine. Thus if he bought white Bordeaux *appellation contrôlée* wine, which was a drug on the market, and non-appellation red wine, he could make a financial killing. He bought cheap white wines with the official paperwork for Bordeaux and sold them as *vin de table*. On this part of the circuit, he made a small loss. He also bought cheap red wine from the Midi, transferred to it the official paperwork for the white wine and sold it, at enormous profit, as Bordeaux rouge. To help him he set up a front company under the name of his truck driver, Serge Balan.

He also arranged for Monsieur Balan to visit the authorities and apply to be issued with the official franking machine, which authenti-cates all the *acquit verts*, the *appellation contrôlée* accompanying documents. (In France, this is available to companies of good repute, on the lodging of a deposit. Whilst Pierre Bert's track record pre-vented his hoping for this privilege, his stooge was welcomed by officialdom!)

Now equipped to carry on business in a big way (and in case of shortage, Bert was always ready to add some water to convert the opulent wines of Languedoc to the lighter-style wines of Bordeaux), customers had to be found. Initially, he had no difficulty amongst the horde of marginal traders in Bordeaux, who exist by picking up the crumbs that fall from the table of the Chartronnais. Some of these were subsequently to appear in the dock, but their relevant lack of importance never attracted much attention.

In April 1973, however, Pierre Bert, no doubt with tongue deep in cheek, presented himself at the Quai des Chartrons office of Cruse. Whether he had done his homework or not has never been made clear, but what is clear is that he picked a company that needed him. The courtship was not easy and he had to come back four times in the same week, before a trading accommodation was agreed upon. Cruse were unhappy about buying from Bert, because of his reputation; from Serge Balan & cie, because they were too recently established, but would buy from Bertrand de Pinos, one of Bert's cousins. (It helps a lot in France to have a *de* in your surname, as La Bruyère pointed out three centuries ago. It gives a hint of aristocratic authenticity to the name.) The final point upon which the Cruses insisted, was that they would only buy *appellation contrôlée* wine from Bert in the same quantities that he would take *vin de table* from them.

The Cruse family thought that they must have made a favourable deal for they were buying Bordeaux rouge at some 15 per cent less than the market price and they were also liquidating their stocks of *vin de table*, wine that they had hoped, without success, to sell to their American customers.

Within days, the wagons started to roll and it soon became apparent that the whole arrangement was too complicated. Instead of exchanging the wine when the tankers arrived at the Cruse cellars, as was in the agreement, why not just exchange the official documents? Time and effort would then be saved and everyone could get on with their work. Once the system began to flow smoothly, the figures turned over became astronomical. In the first two weeks in June, according to the paperwork, Cruse purchased 4,000 hectolitres of Bordeaux from the combine, the equivalent of 25 tanker loads and almost five times the capacity of the warehouse from where it was officially coming.

In the following week, the Cruses decided that the system was reliable enough even to buy some 'better' wines, some Saint-Emilion, and to avoid complicating the system, they were prepared to buy directly from Serge Balan, whose reputation for probity had no doubt been proved over the intervening period. It was not to last; on the doorstep waiting for the offices to open at 9 a.m., on 28 June, were the inspectors from the tax authorities, tipped-off that something illegal was going on.

That they should have had to rely on an informer to move in appears strange, for the very scale of the operation must have raised some eyebrows. According to the authorities, from nothing, within the space of four months, Serge Balan & cie. sold almost 30,000 hectolitres of wine—and that was what the authorities were able to trace. In addition, the numbers of people involved and the little effort made to ensure secrecy leads one to think that the whole operation was grossly incompetent, or that the perpetrators had no respect for, or fear of, the authorities.

Even stranger was the fact that the inspectors went through Pierre Bert's books five days before they visited the Cruses—and he did not give them any warning as to what had already happened. When the inspectors did arrive at the Quai des Chartrons, they were not certain what they were seeking and they were received in a cavalier fashion by Lionel Cruse, who said it was inconvenient for them to arrive at that time of the year, as they were about to close for the holidays. When this failed to deflect the interest of the authorities, he simply refused them access to the cellars.

Also involved in the processes were two distinct political threads: one was local concerning the wine-trade; the other was on a national scale. A close friend of the Cruse family was Jacques Chaban-Delmas, the mayor of Bordeaux and a candidate in the forthcoming presidential election. The French satirical magazine *Le Canard Enchaîne* was tipped off about the scandal, and within a short time the whole story was built up as being part of a plot to implicate Chaban-Delmas, hatched up by his opponent Valéry Giscard d'Estaing. To the average Frenchman this was red meat and the whole story became totally confused during the silly season of the summer holidays.

In the meantime the Cruses made little effort to cover their tracks, but rather complained, to any journalist who would listen, that they were being as cruelly persecuted as Richard Nixon—for the Watergate saga was running at the same time.

On a local level, the merchants in Bordeaux first of all rallied round the Cruse family saying that the action of the authorities was in grave breach of the Bordeaux Agreement of 60 years earlier. It is probable, too, that many of them would not have been happy if there had been a general inspection of trade records. In due course, however, they chorused that the action of the Cruse family had gravely damaged the noble reputation of Bordeaux and its wines.

By the end of August, and the end of the holidays, the authorities had a reasonable idea as to how the fraud was perpetrated and the inspectors, this time from Paris, descended on the Cruse cellars again on 27 August. It seems incredible that the Cruse family still thought that they could deal with the matter in an offhand manner. Their books which they left available for inspection spoke openly of wines of the Burgundy and Côtes du Rhône types, and they were prepared to admit that any losses in the casks were topped up with ordinary table wine. (In theory the topping up, or *ouillage*, should be carried out with wine of the same kind as that in the cask, but with perhaps hundreds of different wines in a merchant's cellar, there must be more who abuse the law than stick to its letter.) It must suddenly have come home to the company that the inspection was serious, for the following morning, some of their records disappeared and others were crudely altered. Subsequently, records as to how the wines had been often illegally treated went missing, though the incriminating chemicals themselves were left.

It took the state more than a year to prepare the case for the prosecution, but in the meantime the case was discussed quite openly around the world, with little respect for the Anglo-Saxon concept that the accused is innocent until proved guilty. Before the trial began, at the end of October 1974, Hermann Cruse committed suicide, overwrought by the unfavourable publicity.

The trial, itself, turned into little more than a farce, orchestrated by Pierre Bert, who adopted the classical role of the *fraudeur* who has been caught out. All that he did had been done for generations by others in the trade, and was common practice in Bordeaux. In any case, what he did was for the benefit of the wine. In 30 years in the trade, no one had ever complained of the quality of what he had sold. The same was said some years later by Bernard Grivelet in one of Burgundy's better-publicised scandals.

Pierre Bert's outgoing personality, and the weakness of the presiding judge, guaranteed maximum publicity for what was said and the real matters at stake soon were buried under a heap of irrelevances. The defence of the Cruse family was based on the concept that when they bought wines that were young, they had to anticipate the final product. However, the prosecution pointed out, with some justification, that the case was clear enough, without the quality of the wine being in question. The way that they conducted their business was plainly fraudulent.

After the 15 months of speculation and gossip about the enormity of the offence, and the undoubted harm that it did to the reputation of the wines of Bordeaux, the final sanctions appear derisory. They themselves were lessened, on appeal, to: remission of a short prison sentence on Pierre Bert; suspended sentence, pardoned by the new President, for the other seven accused found guilty. There was also a substantial tax imposition, but no one ever expected this to be paid. To rub salt into the wounds, Pierre Bert wrote a best-seller, exposing all, called *In Vino Veritas*, which made him a great deal of money, whilst holding the traditional Bordeaux merchants up to ridicule.

Whilst it is easy to laugh with Pierre Bert, one must be sad that the penalties imposed were ultimately so slight. Regularly, in France, one has the opinion that the authorities consider wine-fraud to be of trivial importance. If dollars can be earned, it is not important how we earn them.

After the excitements of Winegate, there is little that cannot seem but an anti-climax, but there are two points about Bordeaux and its wines that worry me, though both of them are perfectly legal. The first is the status of the vineyard name. In any other part of France a vineyard is a portion of land marked on a map that is lodged at a local town hall. Thus, for example, the vineyard of Blanchefleurs, in Beaune, consists of plots CE 1974, 5 to 8, 14 to 17, 22 to 25, 89, 97, 99, 102, 103, 106, 107, 110, 111, 114 and 131 to 134. Of these, the portion 97 has the right to the appellation Beaune Premier Cru, whilst the rest can be called no more than Beaune. In Bordeaux, however, the name of a château is little more than a brand-name that is attached to the *appellation contrôlée* of the village or region.

Let us look at some examples as to how vineyards of repute can vary in size over the years. According to Cyril Ray, in 1908 there were 75 hectares under vines at Château Lafite; in 1992 the figure was 70 and during the slump of the 1930s it was as little as 50. In 1978, Cyril Ray quotes it as 95 hectares and three years later, Serena Sutcliffe as 88. Whilst there might well be some land lying fallow at any given moment, the variation is quite wide in an estate whose total extent is 123 hectares. One must assume that certain soils on the estate give better wines than others. The corollary of which is that there are certain soils which give worse wines. Nevertheless, the vineyard is classed as a first growth no matter from which part of it the wine comes.

Another example is the vineyard of Château Gloria at Saint Julien. This vineyard did not appear in the 1855 classification, which is scarcely surprising as it did not exist until 1942, when Henri Martin created it with 6,000 square metres of land under vines which he bought from Monsieur Cazes of Pauillac. From that humble beginning has grown a 50 hectare vineyard, that will be rated highly when there is any new classification of vineyards of the Médoc.

The final example is that of Château Pétrus, the Pomerol wine that is often the most expensive in all Bordeaux. Over the past years the size of this vineyard has increased from just seven hectares to approximately twelve. This increase in size has come about by the purchase of neighbouring vineyard land of the same soil structure. By being transferred, this land now produces wine that will sell for approximately three times as much as it did hitherto. By becoming Pétrus is has taken a majestic leap in value.

In none of these three cases do I claim that the owner is making wine not worthy of the name, and the price under which he sells it. Surely, though, there must be something wrong with a system which permits a vineyard to increase in size according to the wishes, and perhaps the finances, of the owner. The system works because it is, at present, in the interests of the owners to maintain high prices for their wines by only having as much wine available on the market as it will absorb at the optimum price. Pétrus does not sell more expensively than Margaux because it is a better wine, but mainly because there is less of it available. The increase of size in the vineyard was a calculated risk that has paid off magnificently; but has the price of the wines of the adjoining vineyard that sold its vines come down now that it has lost its, presumably, best plot? I very much doubt it.

In all fairness, the whole situation can work in the opposite direction. Take the switchback career of Château Lagrange, at Saint Julien, for example. In the 1855 classification its reputation was high enough for it to be rated a third growth, a status that it has retained, even though, under the ownership of a Spaniard, Señor Manuel Cendoya, a rapid decline set in following the financial slump of 1929. Over the following 54 years, much of the vineyard was sold off, and it became notorious for the quality of its wine. In December 1985, it was purchased by the Japanese Suntory group and since then they have spent more than 150 million francs in restoring the vineyards, the cellars and press-house and the château. More important, they have invested in the finest brains to ensure that the quality of the wine will be restored to the position that it held more than 130 years ago. It is possible for reputations to be restored in Bordeaux — but it does not often happen.

This system works only as long as it is carried out by honourable men. It is optimistic to think that Bordeaux has none but honourable men. I can foresee that someone will take over a classified growth and buy a considerable number of lesser vineyards around about to increase the production. If I can give a tip to that speculator, I suggest that he goes for a vineyard like Cantemerle. With the appellation Haut-Médoc, that gives enormous scope for extending the holding within the same appellation!

The growers of Bordeaux claim that their wines owe their greatness to the soil of their vineyards, yet I have just shown that the soil can be varied at the owner's whim. On the one side they do their utmost to protect the mystique of their wines, but on the other some of them do not hesitate to exploit them for wider commercial purposes. The prime example of this is the branded Bordeaux wine Mouton Cadet. Nicholas Faith tells how this was created as a second label for Château Mouton-Rothschild in 1931. The wine was sold with the appellation Pauillac, and even when I joined the trade in the 1950s, it was suggested that if not totally from the vines at Mouton, they provided a solid base. It was a full member of the Mouton family — as was Château Mouton d'Armailhacq. The impression is confirmed by the sheep on the label and by the meaning of the word Cadet. My dictionary gives this as: 'Younger, junior and (familiarly) the youngest in a family.' The name of the company that produces it, La Bergerie (sheepfold), continues the whole theme.

Over the years the nature of the wine has changed. Whereas its opening appellation was Pauillac, the more successful that the wine has become, the lower in the hierarchy, its source. Now, it is just a plain Bordeaux. However, the very success of the brand has led to a swing in the other direction and there are now a number of speciality wines under the label: a Médoc, a Saint-Emilion, a Pomerol, a Graves and a Sauternes.

In an interview for *Impact International* magazine, Philippe Cottin, the joint managing director of Baron Philippe de Rothschild S.A., said: 'People ask me what is Mouton Cadet? I say it's a Schweppes bottle and it is.' It is a Schweppes bottle that sells to the tune of more than one and a half million, twelve-bottle cases a year. I respect the marketing skills that have created and expanded this brand, but the relationship between the name of what is now a first growth and a branded wine is too close for my comfort. As Nicholas Faith points out in *The Winemasters*, their label design, according to the present management, 'would today have had them sent to prison, because it was so close an imitation of the normal Mouton label'. Because something has been established, and accepted, for many years, it is no reason why it has to be accepted with today's perspectives.

The other danger of permitting the continued use of Mouton Cadet, is that its success will encourage imitations. This is already happening. The Bass Charrington group own Château Lascombes, a classified growth in Margaux, which is particularly well known in the United States, as it peviously belonged to the writer Alexis Lichine. They are now producing a wine called Chevalier de Lascombes, which has no pretensions to relying upon the château as a source. Surely the sole intention of creating this brand must be to cash in on the reputation and the high prices of the vineyard. To me, this is on the fringes of selling under false pretences. This use of a vineyard name must be compared unfavourably with the 'second' wines that are now made by many of the Bordeaux classified growths.

Bordeaux is one of the great wine-producing areas of the world; the one with perhaps the highest of all reputations. It is not that there is any more in the way of fraudulent practices carried out there than anywhere else in the world, it is just that when, and if, they come to the attention of the public, the spotlight shines upon them. That is the ever-present penalty of fame. For many reasons, the bad publicity generated by Winegate appealed to the newspapers of the world. That two of the greatest reputations in the world, the presidency of the United States and the wines of Bordeaux, should be shown to be fallible, was a parallel that was reflected not just in the names given to the scandals. The recent Contra hearings in Washington have shown that not too much has changed there since Watergate. I hope that Winegate does not have it successor in Bordeaux.

Burgundy — from here, there and everywhere

It may be because I know Burgundy better than any other wine region, that I view it as being more complex. It may be because I love Burgundy better than any other wine region, that I am more aware of its faults. Nevertheless, however prejudiced I might be, there is no doubt that there are certain aspects of Burgundy and its vineyards that put it apart from any other wine region of France, and which, in some ways, lay it open to fraudulent practice. The first problem is the small extent of the vineyards that make the great wines of Burgundy, and tied in with this is the high reputation that they have throughout the world of fine wine buyers. The second problem, and this ties in with the first, is the structure of the vineyards and their ownership. The third is the question of the climate, for this does not permit great wines to be made each year.

It should be said that whilst the vineyards of the viticultural region of Burgundy spread over the four *départements* of the Yonne, Côte d'Or, Saône et Loire and the Rhône, this chapter will deal almost exclusively with the wines of the first two, where the prices tend to be higher and the production smaller. This is not to say that there can be a completely clean bill of health given for the wines of the Mâconnais, which come from the Saône et Loire, or the Beaujolais, which for the most part come from the Rhône, but there the most regular breach of the law is probably about over-chaptalisation, and that is dealt with elsewhere.

To put everything in perspective, it might be constructive to make some direct comparisons with the other great region for the production of still wines in France, Bordeaux. The area under vines in the Bordeaux region is approximately 98,000 hectares; that in all Burgundy approximately 38,000 hectares, and, if one talks only of the Yonne and the Côte d'Or, no more than 10,000 hectares. In Bordeaux, the total average production is something over three million hectolitres; in Burgundy, it is, all told, just about two million hectolitres, but in the Yonne and the Côte d'Or no more than 440,000 hectolitres. Perhaps it is instructive to make some more detailed comparison at the level of individual villages of comparative reputation. Pauillac, which includes within its boundaries three of the first growths of the Médoc, has about 900 hectares of vines. The village of Gevrey-Chambertin, which includes no less than eight of the *grand crus* of Burgundy, but whose vineyards also include some that physically lie within the boundaries of the neighbouring village of Brochon, has no more than 445 hectares of vines. Whilst one can say that the wines of Burgundy and those of Bordeaux have approximately equal reputations, there is a great deal more of the latter available to connoisseurs than of the former. If supply cannot meet demand two things happen; prices rise and the interest of the fraudsters is whetted.

Also of importance, in seeking to understand the organisation of the trade in Burgundy, is the fact that vineyard holdings are, for the most part, very small, and are generally spread out amongst a number of separate vineyards, often over two or more villages. The reason for this is that in Burgundy, more than apparently anywhere else in France, the Napoleonic Law of Succession has wreaked its full effect. By this, at one's death, the majority of your property has to be shared equally amongst your children. It is not difficult to see that over the generations this works in a form of geometrical progression with, in theory, holdings becoming smaller and smaller. In Bordeaux most of the major vineyards are now operated as limited companies, so that it is shares that change hands rather than vines; in Burgundy this is still quite rare. The situation is not, however, as bad as it might seem. For tax purposes, it is frequent that a number of members of the same family will make separate *déclarations de récolte*, whilst effectively they will tend their vines and make their wines together.

A further result of this system is that it is rare for a vineyard to belong to just one owner. To illustrate the point, it may be worthwhile to take the extreme example of the *grand cru* vineyard Clos de Vougeot. From the time when the vines were presented to the Cistercian order of monks in 1110 until the time of the French Revolution, it remained as a single property in their hands. It then passed rapidly through the possession of a number of owners, until it was purchased in 1818 by a Monsieur Ouvrard, who, in modern day parlance, would be probably described as something of a wide boy, having made his fortune from speculation during the Napoleonic

Wars. He later burnt his fingers in Bordeaux, and, after his death, the property was sold in 1889 to 15 different purchasers, all involved in the wine-trade, but with bases ranging from Dijon to Chalon-sur-Saône. The latest list that I have names 85 names, with addresses as far apart as Paris in the north and Avignon in the south. Each one of these will probably make his own wine; many of them will sell it under their own label; some will sell it in bulk for bottling under the label of a merchant, who might even blend together the wines of two or more growers, before bottling it under his name. Thus, from one vineyard, of just over 50 hectares, there will be, in any one year, a minimum of 80 different wines on sale, of varying styles and qualities. Compare this situation with, shall we say, Château Latour at Pauillac, which has approximately 60 hectares of vines. It is true to say that in most vintages two wines are made at the château, but only one of them is labelled as Château Latour. Thus in the 1982 vintage, for example, we know what we can expect from Château Latour. Whilst an individual bottle might have been kept well or badly, the original wine in the bottle is the same. With a Clos Vougeot 1982, on the other hand, it might be almost anything, from the sublime to the . . .

This multiplicity of owners in Burgundy, and fragmentation of the vineyards, has led to the important role of the *nêgociant* or merchant in the commercial life of the region. He will buy wine from a broad range of sources, blend wines of the same appellation together, if necessary, age them in his cellars, bottle them, and sell them under his own label. Whilst the figures vary from year to year, as a rule of thumb, no more than 30 per cent of Burgundy is sold under the label of the man who owns the vines that gave the wine. This proportion is increasing slowly over the years, but nevertheless it shows the important role that merchants play.

The very smallness of the production of Burgundy makes it difficult for merchants to exist by selling nothing but wines from the region. Many of them sell table wines that they blend from wines from elsewhere. There is nothing new about this. Chanson Père et Fils, for example, have records showing that such wines formed an important part of their business 200 years or more ago. Many companies will also offer a range of wines from the Rhône Valley, and now even from the south of France. In order to satisfy the demand for fine wines made from the Chardonnay grape, for example, the highly respectable house of Louis Latour has planted vineyards in the Ardèche. Wines from outside Burgundy have for long played an important role in the turnover of the merchants of Beaune and Nuits Saint Georges. As they expand, and the production of Burgundy expands more slowly, this role must become ever more important. To my knowledge, only one of the major merchants of Burgundy, Joseph Drouhin, now deals solely in the wines of the region. The full implications of this situation I shall discuss in more depth shortly.

There is one more aspect of the fragmentation in Burgundy that is of importance, and one created by the growers in the hope that it might increase their income. This is the question of the *appellations contrôlées*, the official names that are strictly controlled by the government. We have already seen that the area under vines in Bordeaux is approximately two and a half times as important as in Burgundy. For the 98,000 hectares of Bordeaux, there are 47 different *appellations contrôlées*; for the 38,000 hectares of Burgundy, there are no less than 104 different controlled names. In fact, to tell the truth, that latter figure is but a fraction of the reality, for in Burgundy, any vineyard that is of *premier cru* status has its own individual AC status. Thus, on a bottle of Burgundy, the label might read Beaune Grèves, with on the next line, appellation Beaune Grèves contrôlée. As explained in the Bordeaux chapter, no vineyard there has its own 'official' status.

To put this more graphically, let us compare once again the villages of Pauillac and Gevrey-Chambertin. Pauillac, though it has twice as large an area under vines as Burgundy, has only one appellation that is exclusive to it, that of the village name itself, Pauillac. Gevrey-Chambertin, on the other hand, has, at a conservative estimate, no less than 36. These are made up of the village name, 27 *premier crus* and eight *grands crus*. The figure could be increased easily, and legitimately, by including the global name, Gevrey-Chambertin Premier Cru, and the host of permitted alternative names for individual vineyards.

With the small scale and the fragmentation of the vineyard scene in Burgundy it is easy to see that controls must be difficult to apply, more particularly since this branch of the civil service is chronically understaffed.

The third problem, that of the climate, is one that is largely beyond the control of the growers. It is true that steps can be taken to try and turn damage aside. For years there were planes on standby duty during the potential season for damage from hailstorms, which could take off when needed to seed the clouds with chemicals so that what fell was rain and not hail. It is always difficult to quantify the efficacy of such a service. If hail does not fall, is it because of the defensive measures taken, or would it not have fallen in any case? Given the obduracy of many of the growers, who preferred to rely on the power of prayer and their insurance policies to protect them, and therefore refused to contribute to the communal charge for the service, it is perhaps unsurprising that it no longer exists. There are sprays, too, which minimise the effect of rot upon the grapes. This probably means that totally bad vintages are now a thing of the past. However, it does not mean that there are any more great vintages over a given period.

At the level of the grower, there is a tendency, in some cases, to adopt a cavalier attitude towards wine-making. Some, and fortunately the proportion is getting less, rely on making 'paper'; they are not worried about the quality of their wine. Because they own so many hectares of certain vineyards, they have a right to produce so many hectolitres of wine under the names of those vineyards. If the names are fashionable ones, the documents that must accompany the wine throughout its life can be worth a lot of money, no matter what the quality of the wine. There are incentives, therefore, to try to produce the maximum amount permitted by the law. As far as the legislation is concerned, great red Burgundies must be made from the Pinot Noir grape. Sadly, within that name there is encompassed the broad family of vines producing higher, or lower, quantity and quality. Take the Pinot droit, for example. There is no doubt that the wine it gives is of inferior quality, though the yield is high. It is permitted, and is therefore grown by many *vignerons* who never sell the wine under their own label, but rather sell it in bulk to the merchants. As Serena Sutcliffe has said: 'Growers should be persuaded to adopt the most successful quality clones, even if they have to renounce the highest-yielding examples.'

The question of using the right clones of vines has an interesting parallel in South Africa. As the quarantine period for new vine-stock introduced into the country is so long, some growers had become impatient and imported some Chardonnay cuttings on their own account. These were planted and in due course South African Chardonnay has appeared on the market.

One of the first of the wineries to do this was the Dewetshof Estate at Robertson. As John Platter has written in his *Book of South African Wines*, about their 1980 vintage: 'An exciting new wine, the first Chardonnay made on this estate, from a grape that needs careful handling and has been avoided by many other vintners.'

Even though Danie de Wet's cuttings came from one of the best white wine domains in Burgundy, it is not surprising that many other vintners had avoided them, for, when leaf-analysis was carried out by the authorities, the vine concerned turned out not to be that Chardonnay, but rather the inferior Pinot Auxerrois.

Perhaps this is the time to explain the declassification system in Burgundy, that has been at the root of many of the scandals, not only in France, but also in the United States and Britain. Up to and including the 1973 vintage, there was no restriction as to how much wine a grower could produce from each hectare of vines in Burgundy. What there were, were restrictions on what he could call it. For example, to return to the village of Gevrey-Chambertin once more, if he owned a hectare of vines in the *grand cru* vineyard Chambertin, the first 30 hectolitres he made, he could call Chambertin, the next five hectolitres Gevrey-Chambertin, or Gevrey-Chambertin

Premier Cru, the next 15 hectolitres Bourgogne, and anything over that *vin rouge*.

Not unnaturally, this gave considerable incentive to the grower to make as much wine as possible, for whilst he could only officially sell a certain proportion of his crop as Chambertin, the rest he could sell at good prices to such markets as Britain, which did not yet fully accept the implications of *appellation contrôlée*, or else, with a bit of a nudge and a wink to private customers, who would realise that the wine might be every bit as good as the wine from the same grower sold with the famous name, and high price, of Chambertin.

From the 1974 vintage, the situation has changed. A grower is permitted only to make such a quantity as is permitted for the appellation. Thus, if the same grower chooses to make Chambertin, he is only permitted to make 30 hectolitres of wine from his hectare of vines, with the proviso that if he makes up to 20 per cent more, the appellation will be granted if the wine passes both analytical and organoleptic tests. He might however choose to make rather more wine and give it a lesser name, be it Gevrey-Chambertin or Bourgogne. At the same time it was decided that the maximum production figures would now vary from vintage to vintage, and even from village to village, according to how the local growing conditions had been during the year. Also, and this does not yet appear to have come fully into effect, all wines would have to be tasted by independent experts before they could be granted the names that they claimed. Certainly this new system does encourage the production of quality wines by restricting the yields, but it is still open to abuse. If the grower makes over the allocation, he can still sell it clandestinely to private customers. They are thrilled to buy it, particularly if they think that they have a bargain. Can you not envisage the scene around many Parisian dinner tables? 'I have a friend who is a small grower in Burgundy and, as a special favour, he lets me have some of his top quality wine at a lower price than normal. Of course the bottle does not have a label on it, but that is just because of the stupidity of the French wine laws.' If the grower wants to cover himself slightly, all he has to do is to buy some *vin ordinaire*, just before the vintage, to slake the thirsts of his grape pickers. For the man who wants to deceive the possibilities seem almost infinite.

There is one other aspect of the grower's trade which has often surprised me. Given the fact that he might be making small quantities of a range of wines, he regularly appears to distinguish between them only as far as the paperwork is concerned. On many occasions in Beaune I have seen brokers arrive in the merchant's offices with small samples of wines from a grower. On the label it tells you what the wine is, or is meant to be. Frequently it will say, 'So many hogsheads of Pommard and so many hogsheads of Volnay', or even, 'So many hogsheads of Pommard vintage A, so many hogsheads of Pommard vintage B and so many hogsheads of Pommard vintage C.'

I always have grave doubts about anyone who can give a detailed judgement on a wine of Burgundy when he tastes it blind. The nuances between neighbouring villages is small and these are often obliterated when the grower may own vineyards in both villages. Then it is more likely that it is his individual style of wine-making that will impose, rather than the village or particular vineyard. My scepticism is increased when one comes across samples from the growers, like those I have just mentioned. They have the paperwork that shows that in their cellars they are supposed to have so many casks of wine A and so many casks of wine B. It is not always important that the wine should actually be what it is offering itself as; it just must match up with the official records.

The difficulties involved in the differentiating between a range of Burgundies are unofficially recognised by those tasting panels which look at samples of all wines that are shipped to a number of foreign markets. The panels are made up of professionals who know their Burgundies, but on the number of occasions on which I sat on the panel, a wine was never rejected because it was not typical of what it claimed to be. Wines were turned down because they were bad wines, but they would have been bad wines whether they had come from Bordeaux, the Barossa Valley or Burgundy. On occasion, polite messages would be sent to the supplier suggesting that his wine lacked typicity and that he should do better in the future.

As the writer Pierre-Marie Doutrelant so aptly says, in his book *Les Bons Vins et Les Autres*: 'In the Burgundian economy, it's the grower who wears the trousers. The merchant follows quietly behind.' Like most good marriages, however, both partners have need of each other. If every vintage produced excellent wine, the grower would bottle all his production and sell it under his own label. Every vintage is not excellent, and in the less good years the grower might find that the merchant is the only customer willing to buy from him. This does not mean that merchants only buy off-vintages. Many have built up the tradition of buying from the same grower year after year. Sadly, some others, as we shall see, care little for the wine that they buy, but are more interested in the paperwork that accompanies it.

The merchant has an important role for the many wines that are not of the highest quality. Monsieur Doutrelant illustrates this with a quotation from a major broker, whom he calls M., 'Forty per cent of the wines of Burgundy are of high enough quality to be sold as they are. Forty per cent need to be slightly "improved". The remaining twenty per cent are so bad that they have to be replaced by wines from other regions.' It is within these various percentages that the merchants in Burgundy seek to make a living.

Over the years it has become fashionable for the merchants of Burgundy to be vilified as being fraudulent rogues. There is nothing new about this. Here is a quotation from a Monsieur Lasseure père, a Burgundian who wrote with feeling on the matter more than 130 years ago: 'One abuse that is essential to mention is that which results from the use of alcohol, and wines from the Midi, or lesser wines from the Côtes du Rhône, wines which are heavy, dull and false, wines that gourmets and true connoisseurs should totally condemn. Thus is prepared, by a diabolical recipe, black, thick, syrupy concoctions with which they pretend to *enrich* the wines of the Côte d'Or by giving to a Savigny, a Beaune, a Volnay or a second class Pommard the look of a Chambertin. At first taste, these unworthy wines can deceive an ignorant palate; but it is easy to recognise them by comparing them with wines of pure origin and authentic quality.'

'The lesser wines of the Côtes du Rhône and certain wines from the Midi have little true nose, but they are *flavoured* and flatter the nose when they are poured into a glass. Boosted by alcohol, naturally they will give body to a would be Burgundy, but they emasculate it with a frightening rapidity. As they age, the wines so prepared become totally false; they take on an unpleasant taste, a sickliness that a man who is used to natural wines just cannot take. What does he do? He puts down his glass and says, "I just can't drink Burgundy any more." It is in such a way that a product is killed.'

At about the same time Auguste Luchet tells a story of how at the end of a magnificent meal, when fine wines were loosening tongues, a wealthy Burgundian merchant was asked how he had made his considerable fortune. 'Quite simply', he candidly replied. 'By always selling the finest names without ever having grown any or bought any.'

More recently, it is perhaps Alexis Lichine who has led the attack on the merchants of Burgundy. In his *Wines of France*, it is a recurring theme for him: 'All this fraud got started in a big way shortly after the Revolution, in 1790, when the vineyards passed into the hands of the individuals. Always handicapped by lack of an outlet to the sea, man began to make a business of the dangerous overland hauling. With more stable times, these wine-shippers began to make Burgundy known, and when Napoleon praised the wines, shippers could no longer meet the demand.'

'Burgundy has never been plentiful, the great wines coming from an area of scarcely 12,000 acres, and the shippers felt the need of blending in order to make the greatness go further. This was profitable, for Burgundy had become a fabled name. It was so rare that few people have ever tasted the real thing, and imitations were accepted as genuine. To a dangerous degree the same condition persists today. Fraud by shippers was helped by the confusion of wine names that exists in Burgundy.'

If you want a genuine wine, according to Lichine, it is essential to insist on one that is bottled by the grower. As he says: 'The man who owns the vineyard bottles his own wine, putting the name of the vineyard and his own name on the bottle as a guarantee of an honest wine.'

Whilst there is much truth in what Lichine writes, the fact that a label on a bottle says 'Estate Bottled' or 'Mise du Domaine' is no guarentee of authenticity. I have already shown that there is potential for fraud at the vineyard level. Naturally, if it is practised there it will tend to be on a smaller scale than if it is practised by the merchant, but for him, too, his label is his reputation. If he believes in maintaining a quality image for himself, there is no reason why he should sell false wine under his own colours. Lichine says: 'Because estate-bottled wines are produced in small quantities, by growers whose holdings are usually small, frauds may be checked easily. Where a large shipper may be able to afford fines, a small grower cannot. What is more, the grower feels that his signature is that of an artist. Proud of his name and wines, he has little incentive to discredit either.'

All this is arguing from one side. I have no wish to defend the merchant or attack the grower, but what is true for one is also true fr the other. The small fraud by the grower would presumably be punished by smaller fines than the large fraud by the merchant. Pride is not just the prerogative of one branch of the trade in Burgundy. There is one other aspect that must be considered, if one is to accept as true the earlier quotation from the broker, and in the trade of Burgundy there is probably no one from whom one is likely to receive an unprejudiced opinion; 40 per cent of the wine made needs some *polishing* before being sold. There is no doubt that the merchant with his laboratory, his range of modern equipment and extensive facilities, is generally in a better position to carry out this *treatment* than the grower. Is it better to have a totally natural and honest wine which does not taste so good, or an *arranged* one that tastes perfect? Somehow, I do not feel that there is a clearcut answer to that question.

Sadly there is a deeper problem about the points that Mr Lichine makes. At the same time that he was writing his book, he was establishing his wine company in the United States. For this company, its speciality, as far as the wines of Burgundy were concerned, was wines from, and bottled by, a small number of growers. This policy may have been decided upon because of the points that Mr Lichine has already made; however, one cannot help thinking that there are very good commercial reasons for his having adopted the one-sided policy in the grower/merchant divide in his book!

Pierre-Marie Doutrelant has tried to separate the merchants of Burgundy into three groups: *les traditionalistes* or traditionalists, *les gros faiseurs* or the wine factories and *les bricoleurs* or small-timers. To these I would add a fourth, indeed Monsieur Doutrelant does mention them elsewhere in his book as 'les gros fraudeurs du commerce', the big fraudsters of the trade, and he even identifies three of them by initials as far as the wines of Burgundy and the Rhône valley are concerned as C., R. and B.V. These initials are recognisable to the authorities and the trade, but the companies have calmly continued on their way over the years with the minimum of disturbance. What part do these companies play in the structure of the trade in Burgundy? They are capable of finding almost any wine that the customer might want to buy at the price that he wants to pay. For the most part, they do not deal in bottled wines but rather in bulk, supplying other merchants. The wines that they supply, and they always seem to have the necessary paperwork, can be useful in bringing down the overall cost of a product.

I can only claim limited experience of dealing with such companies, but I can remember, many years ago, wanting to purchase a large quantity of Beaujolais. I visited a certain company in that region who asked me the price I wanted to pay, and made it quite clear that they could supply any quantity, from a single cask to rail tankers, of any wine from the region at any price, with or without the governmental paperwork, the *acquit vert*. (It must be pointed out that this was before *appellation contrôlée* meant anything in Britain.) Quite amusingly, not very long ago, I was invited to visit the company again, because they could not understand why I regularly wrote unfavourably about their wines. I supposed that I must be prejudiced against them ever since that first visit.

The consumer is much more likely to have access to the wines from the 'wine factories', even though they number only a few. Generally speaking they have a broad range of names under which they trade, so that any potential customer can be satisfied. They are particularly interested in buying from the growers the 'paper'. That is to say they will buy wine cheaply, because of the documents that go with it. They will then 'arrange' the wine to a greater or lesser extent. In this they were tacitly helped by the authorities, who for long accepted the Tunnel System. That is to say, as long as the same quantities of each wine came out of a cellar as went into it, there was no control as to what happened in the cellar itself.

The medicinal role of the Burgundian merchant could be very profitable. In his pharmacy he would have a range of wines from the Rhône Valley and the Midi. Algeria, too, until it gained independence, might well have been represented. With the coming of the Common Market, there might be a phial or two of Italian wine. Genuine wines, which might be lacking in colour, body or richness, would be treated to meet the customers' requirements. To compensate in the books, there is no doubt that much Burgundy, that arrived in the cellars with its paper pedigree, would be blended off and sold as up-market *vin de table*. As has already been said, many companies have a long tradition of selling branded table wines which, because of the name of the producer on the label, have been able to command high prices. The economics of the operation are not hard to understand. For the wine sold under the Burgundian name, the raw materials are cheap wines with the necessary appellation (cheap because they are of otherwise unsatisfactory quality) and full-bodied, rich wines, bought at minimal cost from elsewhere. Thus a bottle which might cost ten francs to produce, can be sold for 35. The profit might be less on the table wine, but that is sold at a much higher price than it would command if it were blended, from the same ingredients, by a merchant with an address in the Midi. Naturally, the table wines are sold in Burgundy bottles and often with heavy lead capsules and parchment labels. In this field, perceived value is the name of the game. Because of the large stocks that they hold, and the flexibility with which they can be used, such merchants can offer, say, a Côte de Beaune Villages, in a variety of styles and at a variety of prices.

Of the traditional companies, there are perhaps about enough to be counted on the fingers of two hands. Whilst they do their utmost to maintain their patrician, or perhaps more correctly bourgeois, image, they are now learning to adapt themselves to the realities of the current wine scene. Nowadays, their price-lists offer a range of appellations that they might have shunned in the past. They are beginning to realise that the customer now has to look beyond the single vineyard wines of the Côte d'Or. Most of these traditional houses are fortunate to have behind them substantial vineyard holdings. In times of increasing demand and rapidly rising prices the vineyard owners held most of the aces. A merchant with nothing to sell has no future. In addition, as it is the role of the merchant to age the wine, many were caught buying at the top of the market, only to find their stock being devalued at the same rate as the dollar. Vines, then, have proved the salvation of many of the more traditional houses.

Sometimes, the relationship between the supplier in Burgundy and the importer abroad can become unbalanced with the latter calling the tune. If the supplier is not careful, it can be his reputation that will suffer. Here is one example, from my own experience, of just this very thing happening to perhaps the most traditional of all the companies in Beaune. For a long time this company had had a substantial market for its wines in Britain, where their importer was the subsidiary of a major brewery group. When the time came for Britain to accept *appellation contrôlée*, as part of the package of coming into the Common Market, a derogation period was given for the selling off of any 'old-style' wines that had been imported before that date. The importer decided that he would import several road-tankers full of wines with the simple appellation Bourgogne, for subsequent labelling under such names as Beaune, Volnay and Nuits Saint Georges. This shipment was to take place in the final week before the introduction of the new legislation.

The quantities ordered were enormous and the company in Beaune found itself unable to cope with the blending of such a variety of wines all under the appellation Bourgogne. Staff had to be rushed out from England to see that they had all the correct recipes. Fortunately for the customer, the wine was of the 1972 vintage, wine that lasted well, for sales came nowhere up to expectation and I think that I am right in saying that the last of the wine was picked up by Marks and Spencer at a bargain price. For them, the wine was relabelled and sold as all that it was entitled to be called, Bourgogne Rouge 1972.

On a slightly lighter note, another patriarchal Beaune company was represented in the United States by a company well-experienced in the wine-trade, but one that never wanted to listen to the other side of a discussion. When, in the early 1970s, the price of Pouilly-Fuissé began to rise astronomically, because of demand from the American market, this importer instructed his Burgundian suppliers to start shipping some Pouilly-Fumé in the incorrect belief that the American consumer would be too confused to notice the difference between the names of the wines, or the fact that the styles of the wines would be dissimilar. I am glad to say that this inspired marketing decision also met with the fate that it deserved—almost total failure.

I see that the latest figure quoted gives the total number of merchants in Burgundy as being 156. Of these, probably two-thirds could be described as being small-timers. Many of them will sell only small quantities direct to private individuals, possibly through the regional commercial fairs that remain so popular in France. Some of them just cater for the tourists that flood through Burgundy in ever-increasing numbers. They find an old cellar in Beaune or Nuits Saint Georges, smarten it up, put some casks on scantlings, spray cobwebs in the corners and welcome any flies that might arrive. Some may be for the most part growers who have broadened their range by buying some wines from their neighbours. Some might just operate on one market, or in one country. Their range is infinite.

Before leaving the world of the merchants, I would like to tell two stories of fraud; the first one is somewhat against myself. A few years ago, I was invited to be a member of a panel for a blind tasting of a range of wines with the simple appellation Bourgogne for *Decanter* magazine. We all decided that by far the best wine was the oldest one in the range, which coincidentally was by far the most expensive. I think that it was of the 1973 vintage and we subsequently discovered that it came from a small company in Beaune, whose speciality was to take the wines from their own vineyards and declassify them for sale simply as Bourgogne, as their Réserve or Première wine. As their domain included a good holding in Chassagne-Montrachet, of both red and white wines, some Beaunes of repute, and a small portion of Chambertin, it was logical that their wine should be good—and expensive. We all congratulated ourselves on recognising class.

Some months later, when the results of the tasting were released, I received a telephone call from an eminent wine-merchant. 'Christopher,' he said, 'I though I must ring you. I have always had doubts about you panels of experts. Now, I know I am right. That wine that you all placed first in the Burgundy tasting; I was there when it was blended. The owner of the company was very proud to show me his formula for the British market: a good basis of Burgundy, a healthy measure of Côte de Rhône and a more than healthy dollop of brandy.' So much for the reputation that this company had built up.

My other story, too, is concerned with reputations. Another company, founded more than a century ago in Beaune, had built up a solid reputation for its wines in Britain, before the introduction of *appellation contrôlée* into the country. His story was based on the premise that nearly all the vineyards in Burgundy produced more wine than they were entitled to sell under their own name. However, there was nothing to prevent this wine being sold to Britain as Bourgogne and the customer there labelling it as Nuits Saint Georges, Chambertin, Montrachet, or whatever. Obviously, such a system leaves great potential for exploitation by fraudulent merchants in Britain, but there is no doubt that the wines that this supplier was providing were excellent.

After the introduction of *appellation contrôlée* it was evident that the system could not continue, as declassified wines no longer existed in the same way that they had in the past. Rather naïvely, their importer thought that he could circumvent the problem, by suggesting obliquely that such wines could be found. He brought out a price-list with down the left side of the page a series of the great names of Burgundy, with a thin red line through each. On the other side of the page was a list of wines with folkloric names. Thus, one side might be le Montrachet, on the other Bourgogne Cuvée de Montferrand. The only one that I can actually remember is Nuits Saint Georges on one side and Bourgogne Cuvée du Dragon on the other. I must admit that it took me some time to work out the connection. Given the new wine legislation, it was not surprising that the attention of the authorities was attracted to this attempt at persuading the customers that nothing had changed. The matter was taken up by the French and the merchant was discovered to have a dual stock-keeping system, one set for the officials and the others for his business. I do not yet know whether he had been misleading his customers before the introduction of *appellation contrôlée*, or whether he just got overtaken by events. Having created a clientele for himself in Britain, he was unhappy to lose it overnight, because he could no longer supply them legally. (If this was the case, he would not be the only one. The agent for a merchant in Savigny, known for its 'traditional' way of making wine(?), was heard to say that the introduction of *appellation contrôlée* laws into Britain would mean the end of his wines on the market.)

If fraud is carried on by the growers and the merchants, it can also be carried on by the importers. It is true to say that this is less likely on those markets which import their wines in bottle, such as the United States, than those where there is still a tradition of local bottling, such as Germany, Holland and, now to a lesser extent, Britain. This is not to say that the American record is clean. Some time ago a San Francisco importer was prosecuted for relabelling Gevrey-Chambertin as Pommard. Many people would consider that this is passing-off a greater wine as a lesser one, but it must have come about because of the average American wine-consumer's lack of knowledge of Burgundy and its wines. The three names that seem to have always come to mind first are Chablis, Pommard and Pouilly-Fuissé. Thus there have been recurrent periods when demand from the United States has led to rapidly increasing prices and added incentive for the *fraudeur*. In the late 1960s, for example, one French company, that aimed its sales efforts specifically at the American market, was in the habit of stretching its Chablis with white wine from the Graves region of Bordeaux.

Another fraudulent parcel of wine from Burgundy reached Miami, under the labels of Chassagne-Montrachet and Pouilly-Fuissé, by way of Holland and Bootle in Merseyside. Even though some of the wine had appeared on the British market, claiming to have been bottled in Burgundy, and though there was a simple mistake on the label where a word was written in Dutch rather than English, what seems to have excited the attention of the local Trading Standards Officer was that what purported to be an official Dutch stamp turned out to be nothing other than the impression of a Dutch coin. *Caveat emptor*—yet in this case the American purchaser of the wine was the subsidiary of a major international spirit company. One would have thought that they would be capable of spotting such a simple fraud—or perhaps they just needed wines with those labels at those prices.

Sadly, in Britain, there has been a long tradition of producing bogus Burgundies. In 1971, whilst resting between engagements, I went to a local wine merchant to look for some work during the Christmas period. I was given a job on the bottling line, and I think I learned more in the two months that I worked for the company than I have during the rest of my 30 years in the wine-trade. There was scarcely a wine that was bottled by the company that legally could bear the label it carried. As far as Burgundy was concerned, and the company carried a full range of generic, village and single vineyard wines, the total dependence was on four vats. These were two of white wine and two of red wine imported from companies in Burgundy. All four wines were *vins de table*, rather than Burgundies. To create the wines on the list, the proportions were varied between the two ingredients for either red or white wine.

Perhaps the most notorious example of this style of Burgundy 'construction' was what came to be called Château Ipswich. This was an establishment created on the banks of the river Orwell at Ipswich in Suffolk by the French wine giant, the Société de Vins de France. For many years this company had dominated the French market for table wines with such brands as Kiravi, Valpierre and Vieux Papes. The first two were traditionally sold in the 'six-star' litre bottle, with the plastic plug and the foil, rip-off top, the last came in a classic Burgundy bottle with a cork and capsule.

The original object of the operation in Ipswich was to import the wine from France by coaster, pump it into vats in the warehouse and then bottle it under the same brand names as those used in France. Commercially, this did not prove to be successful and what subsequently happened attracted the attention of Nicholas Tomalin of the *Sunday Times*, and the results of his investigations appeared in the issue of 27 November 1966.

Whilst it appeared that the English wine-merchants were not interested in selling a range of French table wines, they were more than happy to take the same wines, or mixtures of them, under a variety of their own labels. Thus what the Frenchman was happy to drink as Valpierre, the Englishman was happy to buy as Nuits Saint Georges. Sadly, for the French company, life was not quite as simple as that. They were stocking a range of eight wines; three white, three rosé and two reds. Few of their customers, however, were prepared to accept a straight wine as a straight wine. Whilst the more expensive of the two red wines in stock, originally imported to be sold as Vieux Papes, 12° vin de table, would have made an ideal Châteauneuf-du-Pape, the English customers found it rather too expensive and asked for a little of the cheaper 11.5° vin de table to be blended in with it. What was one man's Nuits Saint Georges might well be another man's Beaujolais. No wonder the French manager of the plant complained: 'You English are such individualists. Each one wants a different blend for a different wine . . . As a result I have to keep halting my bottling line, pumping wines from tank to tank . . . just to satisfy old-fashioned quirks. It was not what this operation was designed to do.'

Nicholas Tomalin had no difficulty in finding quotable sources from both sides of the Channel in support of what was an open breach of the law. An anonymous man, described as 'one of the most famous Burgundy shippers', admitted to making his Beaune with up to a third of Côtes du Rhône in it (at least that would be a more expensive recipe than the one from Ipswich). 'You English like it that way, so I make it that way for you.' The corollary was expressed by one of his competitors: 'Take a Nuits Saint Georges. The Englishman has come to expect a round, full-bodied wine bottled under this name. A real Nuits Saint Georges, hard and dry, would not be to his liking at all.'

Whilst these French expressions may well seem cynical, but commercial, there is no excuse for the opinion expressed by an official spokesman for the British wine-trade, the secretary of the national Wine and Spirit Trade Association. For him, and I hope that it did not truly represent the feelings of the bulk of his members, 'To the Trade there are very clear advantages in having a standard product and the general public would be appallingly confused if they had to cope with a myriad of tiny commune names.' Then, perhaps going off on some thought tangent of his own, he added, 'Please remember that the trade is extraordinarily honest. It takes only the smallest of profit margins.'

It may well be that there is still a substantial number of people, in the trade in Britain, who think that *appellation contrôlée* is a confection of the devil. There are still those who are happy to exploit the traditional idea of what is wanted by the consumer in Britain as far as a Burgundy is concerned. The first thing would seem to be a recognisable name on the label and then, some way afterwards, a wine that is full-bodied and easy to drink.

Whilst I was still working in Burgundy, one of our major English customers complained that our price for Nuits Saint Georges was unrealistic. In Britain one source was offering the wine at £20-£30 a case less than he could afford to, even taking a very small margin. The next time I saw him, he opened a bottle of the wine in question and gave me a glass to taste. 'Whatever it is,' I said, 'it certainly is not Nuits Saint Georges.' Some eighteen months later a merchant, based in Ealing, was prosecuted for defrauding another merchant, this time in the West End of London, by selling him large quantities of Bourgogne rouge as Nuits Saint Georges. This was the wine which I had been shown the year before. Apparently it had been sold in good faith by a merchant in Nuits Saint Georges, as plain red Burgundy. The merchant in Ealing had then relabelled it as Nuits Saint Georges and had passed it on to the West End distributor, making a tidy profit on the way.

On the basis of the opinion that I had given some months before, I was called as a witness for the defence. The idea being that if the wine was patently not Nuits Saint Georges, no reputable wine merchant would have bought it thinking it to be so, particularly at that price. Since the purchasing company had two Masters of Wine on their board, they should have been able to recognise a Nuits Saint Georges when they saw one. If they had good reason to believe that it was not Nuits Saint Georges, but were attracted by the price, it clearly was not a case of fraud—whatever else it might have been. This rather bizarre logic appeared to appeal to the court, but it lost its full relevance, and the case of the prosecution was substantially weakened, when it was alleged in evidence, that one of the directors of the purchasing company had received a sweetener from the seller of so many pounds for every case of the wine that he bought.

One would like to think that the vendor in this case might consider himself rather lucky to have been found innocent—of fraud—and that he then settled down to an honest life in the wine trade. However, it was not very long before he was up before the court on another charge. On this occasion he had imported a small quantity of genuine Nuits Saint Georges with the necessary documents, and a vast quantity of plain French red wine, a small quantity of Chablis, with the necessary documents, and a vast quantity of plain French white wine. He then proceeded to label the ordinary red wine as Nuits Saint Georges and the ordinary white wine as Chablis. His thinking was that if he was ever challenged by the authorities, he could show them the official French documents for the genuine wine that he had imported. To add to his problems he drew the attention of the police to himself by the rather forceful way in which he demanded money from one of his customers who had been rather slow in paying. On this occasion he was found guilty of selling fraudulent wine, and subsequently has been in further trouble for trying to defraud the tax authorities; and in fact in front of me I have a current newspaper in which a judge describes him as 'a crook of some dimensions and a con-artist'.

For my final Burgundian fraud, I would like to return to Burgundy, to a story of domain-bottlings, of *vins de table* and of high prices, the story of perhaps the most audacious attempted Burgundy fraud in the United States, the story of Monsieur Bernard-Noel Grivelet. The Grivelet family had been well respected in the Chambolle-Musigny for some years, and earned the burden of the family motto 'Only perfection attracts me'. Bernard-Noel's father, Fernand Grivelet, was mayor of the village and was an ardent supporter of the Confrèrie des Chevaliers du Tastevin, when it was founded shortly before the Second World War. The family had substantial vineyard holdings, but much of these were sold as a result of financial problems during the 1950s. By 1979, Bernard-Noel Grivelet was in his sixties and living in some affluence at one of the two châteaux in Chambolle. He had married four times, his last wife being Lebanese.

In 1979, the demand for fine Burgundy was increasing rapidly on the other side of the Atlantic and Monsieur Grivelet took a series of full-page advertisements offering for sale a restricted number of bottles of high-class Burgundy from his own vineyards in Chambolle-Musigny and from Morey-Saint Denis and such prestigious names as Chambertin and Bonnes-Mares. The bottles were individually numbered and there were also offered a substantial number of jeroboams and magnums. In all, something over 5,000 cases of wine were shipped to the United States as a result of this campaign and more than three-quarters of the total had either been consumed or otherwise disappeared by the time the authorities discovered what was happening.

What was happening was that, in his capacity as a merchant, Monsieur Grivelet had brought into his cellars substantial quantities of non-appellation wine, and it was as such that he shipped the wine to the United States. Thus, as far as the French government was concerned, the jeroboam of Chambertin that the wealthy wine-buff in Mount Kisko might have purchased, had left France as a rather over-size bottle of *vin rouge*. Quite what profit Monsieur Grivelet made from this confidence trick will never be known, but the local paper, the *Bien Public*, calculated it, in a rather haphazard way as being a million francs. I, personally, would put the gross profit of the operation at a substantially higher figure than this.

When the charges were first brought, Monsieur Grivelet was not in the least abashed. In an interview that he gave to Craig Goldwyn, the wine correspondent of the *Chicago Tribune*, subsequently reported in the *Wine Spectator*, he claimed that he had been made a scapegoat by the French authorities and that what he had done was 'widespread throughout the district' and that if he was not left alone, he would 'blow the whistle on his neighbours'. What he said he had done was to use declassified wines from the sources that were mentioned on the label. This was the tradition in Burgundy and the laws were stupid because there were the same maximum figures for production, no matter what the climatic situation. Unfortunately his defence, which was fully accepted by the correspondent, was wrong in two ways; first, since the 1974 vintage, declassified wine, as he used the term, no longer existed and, also since that date, the production limits for each vintage were fixed in conjunction with the local growers. As the wines that he was claiming to sell came from the 1976 vintage, the situation was even less likely, as that was a year with a small crop and no excess production.

I was asked by an English magazine to try to contact Monsieur Grivelet for his version of the story and, to my amazement, he not only answered the phone but spoke to me, and spoke to me, and spoke to me . . . According to him it was all the fault of 'les salopards de l'administration' who were out to get him. (My French dictionary is too polite to give a translation for the word *salopard*, so it is perhaps better to leave it to the imagination of the reader as to what he might have thought.) He claimed that in 15 successive blind tastings his wines had been considered the best and that the authorities were being selective in the manner in which they applied the new wine laws. For example, part of the law stated that all wines of AC status had to be submitted for analysis and tasting before they could gain the necessary certification. According to him, the first such tasting on the Côte d'Or, took place, with his wines, on 12 June 1979. All his wines were proclaimed excellent. He also claimed that the publicity had done him an enormous amount of good, for his sales were now three times what they were before, and that he was just on the point of leaving for Brazil, where the President had invited him to advise the government on the making of quality wines!

Despite all this, in a very short time he was criminally bankrupt and his stock was purchased by a Parisian finance house for some derisory sum, rumoured to be less than nine francs a bottle. A panel of officials had to be summoned to the cellars to reclassify all the wines and it has to be said that the majority of them came out of the tasting with a clean bill of health. I have just drunk the last bottle that I purchased from that cellar. It was really most enjoyable. To what extent Bernard-Noel Grivelet was a fraud, we shall probably never know. Whatever else he might have done, he has given me many bottles of enjoyable Burgundy (?) at reasonable prices.

The answer, 'Well, everybody else was doing it, anyhow,' is by no means restricted to Frenchmen stretching the rules. One of the most successful, and best, standard red wines in Australia is the Long Flat Red from Tyrrell's Winery at Pokolbin, in the Lower Hunter Valley in New South Wales. This was labelled as being a Hunter Valley wine, a statement that has a considerable amount of cachet in Sydney, if less elsewhere.

As a brand becomes more successful, there is quite naturally more pressure on its source, or sources, of supply and this is what happened with Long Flat Red, with a television company exposing the fact that a considerable part of the blend came from elsewhere.

Murray Tyrrell has a reputation for dealing shortly with 'so-called wine experts'. As he says: 'Wine is such a serious business it is a shame that it is left to the wine critics to stuff it up.' From such a man, 'Well, everybody else was doing it, anyhow,' comes as a pallid excuse!

Monsieur Grivelet stated that what he did was just the tip of the iceberg. Is this true? Just how much fraud is there in Burgundy? Of out and out fraud, I feel that there is comparatively little; certainly no more than in any other wine region in France. Because of the fragmented nature of the wine hierarchy, there is certainly scope for manipulation and this is probably encouraged by the customer's often demanding either a style of wine that the region does not produce or a quantity of wine that it cannot produce. Certainly before the rapid expansion in the area planted under vines in the Chablis region, there was much more sold around the world under its name than it could possibly make, and this is discounting such regional aberrations as the Californian Chablis.

As for the style of the wine, Stephen Gwynn, who must have been one of the most educated men of his age, and who wrote one of the earliest books in English on Burgundy and its wines, said of Côte Rotie, Hermitage and Châteauneuf-du-Pape: 'These wines resemble Burgundy in their strength and their general character; but they have neither the exquisite richness of colour, nor of perfume, nor of bouquet that is only granted to places where the wine is not so easily grown.' Here are two of the problems of Burgundy side by side. Too many people think that they taste like wines from the Rhône, and it is, climatically, not easy to make good Burgundy.

Increased conscientiousness on the part of the growers and better treatment of the vines are helping to make poor Burgundy a thing of the past. At the level of the merchants, higher awareness of what is wanted is also raising standards. In Burgundy, though, more than in any other wine region in the world, it is not just a question of knowing which are the best vineyards, one also has to know who are the best growers and merchants.

Is calling a wine from California, Australia or New Zealand Chablis or Burgundy fraudulent? There are many who would say that it is. At best it is borrowing the clothes of another region to disguise what is lacking in your own. Fortunately, the habit appears to be becoming less prevalent. Pressures from the Common Market are one factor, realisation that for wines to be considered seriously they must develop a recognition for their own personal names is another. Burgundy has been abused enough from within for it to have no need for artificial competition from outside. As Anthony Hanson opens his book *Burgundy*, a book that gives praise where it is due but that also does not hesitate to criticise, 'For centuries Burgundy has produced some of the finest wines in the world, wines steeped in tradition and praised wherever wine is drunk.' Let us hope that that tradition can be continued.

4

All that sparkles . . .

'It is, however, necessary to impress on readers that champagne making cannot be done casually. The work is a labour of love, and this can only be achieved when one becomes dedicated to champagne making as a hobby in its own right, and not just as a means to an end.' This is not the translation of some eighteenth-century French manual for the instruction of wine-makers in Champagne, but rather an excerpt from a book entitled *Making Wines Like Those You Buy*, which first appeared in 1964 and has now apparently sold more than 350,000 copies. I first came across it some years ago in a second-hand bookshop in San Francisco and dismissed it as being a relic of the times when wine names had little or no protection. The copy that I have before me is the fourth impression of the third edition which appeared as recently as 1985. It appears that, in England at least, the amateur wine-maker can make whatever he likes and call it whatever he likes. Champagne is not the only wine to suffer; as the blurb trills 'They [the authors] tell you how to make at home wines "like those you buy", your own sherries, ports, vermouths, white, red, and rosé table wines, Sauternes, hocks, Moselles, Madeiras and champagne.' (I am intrigued by the choice of wines that earn a capital letter!) Whatever one may think about the legalities of such descriptions, there is perhaps some justice in the fact that the reader should be invited to make, at home, his own 'champagne'. It was in England that Champagne, as we know it, was first created.

Most books on Champagne will tell you that Dom Perignon, of the Abbey of Hautvillers, was responsible for the three important factors that go to make Champagne: fermentation in the bottle, the use of corks as bottle stoppers and the realisation that wines blended from the various parts of Champagne make a better end product than a single wine. The worthy monk may well have been responsible for the last of these practices, but there is little doubt that the first two adopted from the wine-trade in London, possibly in an effort to protect the reputation of the wines of Champagne from the malpractices that were common in that city.

The high reputation of the wines of Champagne is a long one. The region had the great advantage of being close to Paris and its court and access to it was easy by barges along the river Marne. For more than a century, the great medical question of the day was whether Champagne or Burgundy was the healthier wine to drink. In the end the learned doctors settled for Champagne, though the decision was hotly disputed. In 1771, there appeared *Hygieine Sive Ars Sanitatem Conservandi*, a seven volume poem in Latin about the health-giving properties of various foods and drinks. The author, Etienne-Louis Geoffroy, places Burgundy first amongst the wines, with Champagne, *vino exhilarans tenui mensas festiva*, second. This cannot have been too controversial a decision as Monsieur Vernage, the censor, says, at the beginning of the book: 'On the orders of the Chancellor, I have read an excellent poem in Latin on Hygiene, or The Art of Preserving one's Health; I found therein nothing that should prevent its being printed.'

The French wine historian, Henri Enjalbert, has written, 'the curious thing is . . . that the first sparkling Champagnes were produced in London. This is one notable success of the "English method" which about 1665–1685 was the most often practised and which was in the doubtful tradition of the "Venetian method". Champagne wine was imported into London. It arrived in cask and was bottled after certain ingredients and spices, such as cinnamon and cloves and particularly sugar, or molasses, had been added. As a result the wine from Sillery or Ay began to ferment once again and became sparkling.'

'The infatuation for these "sparkling wines" was such that they dreamed of making them in their country of origin. First it was necessary to have sound glass bottles, like the English model patented in 1662 and cork stoppers as were commonly in use at the time in London. Both these things only became common in Reims and Epernay between 1695 and 1700.'

Confirmation of how this happened in the London cellars is given in a paper presented to the Royal Society by a Doctor Merret as early as 1675, when Dom Perignon was 36 and some 40 years before his death. 'Our wine-coopers of latter times,' wrote Dr Merret, 'use vast quantities of sugar and molasses to all sorts of wines, to make them drink brisk and sparkling, and to give them spirits, as also to mend their bad tastes; all which raisins and cute and stum [boiled wine and unfermented or partly fermented grape-juice] perform.' No particular mention is made of the wines of Champagne and the information is given just before the fact that 'Countrey vintners feed their fretting wines with raw beef', which gives a vivid picture of zoo-keepers throwing chunks of meat into the cages of savage animals!

Like most fashions, the new vogue for sparkling wines split the wine-world in Champagne with the traditionalists condemning the wines soundly, whilst others were just as strong in their support. The trade in bottled wine increased to such an extent that the Mayor of Reims, in 1725, had to petition for the right to despatch wine to Normandy in wicker baskets, and then ship to foreign markets from the ports of Rouen, Caen, Dieppe and le Havre, which were given the monopoly in the trade. Apparently it was the 'head' mistress of Louis XV, Madame de Mailly, who caused sparkling Champagne to become fashionable at court.

Whilst there was controversy as to whether this new wine was acceptable or not, there was also considerable controversy as to what caused the wine to sparkle in the bottle, and it may be that, even in Champagne, early Champagnes may not have been totally natural. The first specialist book on the wines of Champagne, written by Canon Godinot, appeared in 1718, under the title of *The Manner of Cultivating Vines and Making Wines in Champagne*. The subtitle suggests that there was a feeling that there was nothing special in the wines of Champagne: *And what one can imitate in the other Provinces to make perfect wine*. Canon Godinot wrote: 'Feelings have been strongly divided on the principles of this sort of wine; some thought that it was the strength of the drugs, that one put in it, that made it foam so strongly; others have attributed the foaming of the wines to the greenness of the wines, because the majority of those that foam are extremely green; others, finally, have attributed this effect to the moon, depending on the time that the wine was put in bottles.'

Certainly the sparkle in the wine caused severe problems to those growers determined to make the new-style wine. One merchant noted that in 1746 he produced 6,000 bottles of a very sweet wine and all but 120 exploded. The following year, he made a less sweet wine and lost a third of his production; in 1748, the wine was more full-bodied and drier, the losses were only a sixth. These figures, quoted by Maumène, seem representative of what was a general problem. The solution of only using the highest quality bottles, was not totally evident. Godinot suggested that the bottles should not be filled, others that cool cellars would be necessary. Life for the Champagne-maker must have been hazardous, with bottles exploding continuously at certain times of the year.

Whilst excessive sparkle was one problem, it is also clear from a work that was published at the end of the eighteenth century, that lack of sparkle also was not unknown and that the wine-makers had to use certain products to encourage it. This is how a contemporary English translator put it: 'For about twenty Years last past, the Gust of the *French* has been determin'd for a frothy Wine, and this they used to love, as one may say, even to Distraction. They have begun a little to come off from that for the three last Years.'

'It is true, there are a great many Wine Merchants, who seeing the great fondness there is for their frothy Wines, oftentimes put in Alom, Spirit of Wine, and Pigeons Dung, and a great many other Drugs to make it froth extremely; but it is certain, by Experience, that the Wine froths when it is any time bottled from the Vintage to the Month of May: there are some who pretend, that the nearer the Vintage-time the Wine is produc'd, when it is bottled, the more it froths. Many do not agree to this Opinion; but nothing is more certain, that there is no time in which the Wine froths more, than about the End of the second Quarter of the Month of March, and this always happens towards the *Holy Week*. There does not need any Artifice at all, one may always be sure to have Wine perfectly frothy, when it is bottled from the tenth to the fourteenth of the Month of March; of this there is such reiterated Experience, that it cannot be doubted.'

The problem of Champagne, from the moment that it began to sparkle, appears to have been one of sufficient supply to meet the demand. The fact that it comes from a limited region, and that the very process of manufacture is not a cheap one, have meant that it has always been something of a luxury item, leaving room for the cheap imitator to creep in at lower prices. By the beginning of the nineteenth century, there was a considerable trade in so-called Champagne which was made from gooseberries or, occasionally, rhubarb. This fraud was helped by the fact that coming out of the Champagne was a very broad range of qualities of wine, at a very broad range of prices. This meant that there was every encouragement to buy the cheapest and then throw the wine away, or blend it off as everyday wine. The bottles, corks and labels were worth almost what had been paid for them with the wine. The bottles would then be filled with gooseberry wine and sold under such means as 'Superior Quality', or even 'Fleur de Sillery' or 'Creme de Bouzy'. For the astute trader, the licensing laws at the time gave much flexibility. The authorities only controlled wine sold in wholesale quantities of a dozen bottles or more, lesser quantities were not related to the quantity of genuine Champagne that had been imported. If you were dealing at the right level, there was the possibility of trading almost indefinitely against an initial shipment of perhaps just six cases of the lowest quality Champagne.

There was, too, a broad web of incentives for waiters to return to the merchants corks and bottles, so that they could be re-used to keep the distribution chain turning. One writer of the time calculates that it was easy to produce so-called Champagne at a price, including the cost of the initial token shipment of genuine, if poor-quality, wine for 21 shillings the dozen, to be immediately sold at a minimum price of 63 shillings a dozen. It is not difficult to see that there was considerable financial benefit in pursuing such a branch of the wine-trade.

There was then, as there is even now, a vast difference in the qualities that were available. The prices too varied considerably, particularly as the wine was generally sold at the risks of the purchaser. It was his responsibility to accept any losses that might come about from exploding bottles. Cyrus Redding gives certain examples: 'In 1818 there were effervescing wines sold (by the producer in Champagne) at from one franc twenty-five cents, to one franc fifty cents, after the first month of bottling . . . These wines were of a very inferior quality, and being sweetened and seasoned with sugar and spirit, could only answer for instant consumption . . . Some of the growers and merchants never keep any Champagne but of the best quality, and never sell under three francs, let the season be as abundant as it may. These are the best persons of whom to buy.' Speaking again of the cheaper wines: 'Those who have any regard for their organs of digestion, should avoid them as a poison, for though good Champagne is one of the wholesomest wines, the bad is more than commonly pernicious.'

Even though there appears to have been considerable production of low quality Champagne within the region itself, there soon were other areas keen to get in on the demand for Champagne. One of the most successful was the Loire Valley. Charles Tovey, writing in the 1870s, tells of seeing 'a very large number of casks of White Loire Wine at the railway station at Ay'. He had not the slightest doubt that they were there for turning into Champagne. Whilst he has much respect for the Loire wines, in their own right, he considers the practice as 'nothing less than a fraud, as the cost of Saumur wine is on an average one-half less than that of the lower qualitites of the growth of Champagne'.

Even though running his own business as a wine-merchant in Bristol, and writing, Mr Tovey fancied himself as something of a detective. For some years he had thought that the reason why some Champagnes were so cheap was because wines from elsewhere in France were being 'sparkled'. It was not until 1865, however, that he stumbled on the truth. Here is the story in his words: 'I had received several samples of Champagne from a merchant who professed to have a house at Ay. His letters were dated from that town, and the labels on the bottles and cork brands gave every appearance that all was correct. The quality of the wine was by no means inferior, and the price was considerably lower than wine of a similar quality. As I had business in Champagne in 1865 during the vintage, I went to Ay to call upon my correspondent, but I found that he had no house there, and that letters addressed to him, when received at the Post Office, were forwarded to Saumur, where he had an establishment for the manufacture of sparkling wines. As I was going South, I took Vouvray and Saumur *en route*. I found my Ay correspondent in the middle of his vintaging operations. On remonstrating with him for giving me a false address, his explanation was that if he offered his wine as any other than the growth of Champagne he should not be able to do business in England. He declared that he sent continually many hundreds of hectolitres and thousands of bottles of his wine to Epernay and Rheims, which no doubt subsequently found their way to Great Britain and other parts of the world. As I objected on principle to such a deception, I made no purchases either at Saumur or Vouvray. I made this circumstance known in a letter which appeared in the Wine Trade Review in November 1865. Subsequent exposures have occasioned the wine to be introduced under its proper name, and in the advertising portion of the Wine Trade Review there is now a list of thirteen Saumur firms, with their London agents, from whom price lists and samples can be obtained.'

Whilst Mr Tovey might have been successful in his exposure, it was not the same for everybody else. In the 1820s, a weekly magazine ran an exposure of a wine company that was offering spurious 'best Champagne'. The merchant sued for libel and won his case, gaining both damages and costs.

The question of wine coming in from outside the area was ultimately to cause the riots which rocked Champagne in 1911. Concern about this problem was not solely expressed by interfering members of the British wine-trade. In 1897, N.E. Legrand, secretary of a local trade association, published in a very limited edition a book called *Champagne*. He is quoted by John Arlott, in *Krug: House of Champagne*, 'A few manufacturers have settled in the centres of our trade who produce sparkling wine with wine inferior in both quality and price which is grown in other districts. Those engaged in this new industry have no scruples about selling those delusive "Champagne" cork-blowers under the counterfeit name of Champagne wine.'

The frightening rapidity with which the Champagne riots developed, and the results of them, have already been outlined in the opening chapter. In some ways, however, the problems of the region have changed little. Whilst sales have been in a steady upward direction, with a hiccough or two on the way, it can scarcely be claimed that efforts have been made to improve the quality. The vineyard area has continually expanded and now includes vineyards, particularly in the Aisne *département* which, at best, produce wine of no more than marginal quality. The yield per hectare has steadily increased and is now the highest in France, outside Alsace, and is disguised by being always quoted in kilos per hectare, rather than in hectolitres per hectare, as in every other wine region in France. According to the legislation it is suggested that yields should not exceed the equivalent of 50 hectolitres to the hectare. It is permitted, however, to vary this figure according to the vintage. It is true to say that yields are now more commonly in the region of 85 hectolitres to the hectare, than the 50 suggested.

Formerly, the first fermentation always used to take place in small oak casks, which gave character to the wine. To my knowledge there are now only two companies where this happens. Stainless steel is now the order of the day. Formerly, individual rotten grapes used to be taken out by hand before pressing, so that only totally healthy fruit went into the wine. Now it is doubtful whether there are even two companies where this still happens. All this is taking place at a time when, in real terms, the price of Champagne is rising. If more care were being taken, one could understand, but sadly this is not the case.

The real problem is that making Champagne is like being on a roller-coaster. As Pierre-Marie Doutrelant has said: 'When the world economy catches a chill, Champagne catches a cold. When it is going well, Champagne sales swell with it.' If international economists have little success in forecasting what will happen, why should the moguls of Champagne do any better? When business is booming, however, the Champagne houses often have difficulty in keeping up. They are tied to a region which is on the very fringes of wine production. They need excessive yields in the good years to balance out the years when the crop fails. Grapes, when sales are expanding, have to be bought, no matter what the price, no matter what the quality. In *Les Bons Vins et Les Autres*, Monsieur Doutrelant gives two telling quotations from directors of major Champagne houses about the 1972 crop. The first one said: 'We should have used no more than half of the 1972 crop, one of the most disastrous years we have ever known.' The other complemented this by saying: 'If one company refused to buy a load of rotten grapes from a grower, there would be ten others only too eager to do so.' The answer to many of these criticisms is that modern technology can eradicate many of the faults that might formerly have been apparent if inferior raw materials had been used. Whilst there may be some truth in that philosophy, it is a very dangerous one to carry to its logical conclusions.

Champagne, now, is a question of brands. Whilst it is true that there are hundreds of small companies and growers producing and selling Champagne under their own labels, the whole trade is dominated by the large companies — and these are consolidating into their own groups. *Marques* as diverse as Charles Heidsieck, Veuve Clicquot, Henriot and Canard Duchêne, all now form part of the same empire. One assumes that as one brand succeeds, another may be left dormant on a market. One must assume that a good reason for such rationalisation in the trade is that stocks can be shared. Certainly the major co-operative cellars have relied for their daily bread and butter on selling finished wine *sur latte* (bottles maturing, unlabelled, in wine-cellars) to the major houses. It is quite possible that two separate and competing brands might have exactly the same wine in the bottles. The whole question is one that the Champenois prefer not to discuss. Certainly it would appear to make commercial sense; the problem is that if it were generally known to be happening it would destroy the credibility of a brand—and somewhere I have seen a figure given that an average major Champagne brand spends up to ten per cent of its turnover on publicity and public relations. In Champagne the name of the game is IMAGE.

One of the penalties of being a luxury product is that of direct passing-off. Just as one can find bogus Rolex watches and bogus Gucci handbags, so one can find bogus bottles of Champagne. To all intents and purposes, the bottle might look like a bottle of Veuve Clicquot, but what is inside the bottle is something completely different. The reason is the particular weakness in the whole sales-pattern of Champagne. Much of it is drunk not because the person doing so enjoys it, but because of its image. Champagne is the product to drink when you have won at the races (and Dick Francis has based a novel on fraudulent Champagne offered on just such occasions); Champagne is what you order when you are entertaining a good-looking, or an ever-willing, girl in a night-club; Champagne is what you drink on the day you get married. Champagne is for one-off occasions. Most people who order Champagne at such moments little know what to expect. Even more so, it is not the time to ruin the moment by sending the bottle back. More often than not, that bottle will be as well wrapped-up as a new-born baby so the label cannot be seen. Sometimes: 'The label has come off in the ice-bucket, sir.' I am sure that more wine is passed-off as being Champagne than any other, under just such circumstances. What I am less certain is how much false Veuve Clicquot, for example, there is. Most companies seem to have a rogue's gallery of bottles labelled to look like their product and in *Impact* magazine, recently, it was stated that Veuve Clicquot, has 'found hundreds of examples of counterfeit goods around the world'. Artificial Mumm Champagne was also said to have been found in Italy. It is difficult to see how widespread this particular fraud might be.

In one way the Champagne producers like to run with the hare and hunt with the hounds. Many of them own wineries in other parts of the world which produce sparkling wines. The reasons for this policy, are, for the most part threefold. First, on the domestic French market, sales of Champagne tend to vary according to the price. Because of its commodity nature, there is a tendency for the price of Champagne to rise and fall according to its availability. When prices are high, there is a movement to the cheaper, lesser Champagnes and the bottle-fermented quality wines of France such as Crémant de Bourgogne and Crémant de la Loire. A second reason is that, in many countries where foreign currency is in short supply, the importation of Champagne is either forbidden or subject to punitive rates of duty. The third reason is that the great Champagne houses, with some justification, consider their *marques* to be quality brand names. Therefore, there is something to be said for producing the highest quality sparkling wines in other prestige wine areas.

For the first reason, there is a heavy implantation of Champagne companies in the Loire Valley, which has developed from being a supplier of source wine for Champagne during the last century, to probably having the highest French non-Champagne sparkling wine image. In addition, it has by far the highest production, outside Champagne, of bottle-fermented wines. In the year 1984, the production of Champagne was approximately 188 million bottles; that of other French sparkling wines 167 million bottles, of which 54 million bottles were produced by the *méthode champenoise*: 24 million of these bottles came from the Loire Valley. Amongst the Champagne interests there are Langlois-Château which is owned by Bollinger, Gratien & Meyer, attached to the Champagne house Alfred Gratien and Bouvet-Ladubay, which belongs to Taittinger.

Of the implantations abroad, it is Moët et Chandon which has perhaps the broadest range of interests. M. Chandon is a top-selling wine in Germany, as is M. Chandón in Argentina. They have production facilities in Portugal and Brazil, as well as the showpiece Domaine Chandon at Yountville in the Napa Valley. At present California and Australia appear to be the two places which have attracted the attention of the Champagne companies, though there are a number of less likely, on the face of it, ventures such as the establishment of a plant in Korea, under the guidance of Champagne Deutz, to make bottle-fermented wines.

One real, and very delicate problem, is that in many of these countries, the generic word for sparkling wine, however it is made, is Champán, Champaña, Champagne, or something very similar. Whilst Spain, having entered the Common Market, no longer calls its own home-produced wines Champán or Champaña, those words are still common on hoardings and, during a recent visit to Barcelona, there were a number of advertisements inviting me to visit a Xampañería, where I could taste a full range of cava wines. In a country like that, or Australia or the United States, where the word Champagne can be used for the domestic product, however it is made, it is essential that the Champagne company from France treads delicately when it describes its locally made product.

Witness just such an example of delicacy used by M. Chandón for their Argentine wines. I quote from *Los Buenos Vinos Argentinos*, by Enrique Queyrat: 'Although I dislike in every way the world *champaña*, I am going to use it when talking of M. Chandón, as the company ever respectful of the laws justly imposed by the Champagne producers, insist that one uses the word *champaña* and not *champagne*.'

Less felicitous is the association between Piper-Heidsieck of Reims and some partners in India, for the production of bottle-fermented wines in that country. Whilst I am told that the wine is excellent, I do feel that the whole approach of the company leaves much to be desired. For a start it is called Champagne India Ltd., and the label that they proposed, read:

MARQUISE DE POMPADOUR
Grand Mousseux
Qualité Supérieure

750ml   12.5% by vol.

Produit en Inde Collaboration avec
CHAMPAGNE   TECHNOLOGIE
REIMS   FRANCE

After some complaints, the label was withdrawn, but it seems strange that a company such as Piper Heidsieck could have allowed it ever to appear. Whilst it is not clear exactly how the wine is made (whether it is fermented in the bottle or in a tank) or at whom the label was aimed, it would appear to be nothing less than a crude attempt to pass itself off as a French product company from Reims. After having had to change the label, the export manager of the company is reported as having said, in a disgruntled fashion, 'We have to settle for a second-rate name for a first-class product.'

One must hope that the label was produced in ignorance. This could hardly be said of a television commercial that has appeared in the United States for a *cuve close* wine from France, called Chantaine. In it a woman, presumably discussing arrangements for her daughter's wedding reception with a banqueting manager, rejected out of hand a number of famous French champagnes, shown in the flesh, so to speak, in favour of the real thing, Chantaine. One can only be amazed that the authorities accepted it. I suppose, if one has a sense of humour and recognises the cheek for what it is, one can be amused; otherwise, it seems sad that Champagne can be abused in such a way.

America's freewheeling attitude towards the use of the world Champagne is illustrated by some random quotations from *The*

Signet Encyclopedia of Wine by E. Frank Henriques, who appears to be a priest with a detailed love of, and knowledge of, wine. Nevertheless, 'In the very strictest sense there is only one true Champagne, and it's of French extraction. It comes only from one particular delimited area of northern France. All other sparkling wines resemble —or do not resemble!—Champagne but call them by some other name . . . America is the major noncomforming nation in this regard. In the U.S. virtually any sparkling wine can be called Champagne, including red wine. Even the French seem to be getting resigned to this as a sad fact of life.' Whether the French are quite as resigned as the writer would have us think, I have my doubts; however, it is essential that in America, or Australia for that matter, the consumer is totally aware of what he is ordering or being offered. Champagne from France has to be French Champagne. If it is not that, it could be anything from something close to raspberry-ade to a truly magnificent wine. Price, and perhaps some local knowledge, will tell.

Back to France, and something that has never been explained to me. By law, there is only one rosé wine in Europe that can be made by blending red and white wines together, that is Champagne. I am not sure that the wine is any worse for it, but it is certainly a cheaper way of going about things than specifically vinifying rosé wines—as one or two Champagne houses do. It is not even as though this special absolution is given to any of the other *appellation contrôlée* sparkling wines in France. A Crémant rosé from Burgundy or the Loire would have to be made from real rosé wine. It seems a slightly strange exemption to be granted to Champagne. At least it is better than what used to happen. It appears that during the nineteenth century, the village of Fismes was renowned for the elderberries that were grown there and used for tinting Champagne to the necessary shade of pink.

Like all other regions producing quality wines, Champagne has a particular responsibility to see that the standards of its wines justify the high prices that are asked for them. There is little doubt that corners have been too often cut in the past; there has been too much reliance on the credibility of the ultimate consumer. This has not just happened in Champagne, we have seen the same in Burgundy and in Bordeaux. For the image of Champagne to be maintained, there must be substance behind it. Champagne has that little something special; as one of Shaw's characters said: 'I'm only a beer teetotaller, not a champagne teetotaller.' To make that man take to drink, Champagne must be special!

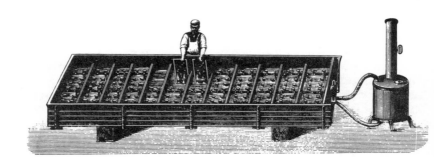

One lump or two?

Some years ago passers-by in that narrow pedestrian precinct off the rue Boissy d'Anglas, in the centre of Paris, the Cité Berryer, may have been surprised to see in the window of the wine merchants Cave de la Madelaine, bottles of Beaujolais, with two sugar-lumps attached to them. Also there was the message to the effect: 'We prefer our Beaujolais natural, but if you like them sugared, you can do it yourself.' The suggestion was that far too many of the wines of the Beaujolais were too heavy; at the time of fermentation, sugar had been added to the must to increase the alcoholic degree.

Many drinkers, and I am one of them, believe that the ideal Beaujolais is a wine that is fresh, light and fruity. For some strange reason, many of the growers and Co-operative cellars think that the wines must be meaty and warming. For me, a good Beaujolais is one that you can open a second bottle of with pleasure and anticipation; not one that leads to worry about headaches to come. A few years ago, I was a guest of honour, with John Arlott, at a luncheon in the Beaujolais and in my speech of thanks, I outlined my idea of the ideal Beaujolais and, in passing, regretted the fact that so many producers in the region relied on additional sugar in making wines that were no more attractive at the end of the operation. No sooner had I sat down at the end of the speech, when the local member of the Chambre des Députés leapt to his feet and accused me, rather viciously, of unjustly impugning the honour of his constituents.

I am pleased to say that, after the meal, a number of people came up to me and congratulated me on what I had said.

The question of chaptalisation, for that is what the addition of sugar to the must of fermenting wine is called, must be a delicate one for the people in the Beaujolais, for Fritz Hallgarten, in his book *Wine Scandal*, tells a similar story. Once again, it was the local MP who turned to the attack. He must feel that all his time is cut out defending the innocent growers of the Beaujolais from the attacks of the perfidious British.

That chaptalisation is a problem in the region, there can be little doubt. It is needed in many years, to some extent, but not every year to the extent that it is utilised. Interestingly enough, it appears that the authorities have recently introduced a maximum degree for some of the wines of the Beaujolais, presumably in a bid to maintain some typicity.

One story from the Beaujolais, from the time when I was working in Burgundy, illustrates the potential dangers for merchants over the whole question of over-chaptalisation. Some years ago, the Mâcon company of Mommessin received into its cellars at the end of the working day a delivery of Beaujolais. Very first thing, the following morning, the government inspectors arrived, analysed a sample of the wine in question and announced that it was over-chaptalised. Mommessin would be prosecuted. No one disputed the fact that they had had no time in which to add the extra sugar to the wine, or, indeed, that it would not have fermented fully if they had. They were to blame, for the wine was in their possession. Even though it was apparent that the wine had arrived in their cellar in that condition, the grower, who had made and sold the wine, was innocent. Naturally, the whole event caused quite a stir, as the merchants felt that it was just another example of their being made a scapegoat, in order to protect the grower. (It must be recognised that in France, the growers' lobby is very important; that of the merchants, irrelevant.) I am sorry that I cannot tell the outcome of this story. I imagine that in the end, the matter was quietly forgotton and never came to court. However, from that moment onwards, the growers found it much more difficult to sell their wines without giving either an analysis, or a guarantee of the legal condition of the wine.

The word chaptalisation comes from Comte Chaptal, whose *L'Art de Faire le Vin* appeared first probably in the year 1800. As well as writing about wine, he also contributed to a book on the production of butter and was the main publicist of the uses of beet-sugar. There is nothing new about the production of sugar from beet. As early as 1575, the Frenchman, Olivier de Serres, had produced a beet sugar which resembled that made from cane sugar. In 1786, the German chemist, Frederick Achard, built the first sugar-beet factory, with the support of the king of Prussia. Two small factories were also built in

France, but the sugar that they made was not of the quality of cane sugar, nor could it be made at an economical price. It was the Continental Blockade imposed by the British, during the Napoleonic Wars, which forced the hands of the French government. The British supremacy on the seas separated France from her colonies and their products, of which perhaps the most important was cane sugar. Within six years after the Revolution the price of this increased tenfold. It must also be realised that France also supplied most of continental Europe with its requirements in sugar.

After the Treaty of Lunéville, which brought peace in 1801, stocks were built up in the country, but Napoleon realised how exposed France might be in the event of a renewal of the war, which, in fact, came about in 1805. The effectiveness of the British control of the seas can be judged from the fact that in 1807, France imported 25,000 tons of cane sugar — and in the following year just 2,000 tons. Several sources of sugar were considered, and each had its supporters. In 1809, Parmentier, perhaps better known for his work in the publicising of potatoes, published *Instruction sur les Sirops et les Conserves de Raisins, destinés a remplacer le Sucre dans les Principaux Usages de l'Economie Domestique*. In this book, one of the suggested uses for grape sugars was in the fortifying and strengthening of wines.

Napoleon, nevertheless, was determined to pursue the possibilities of beet-sugar and in 1811, 45,000 hectares and a million francs were put on one side for a massive research programme. The leader of this was Benjamin Delessert and on 2 January, the Comte Chaptal took Napoleon to visit Delessert's factory at Passy. Here the Emperor was presented with the first loaves of beet-sugar and, as legend would have it, was so impressed that he took the ribbon of the Légion d'Honneur from around his own neck and put it around that of Delessert.

Delessert may have saved the day in the short term, but he was to create a problem that is with us up to this day — that of over-production. When the war ended, new uses had to be found for the excess sugar. The Comte Chaptal, who came from the South of France, perceived that much of it could be used in strengthening many of the wines of his own region and elsewhere. Whilst the Midi might have the perfect climate for the production of wine, most of its vineyards have traditionally been planted with vines which gave a high yield of wines of generally low quality and, often, low alcoholic degree. Such a variety is the Aramon, which is capable of giving a yield of 250 hectolitres or more of wine to the hectare; a wine, however, which will have as little as between 7° and 9° of alcohol. With vines like this, and the possibility of bringing up the strength, by the addition of limitless quantities of cheap, home-produced sugar, Chaptal thought that the problems of the vine-grower in his home region were at an end.

It did not take long for the idea to be extended further afield, to those fine-wine areas, which were incapable of producing good wines every year due to the fallibility of the weather. Burgundy was a prime example of this and, in France, this is the region which has come to be most closely connected with the concept of chaptalisation, and its abuse.

Whilst the introduction of beet-sugar in commercial quantities gave a spur to the idea of adding sugar to wine, it was not a new concept. Camille Rodier tells how the Cistercian monks of Clos Vougeot used to add loaves of sugar to the must, in the final years before their properties at Clos Vougeot, and elsewhere, were sequestrated at the time of the French Revolution. Certain writers claim that the first to use cane sugar for wine-making was a chemist called Marquet in 1776.

In *Le Parfait Vigneron*, which was published in Turin in 1783, the anonymous author spends some time in dealing with the question of what to do with a problem vintage, particularly one when the picking takes place in the rain. Excess water can be removed either by evaporation or by freezing; syrup, made from concentrated grape juice can be added to the must, or, when the grapes are being put in the fermenting vat, a proportion of boiling wine, one part in 20, can be added to the must.

Later, the author tells of how to make a full-bodied wine. 'Any matter which is by its nature sweet and sugary can be used. Honey is the sweetening agent that always succeeds in making the wine perfectly. It is even, notwithstanding the advantage of its low price (at least in the South of France), to be preferred to sugar for this purpose, to manna, to cassia, to mollasses etc.' (It appears that manna was a sweetening agent obtained from excisions in the bark of a certain member of the larch family and cassia a similar product from a member of the cinnamon family.)

In his book, Comte Chaptal clearly states his reason for recommending the addition of sugar to the must. This has 'the double advantage of considerably increasing the spirit of the wine and of preventing the acid degeneration to which weak thin wines are liable'. His promotion of sugar, as opposed to the grape syrup of Parmentier, won the day and was rapidly adapted as a technique, before even beet-sugar became readily available. Vizetelly in his *A History of Champagne* quotes a letter written just a year after Chaptal's book appeared. In it Nicolas Perrier, of Épernay, claims that the addition of sugar to the must has so improved the second quality wines of the village of Ay, that their price has risen in an unprecedented manner. Indeed, Chaptal is credited by some with having allowed Champagne to become the quality wine that we know today, in quantities that allow for broad distribution.

Chaptalisation was not, however, universally welcomed. A viticultural conference in Dijon in 1845 studied the whole question in depth, looking at such other sweetening agents as sugars from starch, as well as beet and cane. The general decision was unfavourable. A resolution was unanimously adopted 'that sugaring denatures wines, taking away from them that which is most precious to them; that incomparable bouquet and delicacy that is their true mark'.

Notwithstanding this criticism, the practice must have become widespread in Burgundy, for Puvis, writing just three years later says: 'Sugaring has been welcomed with enthusiasm in Burgundy; they have used it and they have abused it; it has been applied to all qualities of wine: to those of the *premiers crus* as to those of inferior quality; the trade asked for wines full of colour, soft, spirituous; sugar gave them all these qualitites, they have been lavish with it; but with it the great wines of Burgundy lost a part of their delicacy, of their inimitable bouquet, and it has happened that the chaptalised second growths have had pretensions to challenging the first growths, the third the seconds, and the ordinary wines the thirds; this has caused total confusion in the trade; some wines have mysteriously changed their names, particularly those from the lower growths, which have presented themselves as having come from a superior level; a discredit has thus come to the wines of Burgundy, which has finished by causing a great deal of harm to the first growths, not to mention the second and thirds, with a resultant considerable decrease in demand.'

'Things have happened just as they normally do in such a case; at first they began with moderate sugaring, perhaps one kilo of sugar per hectolitre, in lower quality wines; the wine was notably better and sold more easily for it was softer and had more body; then they doubled and tripled the dose; then in the bad vintages they wanted to give the same advantages to the first growths by heavily dosing them with sugar, but these doses finished by being more harmful than useful; the chemists said to the growers "Add sugar until your musts have 15 degrees, rather than ten", then we had wines where the yeasts were out of balance with the sugar and which were sold without the fermentation being able to be completed; the wines were soft, full-bodied and agreeable; but in the long-term, the residual sugar set up a further fermentation which changed the wine; then one thought of imitating something that has gone on for a long time in Sicily and Madeira; the cellars were turned into ovens and the sweet wines were subjected to a further fermentation which had the twofold advantage of ageing the wine and of turning the sugar into alcohol; but these forced wines did not always turn out right; in order to avoid problems, some casks of wine were very heavily sugared up to 20, 30 or 40 kilos per hectolitre; they were then put in the oven to make what is called an *arranged* wine, which, mixed in different proportions with the various *crus* seemed to improve them; but this mixture has not always had happy results as there has often been a fermentation that has radically altered the wine.' To sum up, Puvis feels that chaptalisation should not be forbidden as a usage, but that abuses should be stamped upon.

Interestingly enough, five years after Puvis wrote, market research was carried out amongst a number of wine-producing villages on the Côte d'Or. The growers' associations of 46 villages were approached with a series of questions, but only 25 bothered to reply within the time-limits given, though Chambolle-Musigny and Morey-Saint Denis did subsequently return their questionnaires. The 56th question that was asked was: 'Is the surgaring of wines an advantageous operation and in what circumstances? How should it be carried out?' The answers appear surprising particularly after what Puvis had written. Fourteen of the villages said that chaptalisation was not used at all by their growers and seven that they could see no use in it. On the other hand, seven said that it would be useful in cold or late vintages. The general opinion appeared to be that the wines sacrificed some of their charm if they were sugared. One specifically said that the practice had been abandoned in their village, presumably because it was found to be unsatisfactory.

Despite the general criticism of chaptalisation, there is little doubt that it continued to some considerable extent and the Burgundian oenologist Vergnette-Lamotte echoes much of what Puvis has already said in *Le Vin*, which was published in Paris in 1867. He sees that it does have advantages in certain circumstances, but he is critical of Chaptal for advocating its widespread use. 'Chaptal, who was born in the Midi, and, as such only valued wine by its alcoholic degree has considered alcohol to be the principal preserving element in wine and it is upon this basis that the sad elements of vinification that govern us today are based.'

Here lies the basis of the chaptalisation quandary. In a region where the climatic conditions are such as not to guarantee satisfactory ripeness in the grapes every year, it is useful to have the possibility of making reasonable wine, even if some of the natural characteristics might, as a result, be masked. Charles Tovey commented on this more than a century ago, when he wrote: 'On my first visit to Burgundy I became accidentally aware that cane sugar was added to the must in making Burgundy, to supply the deficiency of grape saccharine. Whilst tasting with a broker some wines belonging to a grower in his cellars in Nuits, I noticed a want of life, finesse and delicacy in all his wines; they were heavy, heady, powerful, but with no nice character. It was a mere speculative enquiry that I made when I asked if sugar had not been added when the wine was being made. Without the slightest hesitation the broker replied in the affirmative. And, further, that all the wines in that cellar were sugared . . . He informed me that wines so prepared were more readily purchased for England than the natural wines.'

The question of what the Englishman expects from a Burgundy is dealt with elsewhere in this book, but it is still largely true that there are many wine drinkers in Britain who prefer their Burgundies to have the characteristics of a chaptalised wine.

Chaptalisation is practised widely throughout the most northerly vineyards of France; Burgundy, Champagne, Alsace and the Loire. It is also permitted in climatically unfavourable years in Bordeaux. However, the abuses spoken of by Puvis are, hopefully, a thing of the past. He talks of wine regularly having its strength increased by 5°; now, as a rule of thumb, the legislation permits an increase of no more than 2° and records have to be kept of every operation of chaptalisation that takes place. Indeed a supplementary tax has to be paid on every kilo of sugar that is used for chaptalisation.

Whilst there was bitter opposition to the process from many growers during the last century, the Burgundian grower now appears to treat it as a regular part of his life. He will chaptalise, except in the very hottest years, such as 1983 (and even then many did). Perhaps Louis Chapuis, a grower in Aloxe-Corton, sums up the policy of the honest grower, when he says: 'To chaptalise is not to make a wine from beetroot juice. Any grower that is worthy of the name sugars the wine within the limits of the reasonable and knows that a Burgundy that is too high in alcohol loses its bouquet and is no longer good. The quantity of sugar that you put in the wine at the beginning of the fermentation depends on the year. In 1974 and 1976, years which were hot and dry, I scarcely chaptalised at all, because the grapes contained enough natural sugar. On the other hand, I chaptalised a little more than normal in 1975 and 1977 because the grapes contained too little sugar.'

On the other hand, there is little doubt that there is a tendency in Burgundy to resort to the sugar too regularly and in excess. Certain growers, and merchants, have created their distinct style which appeals to many consumers. It is easy to say that the legislation restricts the amount of sugar that may be used, but here there are two weaknesses. First, whilst it does restrict the amount that may legally be purchased, or used, for sugaring the must, it is only too easy to buy sugar over the year from the local supermarket to build up sufficient reserves for the vintage time. Indeed, I ask myself whether this is really necessary. I can remember a visit to a hypermarket in the Languedoc region, where chaptalisation is forbidden, at vintage time. There were great sacks of sugar on display 'for jam-making'. What sort of jam was not specified.

The other weakness in the current law is that in many regions the climatic condition is not taken into consideration. Thus, even in the finest years, the majority of growers will chaptalise — even though the wine does not need the extra boost. It is a move in the right direction that maximum degree levels are now being introduced for certain wines—le Montrachet and Beaujolais, already mentioned, are two examples.

The question does raise a great deal of heat in Burgundy. In contrast to what Louis Chapuis has said, is the view of wine-writer and wine merchant, Anthony Hanson. His book, *Burgundy*, is severely critical of many aspects of wine-making in the region. Chaptalisation is one of his particular targets. 'Heavy sugaring is a policy which has been adopted from one end of Burgundy to the other, by great estates and lowly—but particularly on the Côte de Nuits. I suppose it is the domaine-bottling grower's answer to the rich, velvety Mediterranean blends sold as Burgundy which have formed the public's palate. But do they honestly call these things fine wine? I am thinking of certain wines from the Domaine de la Romanée-Conti, of some of Armand Rousseau's 1972's, of Clair-Dau's Gevrey-Chambertin Clos Saint Jacques 1971, of Georges Roumier's Bonnes Mares 1969, and of many more. Given the example that is being set by prestigious estates, it is not surprising that the practice is so widespread.

The names that Anthony Hanson names are those of the best-known growers in Burgundy; those whose wines regularly command the highest prices. On this question, I have only discussed the matter with one of those mentioned, the Domaine de la Romanée-Conti. Regularly, excessive use of sugar is an accusation that has been levelled at them. They deny this and state categorically that the fullness of their wines is due to the fact that they pick their grapes later than the other growers, thus having more sugar in the grapes— and a higher degree of alcohol.

Also, interestingly, the vintages mentioned are amongst the finest of recent years. In 1971, for example, the vintage was over almost two weeks early because of the exceptional weather. In such a year chaptalisation should have been unnecessary.

There are other results of chaptalisation. One of them is mentioned in a speech made by a Monsieur C. Decombe, as a representative of the growers association of the Médoc, which was reported in the crusading newspaper, the *l'Avenir du Médoc*, in its issue of Sunday, 6 July 1930. The theme of what he had to say was that the Bordeaux growers were suffering a financial crisis due to the fact that 'seventeen times as much Médoc is drunk round the world, as is produced' (a recurring complaint for a number of *appellations*; just the multiple changes), and that the quality of much of the wine that was produced in the region was poor and reflected no credit on the great reputation of the name. He called upon the authorities to introduce seven measures, of which the first was 'the suppression of chaptalisation, which, under the cover of being used to improve the degree of alcohol in the must, tends rather to increase the total quantity of wine produced'.

It is interesting that this criticism is one that comes in Bordeaux, for it is one that I have never heard mentioned in Burgundy. Nevertheless, it is one that is justified, for if a grower has the right to increase the strength of a wine by chaptalisation, he must also be tempted to increase the yield by then stretching it with water. This is a problem that is more peculiar to Germany, and which will be looked at in more detail in the next chapter.

It would seem that chaptalisation is now widespread, and generally accepted, in Bordeaux. David Peppercorn, in his book on the wines of that region, states that permission has to be given every year, but that 'there is a tendency in recent years for permission to be given more frequently'. In talking to him, however, he did make one very important point that might otherwise be overlooked. Whatever one might say about the sugaring of musts, the habit has had a profound effect on the style of the wines produced. From his experience, clarets that were made at the middle of the last century probably, in a good year, weighed in at about 10.5 per cent alcohol; now they average approximately two per cent more. Some of this increase in strength is no doubt due to improved techniques in viticulture, but for the most part, it must be due to just one factor, sugar.

In passing, it might be interesting to mention my first encounter with chaptalisation, and illegal chaptalisation at that! During the 1960 vintage, I was picking grapes at Château Cantenac-Brown, a classified growth in the Médoc. In the evenings, as I was a trainee, there to be used to the full, I was expected to help in the press-house. That vintage was a particularly difficult one, for there was heavy rainfall during much of the picking and many of the resulting wines were short on both colour and alcohol. One evening, I was asked to stumble when I passed a certain problem vat and, just by chance, empty the open sack of sugar, that I happened to be carrying, into it. The reckoning was that they could always blame it on a communications problem with a simple-minded Englishman, in the event of any come-back.

Another quite amusing happening at the same time was the confusion in the mind of one of the local sugar-merchants between the two properties Châteaux Cantenac-Brown, where I was working, and neighbouring Château Brane-Cantenac. The confusion was increased by the fact that one, at the time, belonged to a Monsieur Lawton, and the other to a Monsieur Lurton. The merchant was under the impression that he was confirming the sugar requirements that year of Brane, when, in fact, he found me on the phone at Brown. Thus it is that state secrets are secrets no more!

Is chaptalisation necessary, and is it a benefit to the world of wine? It might be said against sugaring that growers managed without it for centuries and it was primarily introduced in a bid to solve the problem of a sugar surplus. On the other hand, in many fine wine-producing regions, which are at the climatic limits for the ripening of grapes, chaptalisation is now the fall-back which enables wine to be made every year. Sadly, from fall-back, it is now considered by many growers to be a necessity, and there is little doubt that the quality of much wine suffers as a result.

As David Peppercorn has written: 'There is still a feeling in some quarters that there is something faintly indecent in sugaring the must. Nothing could be further from the truth, provided that it is not overdone.' That is the point. I feel that a wine should be as natural as possible. In bad years, with some wines, it may be that nature has to be helped. A direct comparison might be made with make-up. There is nothing more beautiful than a pretty woman with a natural complexion. On some, though, a hint of make-up might improve on nature. There is little more repulsive, however, than a wizened beldam, rouged and powdered to the point of hideousness.

There is one suggestion that I might make to the growers in those parts of France where it is felt that chaptalisation is necessary. Why do they not follow the example of the Germans? (Go no further, I can hear their saying already, we can accept no wine practices from those chemists.) What I am suggesting is that for any wine above that of a village level—a château in Bordeaux, or a *premier* or *grand cru* in Burgundy, the wine must be natural; it must not be chaptalised.

To me, wine should be as close to the natural juice of the grape as possible. That sugar may be needed in certain cases, I do not dispute. Sadly, the whole process of chaptalisation is now widely abused. It is difficult for the authorities to limit it. It may still be reasonable in Bordeaux; it has got beyond that point in Burgundy. Whilst I am not for ingredient listing on wine-labels, I think that we might all be disagreeably surprised if we were to learn just how many producers add how much sugar. It might be claimed that sugar is naturally present in wine, but this is grape sugar, not beet-sugar. There are more natural ways of achieving the same effect; one was suggested by Parmentier, the addition of grape syrup. Indeed, something similar is practised in certain properties, where either concentrated must, or extra-, and possibly artificially-, ripened grapes are added to the fermenting vat. Both the practices are, however, much more expensive ways of giving extra body to a wine.

Chaptalisation is here to stay. Let us try to control it before it gets out of hand.

A spoonful of sugar helps the Liebfraumilch go down . . .

It is interesting to see how fashions in wine-drinking change over the years. During the Victorian times, German wines were appreciated, but there was a vogue for fuller-bodied, sweeter wines, and these were, for the most part, supplied by Austria and Hungary, and even Greece. James L. Denman, who was not only a wine-merchant, but also a writer on wine, offered in his list of 1865, 19 different Hungarian wines by name; his German wines, and there were 30 of them, appeared simply under descriptions like HOCK, still, and MOSELLE, sparkling. The fact is, that whilst the vineyards of Germany were capable of producing great sweet wines, they could only do this in the best vintages; for the vineyards of Germany are amongst the most northerly in the world. Naturally it is more easy to produce fuller wines in the warmer climate of middle Europe.

The wine companies of Germany have created a problem for themselves, though they are victims, to a certain extent, of German drinking habits. In Germany, more than perhaps any other country in Europe, wine is drunk outside a meal, in a purely social context. The Burgundian wine-maker makes wine to accompany the hearty food of his region. It needs to be full-bodied and with a certain amount of acidity and tannin to accompany the rich sauces and heavy meats to which he is accustomed. The German wine-grower is asked to make wines which are lower in alcohol and with some residual sugar, wines which can be drunk easily by themselves, in large quantities. With the German climate, there is no difficulty at all in making wines that are low in alcohol, for naturally they are amongst the lightest made in the world. On the other hand to achieve even this degree of alcohol, in all but the very best years, the sugar has to be fermented out totally, with the resultant wine being, too frequently, mean and acid. This is where sugar begins to play a major role.

The style of wines for which Germany has become known, light and slightly sweet, has been appreciated by many emergent countries in the world of wine-drinking such as Great Britain, the United States and Japan. Demand from these countries has increased production pressures, particularly as the demand exists almost entirely at a low price-level. For the most part, the new wine-drinker is unhappy to invest much in a bottle about which he knows little. Another side-effect of this is that there has been a concentration of the names under which German wines are sold. Until July 1971, there were more than 30,000 recognised vineyard names in Germany. Even now, there are more than 2,500. For the average foreign consumer even these present too complicated a picture and he tends to rely on a name that he recognises, which by the nature of the business must be at a lower level. For the majority a liebfraumilch suffices and this is nothing more than a blended wine, of a certain quality, from one or more of the German wine regions—Rheinhessen, Rheinpfalz, Nahe and Rheingau. To give some idea of the importance of liebfraumilch in a world-wide context, the leading brand sells over two million cases a year in more than 80 different countries. Yet less than one per cent of these sales of Blue Nun takes place in Germany itself. Similarly, the second name, Black Tower, which has annual sales of more than 1,300,000 cases, does not sell at all in the country where it is produced.

To maintain consistent quality in brands on such a scale must present great difficulties, particularly in a country where it is not always easy to produce good wine. I was once asked by a director of the company that produced Blue Nun why I did not buy it. I replied that I felt that with a product with such enormous sales, there must be an eventual lessening of quality. He replied that I would be surprised at the quality of some of the wines that went into the blend!

To many, it comes as something of a surprise to learn just how little wine Germany does produce. It is not always easy to get accurate statistics, but if one takes as a guide Hugh Johnson's *The World Atlas of Wine*, Germany is fifteenth in the world table of area of vineyards, coming lower in the league than such countries as Greece, Romania and Chile. On the other hand, it is as high as seventh in the table of total production of wine, coming immediately below the United States and above South Africa.

The most surprising figure of all is, however, reached by dividing one set of figures by the other, thus giving the average production in hectolitres per hectare of vines. It should also be borne in mind that, whilst there is no hard and fast rule, it is widely considered that low yields give better wine and that high yields give poorer wines. In this table Germany comes first, with an incredible average yield of over 129 hectolitres per hectare. Not only does Germany come first, but it leads by a distance, with the second and third countries being South Africa and Argentina respectively with 91 and 76 hectolitres.

It is true to say that these figures are not directly confirmed by other sources such as the Impact Databank, but in their recent analysis of ten leading wine-producing countries, Germany is shown as regularly having the highest yields per hectare—with the figures for the 1983 vintage, for example, being remarkably close to those quoted by Hugh Johnson.

The image of the German vineyards has, for long, been of steep riverside hills, where the vines cling precariously to life, where the farmer can only work on foot and where the yields are minuscule. Yes, there are vineyards like this, along the banks of the Rhine, the Mosel and the Nahe. Yes, the yields of these vineyards are small, yet they all go into the overall average figures. The mind must boggle at the annual production in some of the vineyards. As the French wine-growers would say of their German colleagues 'Ils font pisser leurs vignes'.

Nevertheless, all this wine is not good wine. On the contrary, much of it would be unmarketable if it were not for the use of sugar. Indeed, even with the use of sugar, there is not enough to satisfy the world-wide demand for wine that is light, white and slightly sweet. The Germans have come up with two answers, one of which is legal, but questionable, the other of which is definitely illegal.

The first reply is the creation of the EEC Table wine. This is a blended wine created by importing base wines from other countries in the Common Market, for the most part Italy, adding perhaps a little German wine and bottling it with a label with a German brand name and a Teutonic style. Only the consumer who really knows what he is looking for is capable of understanding that it is not a German wine. In fact, the outcry within the wine world was so large that legislation was introduced to try and prevent any misunderstanding. Nevertheless, one will find in just about every wine shop German bottles, in the names of German merchants, with German brand names. As I write this, I have taken some wine-lists from the shelf behind me and I find that I can have St. Jacob Haus Wein, Keller's Wein and Sonnenstübchen Tafelwein. None of these is a German wine, though all come from German merchants and all have a German name. Two of them are listed correctly as being EEC blends, the third, from a very well-known merchant, comes under the general heading of Germany, with the sub-heading Tafelwein-Weiss and a reference to page 62 on their previous list which had been sent out some six months earlier. Now this last wine might be a German table wine, but I doubt it, as there is one which is correctly described elsewhere on the list.

Of course, with so much wine coming into the country for legal 'Germanicising' it is not difficult to see that much of it might be re-baptised in the process. Indeed this would appear natural when one considers that much of the basic German wine is already of poor quality.

Here lies the other problem. With so much of the German wine being of poor quality, what can be done to make it marketable and acceptable to consumers around the world? The problem is even more serious, when one considers that this wine has to be aimed at the bottom end of the market which is open to wines from all around the world. Prices have to be competitive. There can be no doubt that this competition has led many growers to cut corners.

Sweetness is present in any ripe grape, for it is this sugar that is converted into alcohol. There are a number of ways of creating sweet wines, some of them legal and some of them not. The finest naturally sweet wines are those which come from the finest vineyards in the finest years. The vineyards might have their own particular micro-climate which enables the grapes to ripen earlier and more fully. In addition, they might be vineyards particularly susceptible to attacks from *Botrytis cinerea*, the noble rot. This attacks the skin of the grape and consumes water that is inside, leaving just the sugar. As one would expect, this means much smaller yields, but of wines with a much higher sugar content. The noble rot is particularly likely to strike in those areas where damp mists are common in the autumn; those areas are often near to bodies of water. These might be rivers, as in the case of the vineyards of Bordeaux and much of Germany, lakes, as in the Neusiedl area of Austria or even irrigation water, as in the Riverina vineyards of New South Wales. As grape yeasts can only absorb so much sugar before they die, the result is wines which might be comparatively low in actual alcohol, but which still have a great deal of potential alcohol in the residual sugar left in the wine. Such are the greatest *beerenauslese* and *trockenbeerenauslese* wines of Germany. In the latter case, the theory is that the pickers might have to go through the vineyards several times during the vintage, to pick the individual grapes that have reached a stage of shrivelled raisinity. The fact is that the status is now given to wines of an exceptionally high must weight, no matter how they were picked.

Alternative methods of making sweet wines rely on the killing of the yeasts, or at least the kidnapping of them before they have consumed all the sugar. The killing can be achieved by the addition of brandy (as it is with Port), of sulphur, as has traditionally been done for lesser wines in France, Spain and Germany, or by sterilisa-tion. The kidnapping can be done by filtering the wine before the fermentation has terminated, through ultra-fine filters. All these processes do run the risk that either the taste of the wine might be affected, or that the yeasts might not be totally removed, with the danger that fermentation might restart at some future date. Because of these dangers the most popular way nowadays is by the addition to the fully fermented wine of concentrated must, or *süssreserve* as it is known in Germany.

Interestingly, Fritz Hallgarten, in his book *Rhineland Wineland*, which was first published in 1951, suggested that this method had largely been abandoned in favour of sterilisation. Nevertheless, since then, there has been a return to the use of concentrated must. This system does, however, have a number of disadvantages. The most important of these is that by adding non-alcoholic juice to what is already a wine of low strength, even after chaptalisation, the result might have difficulty in reaching the minimum degree accepted by the Common Market as being wine, seven per cent. Indeed, whilst *süssreserve* is sweet, a great deal of it is needed to bring wine up to the degree of sweetness demanded by the consumer.

Would not the addition of liquid sugar be a good solution? Indeed it would, for it adds sweetness in a much more concentrated form, and it is much cheaper. There is, nevertheless, one major disadvantage; the practice of adding water to the wine is illegal. But there is also the added bonus, that the addition of invert sugar solution is a most effective way of de-acidifying the wine, and also of increasing the total quantity produced.

One may consider the Germans to be basically a law-abiding race, but what came to be known as the invert sugar scandal was on a monumental scale. The stakes were large for with just one kilo of invert sugar, 46 bottles of humble *tafelwein* could be converted into aristocratic, and expensive, *auslese* wine.

The situation was made much easier for the fraudsters by the federal nature of the German government. This meant that every one could rely on his friend in authority to cast a blind eye, when there were grounds for suspicion. Whilst the fraud is not an easy one to detect, there must have been widespread knowledge amongst the authorities in the various *länder*. Amongst those who were prosecuted, apparently as the result of a voluntary confession, was the President of the German Winegrowers' Association. As much as four years previously, a government wine-chemist had told her superiors that she suspected that this man's wines were fraudulent. She was warned against mentioning her findings to the prosecuting authorities and received anonymous threats upon her life.

The scale of the fraud is mindblowing. One Mosel company alone is thought to have produced more than 13 million bottles of illegally sweetened wine in a three year period. It was calculated that in the two and a half years up to October 1980, more than 4,000 tons of invert sugar were sold to wine-makers in just one region, the Mosel-

Saar-Ruwer, another thousand tons in the Rheinhessen and smaller quantities in the other wine-regions of Germany. So widely did the practice become known, that the habit is also supposed to have spread to the West, to the vineyards of Alsace and Luxembourg.

As in many other scandals, the government took the decision that in the interests of the reputation of their wine-trade, efforts should be made to keep the magnitude of the abuse under wraps. This is hardly surprising when one considers that on the evidence that was produced in court, enough sugar was used to 'convert' from the lowest quality of all to top quality wine something over 260 million bottles of wine. The real figures must have been much higher for two reasons. First of all, it is unlikely that the whole iceberg was ever revealed, we may only have seen the tip. Perhaps more important is the thought that it is most unlikely that much of the sugar was used to raise the quality of the wine more than one step. It would be rare to convert a *tafelwein* into an *auslese*. Much more frequently it would become a Kabinett; the Kabinett might become a *spätlese*, and so on. It should perhaps be mentioned that in Germany there is a distinct hierarchy, dependent on the amount of sugar in the grapes at the time of picking. First there are the basic wines, then those of Kabinett, *spätlese*, *auslese*, *beerenauslese* and *trockenbeerenauslese* quality.

In more human terms, more than 2,500 wine-growers were prosecuted, with each of them facing a potential jail sentence of three years and a fine of some £17,000. Even if the maximum penalties had been applied, given the scale of the offences, many of the growers would have still had a healthy nest-egg when they came out of prison. In the event, the majority of the prison-sentences that were imposed were suspended and maximum fines were applied in a small proportion of the offences. Perhaps the judges thought that the accused had, in fact, been helping the Common Market to solve two problems; the chronic excesses in production of both sugar and wine. In this case, much of the wine would otherwise have been unsaleable and the sugar have gone into long-term store.

The question of the excessive production of marginal wine in Germany is one that is still with us. With the perennial shortage of sun, with the possible exception of, at most, three years in ten and with the excessive yields of the majority of the vineyards, often from grape-varieties that give mediocre wine, it is not surprising that the growers are forever looking for ways to sweeten their wines artificially. It is no coincidence that a number of German wines were found with appreciable traces of diethylene-glycol in them after the Austrian wine-scandal. The importers just could not resist the possibility of 'improving' the German wines, by adding in sweet Austrian wines, that were often higher in alcohol, richer in sugar and lower in price than the German equivalents. Whilst the first defence might have been to suggest that the traces remained in the bottling equipment after the perfectly legal bottling of Austrian wines, on inspection, that line of defence relied too much on the credibility of the authorities.

It must not be thought that the sugaring of German wines is a new habit, or even that there is something new about the addition of sugar and water, as an extract from *The Times* of 15 August 1874, quoted by James Denman, shows: 'The Cologne Chamber of Commerce, in its yearly report, which has just been issued, complains of the adulteration, or rectification, as it is called, of German wines. This, it says, assumed alarming proportions last year among nearly all the vineyard proprietors of the Moselle, and among many makers of the Palatinate. Unsugared natural wines are now scarcely to be met with in the Moselle district, and the addition of sugar goes hand in hand with liberal dilutions of water, and the usual ingredient of spirits. The mixture is formed with grape husks; it is then styled wine. Last season 18,000 centners of common potato sugar were despatched from Coblentz up to Moselle, and considerable quantities were sent to the Upper Rhine; so that many cellars now contain more 1873 wine than the vineyards actually produced.'

The finest German wines are truly great. They come from the best vineyards in the best years. Most of what is made is at best un-distinguished, but nevertheless it appeals to the consumer, who has come to recognise that he can find a style of wine that he likes under names as Liebfraumilch, Niersteiner and Piesporter. This simplicity on the part of the consumer was cynically exploited by the authori-ties, when they revised the German wine-laws in 1971. At all levels, there has been an increase in the areas allowed to label their wine with the fashionable names. Take as an example the Schwarzlay. This was a specific vineyard that was shared by the Mosel villages of Zeltingen and Ürzig. Now it is a name that can be used not for wines from those two village, for Zeltingen has lost the right, but also for wines from Erden, Kinheim, Traben, Trarbach, Enkirch and a number of lesser villages, not to mention Ürzig. Similarly, for a wine to be called Bereich Bernkastel, it can come from Bernkastel, or perhaps a hundred other places on the Mittel-Mosel. Even at the very highest level, the Bernkasteler Doktor vineyard has more than doubled in size. The official reason for these changes is to simplify things for the customer.

I must confess that in matters of German wines, I, for the most part, remain confused. For a deeper look into the depths of the murkier German habits, I would commend Fritz Hallgarten's *Wine Scandal*. It seems sad that his family firm should have been sold to a company, Pieroth, whose reputation has come under attack over the years. Indeed, Fritz Hallgarten, himself, once initiated a prosecution against Pieroth for the illegal labelling of wines—and won.

If one is surprised at the extent of watering and sugaring of wine that has gone on in Germany under the eye of the authorities, one is perhaps more surprised to learn that there is one major wine-producing area where both practices are legal and, indeed, are at the base of much of the local wine-production. This is the Finger Lakes area of New York State. Here, the climate is Continental, with exceptionally cold winters and hot, humid summers. Historically, the main grape varieties that have been used are American hybrids, that give rather weak wines, high in acidity and with a pronounced flavour, that is sometimes described as being foxy. To me it is just plain unpleasant. It is once again the German problem, largely unsuitable raw materials have to be adapted so that palatable wine can be made.

Federal law, in the United States, has been rather more generous than Common Market law. Outside California, wine can be made, and given a state name, for example New York State Wine, with the addition of up to 25 per cent wine from elsewhere. On top of that blend can be added up to 35 per cent sugar and/or water. Thus, if you blend 75 gallons of New York State wine with 25 gallons of Californian wine and add to the mixture 35 gallons of water, you finish up with an end product that is only 55 per cent of what it says it is on the label. To me, this is liberality in labelling carried to excessive extremes.

The reasoning behind the apparent laxity is explained by Peter Quimme, in his book, *American Wines*. 'When looking at the wine-making processes in Eastern U.S. areas, it is important to note that what would be a process detrimental to quality in the making of *vinifera* wines would not necessarily by detrimental to quality in making *labrusca* wines. Federal laws, it is often pointed out, allow the addition of sugar and water to musts in the East in order that the very low sugar/high acid *labrusca* grapes can be made into a balanced wine. While the addition of water to any *vinifera* wines would simply be watering down the product, adding water to some *labrusca* wines undoubtedly produces a blander, but more palatable product.'

This situation has not gone unchallenged, even amongst the local growers. The leader of the opposition is Walter Taylor, whose family founded one of the largest New York State wineries, for which Walter worked for a number of years. Perhaps rather rashly, from this position, he attacked what he called the 'adulterators' in the trade. Not surprisingly, perhaps, the minutes of a board meeting, dated 22 April 1970, read: 'The board's attention was called to the recent newspaper articles, press releases and public statements in which Mr. Walter Taylor had unfairly attacked the New York State wine industry. After a thorough discussion of his past conduct, which was deemed to be persistently in conflict with and detrimental to the interests of the company, it was moved, seconded and un-animously voted that the employment of Walter S. Taylor be immediately terminated without further compensation.'

The answer of Walter was to reconstitute a small winery and make his Bully Hill wines from a variety of European hybrid grape varieties. Certainly I would be happier if he was more truthful in his own promotional material. The wines he makes are good, but to claim that the Baco Noir is a grape variety used for making the finest Burgundies is plainly fallacious and in its way as deceitful as the labelling that he criticises in other New York State Wineries.

It must be pointed out that there have been moves to make wines from such *vinifera* varietals as the Chardonnay in New York. The leader in such moves was Charles Fournier, a Frenchman who had peviously worked at Veuve Clicquot. He was originally brought to America to make New York State 'Champagne' for Gold Seal Wine Cellars, but became determined to improve as well the character of many of the local still wines. To help him in this, he employed Dr Konstantin D. Frank, a Russian exile with experience of making wines in the severe Continental climate of the Ukraine. In due course he left to establish his own winery Vinifera Wine Cellars, at Hammondsport. Despite criticism from the local agricultural advisory service he has successfully made wine from a range of European grape varieties, including the Chardonnay, the Cabernet Sauvignon, the Pinot Noir and the Riesling. From this last he has made a variety of wines up to a *trockenbeerenauslese* quality. I hope that he did not rely on invert sugar solution to produce that!

It must be stressed that there is nothing fraudulent about the way New York State wines are labelled. They conform to the local laws. On the other hand, such wines would not be permitted within the Common Market and, even by the standards of the invert sugar scandal in Germany, their method of production appears flamboyant. Whilst they might be legal, and legality, as has already been said, must vary from country to country and region to region, it seems sad that a wine may be labelled as such when only 65 per cent of it might actually be made from grapes and with a specific source, and when as little as 55 per cent may come from that state.

~7~

Tales from the Vienna Woods

Memories are short in the wine-trade and when the Austrian Wine-Scandal broke upon the world in July 1985, few people's minds went back just twelve years or so to a story that illustrated the happy Austrian philosophy that wine-laws are there just for the record; if there is money to be made by ignoring them, conveniently do so.

One of the cleverest wine-brands to be created is that of the Bass Charrington brewery group, Hirondelle. Its commercial strength is that it has not become attached in the consumer's mind to any source of supply. I have already shown the dangers that success can bring. Mouton Cadet has had to lower the standard of its base wines over the years. There has been pressure on the big German wine companies to find adequate supplies for their internationally known liebfraumilchs. Bass, however, have been rather more clever, they have always bought from those countries that could provide the right wine at the right price. Hirondelle, over the years, has come from a number of sources including France, Iron Curtain countries, Cyprus and, in the early 1970s, Austria.

The company that supplied the wine, Lessner and Kamper, produced excellent wines in apparently unlimited quantities. I imagine that there were preferential rates of duty as an added incentive, for both Britain and Austria were, at that time, members of the European Free Trade Area. Hirondelle rapidly became a very successful brand for its taste was suited to the new generation of wine-drinkers, those who had probably first tasted wine on a foreign holiday and were happy to drink wine at home if it were not too expensive. Hirondelle filled an important slot and sales increased rapidly.

It was the *Sunday Times* who drew the attention of the public to the fact that the consumption of red Hirondelle, sold as an Austrian wine, now exceeded the annual production of the whole country in red wine. Into one loading bay came tankers laden with East European wine, from others departed loads of officially baptised Austrian wine. Hedges and Butler, the wine arm of the Bass empire, pointed out, with some justification, that they insisted that the wine be accompanied by the official government documents that guaranteed the wine's authenticity. They must have seen the quantities of foreign wine that were coming into Lessner and Kamper's cellars. They must have known, too, how much Austrian wine came in and went out. Perhaps the officials were not strong on mathematics; perhaps they were told that it would be a pity to spoil a major source of foreign revenue.

In *The Times* of Monday, 19 August 1985, Richard Bassett, their Vienna correspondent, wrote an article showing how corruption is endemic in Austria. He quoted Metternich's famous saying that the 'Balkans begin at the gates of Vienna'. It was only after I visited Austria after the great wine-scandal that I realised how true this is. Of course, the Austrians recognise that this is true, but they are unhappy with the metaphor; it is too close to home. One well-known Austrian wine journalist described the Province of Burgenland as being 'the Congo of Austria'. Graft and corruption had come to be accepted there as a matter of course, and it was in the wines of the Burgenland that what came to be called the Austrian anti-freeze scandal was rooted.

It is important, however, to get two facts in perspective. First, the additive that drew all the attention, diethylene-glycol, had comparatively small toxic properties. The only recorded deaths from the substance were after massive doses, totally unrelated to wine. Indeed, the scientific press were not slow to point out that the alcohol in the wine was potentially more dangerous than the amounts of diethylene-glycol that were traced in all but a very few samples tested. To the best of my knowledge, there were never any reports of anyone suffering from drinking the wine to any more extent than having a headache—and that is an occupational hazard of drinking wine at the best of times. The dangers of drinking Austrian wine were blown up out of all proportion if one compares the publicity given to the Austrian scandal, when no one suffered physically, with that given to the later Italian story, when more than 20 people died from drinking branded wines fortified with industrial alcohol. Austria is still the butt of wine jokes, yet Italy only suffered temporarily.

The other myth that it is as well to explode is that of diethylene-glycol being an ingredient in anti-freeze. This seems to be just a matter of chemical confusion, for it is ethylene-glycol that is used each year to keep your radiator free. Despite this fact, the BBC in a television programme had the audacity to suggest that Austrian wine, and they showed a specific bottle of a brand that had never been found to contain diethylene-glycol, might be useful in keeping airport runways free of ice. In fact it is true that wine, and not particularly Austrian wine, freezes at a lower temperature than water and thus might be said to have anti-freeze properties, but it seems foolish, if not libellous, of the BBC to make the connection on such a sensitive matter. (In parentheses, when I was frozen in recently at Bordeaux airport, the authorities used animal urine to clear the runways.)

Whilst the attention of the press was drawn to just one aspect of the venal state of much of the wine-trade in Austria, they seem to have ignored other, perhaps graver, practices that were widespread at the time and which played an important role in the creation of the circumstances that led to the final explosion. The root problem in Austria has for a long time been the gross over-production in certain vineyard areas. As the Austrian wine-laws in no way controlled the amount of wine that could be produced per hectare, this, in itself, led to a number of abuses, some of which the authorities must have condoned, if not openly encouraged. There was widespread trafficking in official accompanying documents, the passport that each quality wine must bear. Thus, wines were being given guarantees of authenticity to which they were not entitled—degrees of nobility to which they had no right.

More seriously, it seems that a considerable amount of the wine sold on the Austrian domestic market had simply never passed through the official records at all. Thus it passed from the producer to the retailer and the customer without ever having to pay any taxes. One leading member of the wine-trade told me that he estimated that at least 40 per cent of all home-produced wines consumed in Austria had escaped the tax net. It is not difficult to see that such a situation put considerable pressure on the honest members of the trade to enable them to compete. They had to find cheaper sources for wine and this, in its turn, put pressure on the growers.

Apart from the diethylene-glycol aspect of the story, there were two other 'chemical' angles to the scandal. The first of these was the widespread use of stabilisers for the sweeter wines, which were, in themselves, dangerous and unstable. One of them was reported as being highly explosive, if not handled with caution.

More serious still was the fact that there was developed by Otto Nadrasky Snr, das Superhirn, or superbrain, as he came to be called, a method of making wine which owed nothing to grapes at all. In itself, this was not a new concept, for it had been carried out in Italy some years before, and it was suggested that Herr Nadrasky received his training from that country. What he did was to refine the recipe so that chemically he produced a substance that, to the consumer, was indistinguishable from wine. This side of the wine life of Austria appears to have been conveniently forgotten in the total sordid quagmire that came to be exposed.

Another contributing factor of some importance was the German market. Since the invert sugar scandal, just a few years before, there had been a shortage of the sweeter wines so appreciated by the German consumer. Austria was a natural replacement source for important quantities of sweet wines were produced there, particularly in the eastern region of Burgenland, up against the Hungarian frontier, where the autumn mists from the Neusiedlersee lake give ideal conditions for the development of noble rot. In Austria, too, the climate is more reliable than in Germany. It is true that there can be big variations in the quantities produced each year, but in each year sweet wines can be of good quality. The levels of residual sugar demanded by the Austrian wine-laws are higher than those for the equivalent wines from Germany; thus an Austrian *spätlese* has approximately the same degree of sweetness as a German *Äuslese*. Many German merchants began to import quality Austrian wines in bulk and bottle them for distribution on the German market. The demand increased rapidly and the business became more competitive. There is little doubt that much of the fraudulent wine began to be sold in Germany at very low prices. This put further pressure on the honest merchants, who found themselves now incapable of competing on the most important export market as well as at home.

Before moving on to the diethylene-glycol scandal and its effects, it is perhaps worthwhile clearing up the question as to why it was added to the wine. Many have suggested that it is in itself a sweetening agent. This is not true. The fact is that Otto Nadrasky discovered that when added, together with sugar, it masks, in analysis, the additional sugar. After the invert sugar scandal in Germany, government chemists around the world were on the look-out for wines so treated. Similarly, the alternative additive to make wines sweeter and more luscious, glycerine, was also well known to the authorities. This was the real worth of Otto Nadrasky's discovery; he had found a substance that would mask the considerable addition of sugar and yet was not being checked for by the government chemists. Whilst they might have looked for it in varnishes or disinfectants, they would never expect it in a wine. As Colin Parnell, the editor of *Decanter* magazine, pertinently pointed out in a letter to the editor of *The Times*: if someone were to add oven-cleaner to an ordinary red wine to give it the characteristics of the greatest wines of Bordeaux, it might be years before anyone would discover, for no one would think of analysing the wine to see if oven-cleaner was present.

There is some dispute as to how long diethylene-glycol had been added to wine before the fraud was discovered. What is true is that some of the contaminated wines that were subsequently discovered in Germany bore labels of the 1978 vintage. This suggests that the fraud had been going at least since the autumn of 1978, or that the fraud was not just connected with the making of the wine!

The official story as to the discovery of the fraud is that it came about by chance, in March 1985. The VAT inspector at the village of Pamhagen, which is about as remote a viticultural corner as one can find in Austria, for it is on the Hungarian border on the far side of the Neusiedlersee, was checking the return of a local merchant, Siegfried Tschida. On this he was surprised to find recurring claims for purchases of diethylene-glycol. He had difficulty in understanding why this should be needed by a wine company and went to consult one of his neighbours, the local food and health inspector. Whilst this story may be true, there is evidence to suggest that the Austrian authorities knew about this illegal practice as early as the previous November. What is absolutely certain is that they warned their colleagues in Germany, in April, that some tainted wines had been shipped to that country.

Between April and the beginning of July there seems to have been a decision taken somewhere that the whole affair should be kept under wraps. Obviously, it was in the interests of the Austrian government to say as little as possible, and it may be that the Germans felt that a scandal involving their wine-trade, even at second hand, would lower yet again the credibility of their wine-companies. The official reason, subsequently given by the German authorities and quoted in *Time Magazine* (5 August 1985), was that 'the Austrians (when they sent the message about the tainted wine) had not gone through the proper channels and that they had failed to sound a sufficiently urgent alarm'.

The news first came to Britain via Holland, on 11 July, and caused comparatively little stir. In Germany, the matter now became a matter of some urgency and *Die Welt*, on 19 July, published a list of 125 wines, most of which had been bottled in Germany, which had been found to be contaminated. On the same day three discreet paragraphs appeared in *The Times*:

The Ministry of Agriculture is to advise British wine merchants to remove all stocks of Austrian white wine from their shelves and the public is being advised not to drink any that they may have bought after samples contaminated with anti-freeze additives were discovered in tests in South Yorkshire last night.

The tests were carried out after a consumer complaint to South Yorkshire County Council. The supplier of the wine, a Georgener Spatlese, was not known last night.

In the past few days thousands of bottles of contaminated Austrian white wine have been found in West Germany.

On another page under the heading 'Medical Briefing' the readers were warned to beware of a pain in the neck and also that 'one hundred milligrams of ethylene glycol (anti-freeze) per litre of wine is considered an acceptable sweetener'. However, the reader should not worry as 'Alcohol is the antidote in cases of anti-freeze poisoning. Even the weakest Austrian wine has enough alcohol in it to neutralise any possible ill effects.' The piece went on to suggest that 'some Austrian growers have been too enthusiastic in the amount of anti-freeze they have added to their wine' and that if anyone drank too much of it there was the possibility of kidney problems.

The response to the story remained comparatively muted in Britain, until the *Observer* printed a well-documented article on the scale of the scandal on Sunday, 11 August. For the first time, many readers began to appreciate to what extent the wines on the shelves might be affected. I say the wines on the shelves, but, by this time, all Austrian wines had been withdrawn from distribution in Britain, for analysis, which was either to clear or condemn them. The *Observer* did however list 13 Austrian wines and five from Germany that had already been confirmed as being contaminated.

The testing of the wines, too, was presenting a serious problem, as an article in the *Sunday Telegraph* on the same day pointed out. The government laboratory at Norwich was suddenly called upon to test a vast number of samples for a substance that they had never before looked for in a wine, and to tolerances that were much tighter than normal. In addition, the analysts were under considerable pressure from the importers of Austrian, and German, wine to clear the wines so that they could be sold again. In the event, even clearance by the chemists did not mean that an Austrian wine would sell—in the minds of the British consumer, the country and its produce had lost all credibility.

In the meantime, what had been happening in Austria itself? Before the end of the month of July, the Austrian Chancellor, Fred Sinowatz, announced that his government would introduce 'Europe's strictest wine-laws'. This led to the immediate response that there had not been too much wrong with the previous set of wine-laws in the country, which had been promulgated as recently as 1972. It was fair to say that there were grounds for improvement, but the real problem lay more with their application than with their content. It was the authorities that were fundamentally to blame. (I have been given one example by a man, whose father was a government wine-inspector. In 1981, he wanted to prosecute one of the leading companies in the country for wine-frauds, but was forbidden to do so by the authorities.)

The Minister of Justice, Herr Harold Ofner, described the scandal as being 'the greatest criminal case of the post-war years' and the President, Rudolf Kirchslager, called for an improvement in the moral fibre of the country; its reputation was suffering abroad. Everybody seemed to want to get in on the moral indignation scenario. Varying figures were quoted for the number of people that were imprisoned, though most of these were briefly on remand and then released on bail.

On what scale was the Austrian wine-fraud? This is almost impossible to calculate, given the nature of the trade in the country, where parcels of wine in bulk seemed to circulate freely and where some companies were implicated because they had sold wine that they had never seen. One such victim was the prestigious house of Lenz Moser, a company that, over the years, had done more than any other to enhance the reputation of Austrian wines to the extent that they were selling more than 1,800,000 cases of wine in a year in 36 different countries. They had bought from a grower and sent directly to Germany a Ruster Spätlese 1984, that was found, on analysis, to have diethylene-glycol in it. Similarly, Döblinger Herrenhaus Kellerei of Vienna despatched to Manchester, direct from a grower in Burgenland, a road-tanker full of Welschriesling 1983, that, too, to the surprise of the importers, was found to be contaminated.

Here are some actual statistics, that have been quoted. In July 1985, the German government announced that 78,000 gallons of wine imported into the country from Austria was contaminated. This represented a total of over 350 different wines. At the beginning of August, the Austrian Justice Minister announced that 38 wine-merchants had been jailed for fraud and that a further 156 suspects were being investigated. Millions of litres of wine were involved and 'this was just the tip of the iceberg'. On 10 August, the Agriculture Minister, who, as events turned out, was not to last for long, stated that 15 million litres of wine had been confiscated.

On a more personal level, in the cellars of one supermarket company, there was found the equivalent of two million bottles of tainted wine. The manager, Herr Karl Siegfried Peer, and his wine-chemist assistant, Herr Thomas Eckert, were arrested. Herr Gerhard Fischler, the proprietor of a chemical company, admitted delivering diethylene-glycol by the lorry-load to the Furst company in the town of Retz, where, I hope coincidentally, the Austrian wine-school is situated. It appears that Herr Franz Schaden, the proprietor of Furst, was in the habit of buying each year enough chemicals for the artificial sweetening of almost three million bottles of wine. Not surprisingly, he, too, was arrested. It was announced that the widely respected company of Gebruder Grill at Fels am Wagram had not supplied a single 'honest' bottle of wine during the previous five years. This may have been connected with the fact that the company had had as their cellar-master for many years Otto Nadrasky Snr, and that it was they who had encouraged him in his research into artificial wines. Herr Richard and Herr Joseph Grill joined the others in prison, one of them for a ten-year sentence.

For the mastermind behind the whole scandal, Otto Nadrasky Snr, it took some time for the authorities to frame charges and he was, for a time, released. The reason for this was that they thought that carrying out research was not, in itself, illegal and they had difficulty in proving that he had actually sold any fraudulent wine or been part of a conspiracy in its sale. Nevertheless, he was finally brought to justice and received a severe prison sentence. (It is interesting to compare the maximum sentence of three years in jail imposed as a result of the German invert sugar scandal, with the ten years given in certain cases in Austria.) Another of the major wine-merchants involved, Herr Hubert Haimerl, received a two and half year sentence, whilst the majority of the others accused received fines and suspended sentences. Perhaps it was felt that the whole Austrian wine-trade might collapse, if too many of its leaders were taken out of circulation.

There were in Austria, some immediate results. Many of the companies involved went into liquidation. These included Gebruder Grill, with 150 redundancies, Hieber, Petermichli, Kleinbauer, Haimerl and Hafner and a number of smaller firms in the Burgenland, including the company that had supplied the enriched Welschriesling that was shipped to Manchester! Sadly, the world-wide collapse in sales led to control of the Lenz Moser company passing from family control to that of Mautner Markhof group, which already had interests in food and beer.

In other countries, the Austrian story also had wide effects. As far away as Japan, where a small number of contaminated wines was found, pronunciation difficulties, particularly by television newscasters, led to widespread confusion. Many people thought that it was the reputation of Australian wines that was at stake and the export manager of one major South Australian winery has told me that this confusion put back the success of his product on the Japanese market by at least two years.

It was perhaps in Germany that the Austrian scandal had the biggest effect. Germany had long been Austria's major export customer. As has already been said, the wines played a replacement role for many of the artificially sweetened German wines that had been exposed by the invert sugar scandal. Whilst there is no doubt that the majority of Austrian wines that were imported were labelled correctly, there can also be little doubt that some of them were used in their turn artificially to sweeten German wines. The companies whose German wines were found to have significant traces of diethylene-glycol in them, were also major importers of Austrian wine in bulk. They argued that the traces must have come through in subsequent bottlings as a result of poor cleansing of bottling lines.

It is evident, however, that they must have been used to stretch German wines. In all, when the analysis figures were correlated by the Common Market authorities, it was found that something over 1,000 Austrian wines had been adulterated, approximately 50 German wines and ten Italian wines. Four German companies accounted for the 50 samples; two from Peter Mertes and the rest from Walter Seidel, Ferdinand Pieroth and Niederthaler Hof. Coincidentally, the last two companies form part of the same group, and both specialise in pressure selling direct to private individuals.

No one has satisfactorily explained how diethylene-glycol came to be found in the Italian wines. The initial reaction of one of the companies involved, Biscardo of Verona, was that it must have come from a chemical spray used on the vines. The Austrians said that the whole concept of diethylene-glycol came from Italy in any case!

As for the British market, Austria has lost most of the small slice of the cake that it had before the scandal. This largely consisted of wines towards the bottom end of the price scale, some of which were bottled in Britain. Some three years later, the Austrian government is beginning to spend some money to promote its better quality wines, but it may be a case of too little, too late. Sadly, and perhaps unfairly, the wines of Austria have now become an object of derision, mentioned as the frosts arrive each winter, in the same breath as anti-freeze.

In Austria itself, the situation has changed quite considerably. The main reason for this has been the introduction of the new wine-laws, though this was against the initial opposition of both Conservative and Austrian People's Party members of parliament. For some time it looked as if the promised 'severest wine-laws in Europe' would never make the statute book. The stumbling-block was the proposed maximum yield per hectare law, which would cut straight to the heart of the free-wheeling habits of many Austrian wine-growers, particularly those from Burgenland, where the vines are mainly planted on the plain and astronomically high yields are not uncommon. For many growers, particularly those with hillside vineyards, small yields were a matter of course. In the end a compromise was agreed upon and, for the first time, the concept of maximum yields had to be taken into consideration.

Many of the other 'novelties' introduced appear logical in any case. If a vintage, a grape-variety or a source of origin is mentioned on the label, the wine must be 100 per cent what it claims to be. In addition, such wines as Gumpoldskirchner and Falkensteiner had to come from the actual villages concerned, not from loosely defined regions around them. Most of the rest of the law had the aim of avoiding, in the future, questions abroad about bottling sources. For example, the higher quality *pradikätswein* would have to be bottled in Austria, and could no longer be shipped in road-tanker to Germany. More controversial was the introduction of the banderole, or slip-label, which was to be put over the top of the cork, under the capsule. As was quickly pointed out, if this was to be put on by hand, it would be incredibly labour-intensive, and it would cost a considerable amount of money to buy a machine to do the job; money which the smaller growers did not have. This and maximum yields were the grounds on which the growers chose to fight the battle.

The new Agriculture Minister, Dr Erich Schmidt, decided that barter would be better than bloody warfare, and it was on such a basis that agreement was reached. If the growers would give way over yields, the Minister would accept that the banderole would only have to be used by those producers who turned over more than 45,000 litres in a year, and on those wines that were being exported. Smaller growers, instead, would have to affix on their bottles a label on the shoulder which would give similar information to the consumer.

To me, it seems to make very little difference whether the label goes under the capsule and across the cork, or whether it is stuck to the shoulder of the bottle. In either case, at the end of the day, it depends on the honesty of the grower. One has only to look at the abuse of the similar system in Germany, the A.P. number, to limit one's faith in the control. As Robert Lehner, the former manager of the Cooperative Cellar at Gumpoldskirchen said: 'I was brought up to believe that the making of wine is a question of morality, but there are many who do not think like me. If I wanted to cheat, I would look for a way to get round the law. Take one example, the banderole: I could get that printed wherever I wanted abroad. Maybe it needs two or three years. All of a sudden there is too much control.'

On a general basis, the new wine-laws were welcomed. It was their application which again caused concern. For those interested in exporting, the new controls seemed insurmountable. One example, given by Robert Lehner at a symposium on exporting, bears evidence of the petty-mindedness of Austrian officialdom. 'For one shipment,' he claimed, 'I have needed two hundred and fifty stamps on the export documents and a corresponding number of signatures. I have had to make several visits to an assortment of offices and the shipment has been held up for two months. My customers abroad can only accept this for so long.'

Indeed many growers decided that it was no longer worthwhile attempting to export their wines. For a start both the 1985 and 1986 vintages were smaller than average and could be largely absorbed on the domestic market. In Austria, too, there was a big hole left to plug, which had previously been filled by the fraudulent traders. No longer, in theory at least, was there the 40 per cent of the wine that did not pass through the system. No longer was there the totally artificial wine. No longer was there the artificially sweetened wine.

Now there was business to be had, on which one could make a profit. Why have the trouble of trying to sell wine abroad when one has to deal with a bureaucracy, that is , in the words of one journalist, 'like something out of Swift, that thinks it is running things when it is merely inventing regulations'.

In Germany, we have seen, one scandal can lead to another. Will the same happen in Austria? One can only hope not. As Alexander Unger, a grower and merchant from Burgenland, who was unfortunate enough to be placed in jail by the writers of the *Observer* (incorrectly, as it happens) because one of his wines was glycolised by another merchant after leaving his cellars, has said: 'No one of our generation will forget this scandal, but good has come from it. Our wines must now be the cleanest and purest in the world. Everything that can be tested has been tested.' There is the voice of the optimist. Rather more pessimistic is that of another Burgenlander, Max Juhasz, from Neusiedl. In a letter to the Austrian daily newspaper the *Kurier*, nine months after the scandal, he complains: 'Have the government now forgotten completely about the wine-farce of last year and the innocent wine-growers that suffered as a result? Can they only now pay attention to the succeeding problems of Voest-Alpina, Inter-trading, Steyr-Daimler-Puch and Merx?' Perhaps this is the problem of having the Balkans on your doorstep.

Still bent to make some Port . . . *

Hilaire Belloc once described Port as not being a wine, and in this he follows a lengthy tradition. There can be no product of the grape that has been so appreciated in Britain over the years, or one that has been so criticised. Port is sometimes called 'the Englishman's wine' and this, to a large extent, is true. Port as we know it was created by the British for the British market and, whilst there may now be countries where it is more widely, and more deeply, drunk, the trade is still largely in the hands of British companies.

To understand Port fully, it is necessary to study history more so than for any other wine. The fact that Port is so popular in Britain is not, for the most part, because the British have a particular liking for the wines of Portugal, but rather because the politicians have forced it upon us. Whenever we have been at war with France, we have been at peace with Portugal. Whenever French wines have been forbidden to us, we have been encouraged to drink Portuguese.

As early as 1353, there were trading treaties between Lisbon and Oporto and England. By the reign of Henry VIII, the rise of the middle classes, who largely made their fortunes from trading, meant that there were already Factories, or official associations of British merchants, with legal status and certain diplomatic privileges, in

---

* Still bent to make some port he knows not where
  Still standing for some false impossible shore
        Matthew Arnold, 'A Summer Night'

Lisbon, Oporto and Viana. Originally, this last town was the centre for the shipment of the wines form northern Portugal, which were often exchanged either for dried fish from Newfoundland, or woollen goods from Britain. The real impetus for the wines of Portugal first came in 1678, when, for a period of eight years, the importation of French wines was prohibited.

The year 1703 saw two treaties signed between the Portuguese and the British. The first, in May, signed by Sir Paul Methuen, enabled troops to be disembarked in Portugal and to cross the country to attack the Spanish. Seven months later followed what has been known since as the Methuen Treaty, which was signed by a different member of the Methuen family, Paul's father, John, who was the British Ambassador. This agreement opened up the Portuguese market in a substantial way for British textiles, and, reciprocally, the British market for the wines of Portugal.

The wines that were made at that time in the valley of the Douro must have been green and rough, perhaps similar to the red Vinho Verde that is so common in Portugal today, but which is considered such an acquired taste that it rarely finds its way abroad. How to deal with this problem had already been discovered by two young Englishmen, who had been on a wine-buying trip to Portugal in 1678. As in many other countries at the time, much of the best wine was made on church properties, and they visited the monastery of Lamego, which lies in the valley of the Douro, some 90 kilometres upstream from Oporto. There they tasted a soft, smooth, slightly sweet wine, totally unlike anything that they had come across so far on their travels. The secret, according to the abbot, was the addition of brandy to the must during fermentation. At about the same time, the merchants had found that the light, acid wines of the region did not often support the voyage across the Bay of Biscay to the wine ports of the south-west of England. The judicious addition of a few gallons of brandy before the voyage, on the other hand, rendered them considerably more stable.

Thus it was that initially the fortification took place with fully fermented wines, as it does nowadays with Sherry. It was only towards 1730 that the concept of adding brandy during fermentation became prevalent, thus giving a sweeter wine. Here then was the wine that the British consumer was seeking—one that was high in alcohol and sweet. Here was to be conceived the root of many years of dispute. Should Port be a natural, light wine, or should it be full-bodied and deep in colour?

In the anonymous *Maxims of Sir Morgan O'Doherty Bart.*, which appeared in 1849, the first maxim of all deals with Port. 'If you intend to drink much after dinner, never drink much at dinner . . . Port, three glasses at dinner—claret, three bottles after; behold the fair proportion, and the most excellent wines.' It is clear here that Port is considered to be a light wine.

In 1863, Charles Tovey, who was a Bristol wine-merchant, as well as being a writer on wines and spirits, carried on a correspondence with George Sandeman, of the Port company of the same name, suggesting that the unfortified wines from the Upper Douro were outstanding wines in their own right, 'full of delicious flavour— Chambertin, Clos de Vougeot, Romanée-Conti, or the choicest Burgundies could not excel them in exquisite character'. Mr Sandeman, for his part, gave details of research that he had carried out in his cellars in Vila Nova da Gaia. 'My first experiment was made with the fine vintage of 1815, when I selected three pipes drawn from the same tonnel, to one of which I put one-third of the usual quantity of brandy, to the second two-thirds, and to the last a full dose of brandy. Recollect this was one of the finest vintages I ever had to deal with, and the tonnel was one of the best of the year. I bottled all the three pipes at the same time, and between one and two years afterwards I found the first pipe becoming sour, and was obliged to start it again into cask and dose it with brandy. In three or four years I was obliged to do the same again with the second; but the third was so much liked that I was offered a guinea a bottle for it. But I kept it "to be drunk on the premises".'

In order to create a wine that was often a picture in the imagination of the British consumer, the merchants in Portugal often had to resort to artificial additives to achieve the desired effect.

There can be little doubt that some of the wines that were coming out of Portugal during the middle of the eighteenth century must have been of very low quality. Consumption was falling in Britain and there were regular complaints from merchants there. As a result, the merchants decided to do what they could to throw the blame on the growers and agents in the Alto Douro. In September 1754 then, the group of merchants at the Oporto Factory wrote to the 'commissaries' at Regua, outlining a number of specific complaints. Of these, the most important were that:

(1) The growers were buying inferior wine elsewhere and adding it to their own.
(2) Too little time was spent on making the wine, with the result that it lacked the full body that was wanted.
(3) Fermentation was stopped by the addition of brandy. This made for unstable wines. In addition the brandy that was being used was of unsatisfactory quality.
(4) Because the red and white grapes were not separated, the wines were deficient in colour. This deficiency was too frequently made up by the addition of elderberry juice.

The commissaries did not dispute the fact that the wines were of low quality, but laid the blame firmly and squarely at the door of the merchants. Whilst the wines had been totally pure and natural, they had been excellent, but the Factory had insisted on artificial, fiery wines. Indeed, not only did they receive the wines that they ordered, but they also interfered with them even more when they arrived in their cellars. One had only to look at the quantities of cheap wines from other regions, low-quality brandy and elderberries, that the merchants purchased directly themselves, to have some idea of the diabolical practices that were being carried on in their lodges. There was probably also, behind their complaints, some feelings of bitterness towards these foreign merchants who had settled in Portugal and were now lording it over the Portuguese growers.

In the event, the Portuguese government found a solution. In 1755, Lisbon was ravaged by an earthquake, and, in the chaos that followed, the man who took on the responsibility for re-establishing life in the city, created such a reputation for himself that he was appointed Chief Minister by King Joseph I. This man was to have a profound effect on the wine-trade in Portgual. His name was Sebastiâo Carvalho e Mela, Marquess of Pombal.

In 1756, he resuscitated the moribund Oporto Wine Company and granted it monopoly rights on the distribution of wines made in the Upper Douro. Amongst the measures that he undertook were the delimitation of the vineyards area permitted for the production of Port. This was the first attempt, anywhere in the world, for a country to establish delimited areas for the production of quality wine. He forbade the use of manure as a fertiliser to increase yields. All elderberry trees in the region had to be destroyed. (According to John Croft, in his *A Treatise on the Wine Trade*, which was published in 1788, the first use of elderberry juice for colouring wine can be credited to Viana merchant Peter Bearsley, whose company subsequently became that which now produces Taylor's Port!) The distillation of brandy became a monopoly of the Company, which also would keep records of the quantities of the wines that were produced by each grower and decide which were fit either for the export market, or for the home trade. In many ways the Marquess of Pombal was ahead of his time, for all that he laid down has later been absorbed into wine legislation around the world. Unfortunately, he was a harsh autocrat and made few friends, either amongst the growers or the merchants.

Sadly, the measures that he proposed did not last long and the Oporto Wine Company folded yet again. As the Victorian writer, and Dublin customs officer, Samuel Morewood said: 'Experience has proved that chartered companies, for the most part, have been productive of injury to trade and commerce, and have tended much to the obstruction of improvement in manufactures, enterprise, and general industry; of this the company just spoken of is a striking exemplification, as it failed in accomplishing any one of its purposed objects.' Pompously said, things soon returned to their previous, lax ways.

By the beginning of the nineteenth century, Port was truly established as the Englishman's drink. According to Cyrus Redding: 'Numbers believe Port wine to be the only real wine in the world, and shiver whenever Romanée-Conti, or Lafitte are named.' He goes on to justify this assertion by quoting some important statistics. In the first decade of the eighteenth century 81,293 tuns of Port arrived in Britain; in the first decade of the nineteenth century, despite the fact, and to a certain extent, because of the fact that Britain was at war for much of the time, 222,022 tuns were imported. Sadly, there can be little doubt that much of the wine was artificially treated both in Portugal, and in Britain. On 12 July 1812, a report by London wine-merchants on the Port wine-trade was presented as a petition to the House of Commons. In it the wines were described as 'pernicious mixtures', corrected with 'elderberry juice, rough spirit and sweeteners'. They were no more than 'confectioned drinks, drained of their natural taste'.

A glimpse of what must have been a regular practice is given in *Wine and Spirit Adulterators Unmasked*. This book must have been widely read for, by 1829, it had reached its third edition.

Port Wine

The most usual mode of adulterating this wine, may be said to consist in admixing the following articles in various proportions, with whatever different qualities and quantities of it in its genuine state, may be required to answer the views of the cheap wine seller.

BENECARLO, a strong coarse Spanish Red Wine, known by the denomination Spanish Black Strap, to be purchased, including duty, at about £38 per pipe of 115 gallons.

FIGUERA, a Red Wine from the province of Estremadura in Portugal, of intermediate quality between Black Strap and inferior Port, bearing a nearer resemblance to the latter, and generally to be bought at £45 per pipe of 115 gallons, duty included.

RED CAPE, which, from its low rate of duty, may be had, including that charge, for about £32 per pipe of ninety-one gallons, consequently forming a profitable ingredient.

MOUNTAIN, a small quantity, if required, to soften, and give an appearance of richness.

SAL TARTAR, a portion to occasion the Compound, when bottled, to crust firm and soon dissolved with a proportionate quantity of

GUM DRAGON to impart a fullness of flavour and consistency of body; and to give the whole a face.

BERRY-DYE, a colouring matter extracted from German Bilberries, and Known under this name,
In addition to these may be introduced,
BRANDY COWE (the groggings of an empty Brandy cask),
which costs nothing, in the proportion of about three gallons to
every hundred gallons of made up wine. Another ingredient that
may also be mentioned is,
CYDER, but as this is only made use of where a second quality of
manufactured Port is required, it may be unnecessary to render
any other illustration than that which I am about to give.

The illustration that he does give is that taking a base of one and a
half pipes of 'Stout Good Port' at £76 per pipe and one pipe of
'Common Port' at £63 per pipe it is not difficult to produce eight
pipes of a

superior Port Wine, made up according to the best and most
approved plan, and which stands our Advertising and Placarding
Dealers only at £50 per pipe of 115 Imperial gallons, every expense
included, and reckoned at the very outside; or should even this
be manufactured at too high a price, to render their profits sufficiently adequate to support that degree of *modesty* for which they
are so famous, a slight variation, in the proportion of any of the
ingredients need only be made, to produce a considerable altera-
tion in their favour.

It is easy to see how considerable profits could be made. Indeed in
some cases, the alchemist's art was a matter of necessity, as the author
says, as many of the 'Wines of the lowest quality, in dock, are by no
means saleable to the Public, until they have undergone a course of
doctoring'.
To make the ideal, even if it be artificial Port, either in London or
Oporto, it seems as though three ingredients were needed: base-wine,
brandy and colouring material. In the middle of the last century,
there appeared to be no shortage of any of these three and there was
always an alternative. One could always ship ready-made 'Port' from
elsewhere. James Denman, himself a wine-merchant, with branches
in Piccadilly and Abchurch Lane in the City, claimed that at a period
when the official imports of Port into Britain amounted to 20,000
pipes per year, something over 60,000 pipes of so-called Port were
consumed in Britain. He gave Tarragona in Spain as being a source
for much of this 'more or less rough, fruity, fiery, rounded and
tawny, cheap drink for the delectation of strong and undiscriminating
palates'. Indeed, some 30 years or so ago, when I joined the trade,
there used to be a considerable consumption in Liverpool, and, for
all I know, elsewhere, of quart flagons of Tarragona, which was

known affectionately as 'Spanish Port'. Indeed, until quite recently, in Spain itself, wicker flasks of Porto, produced in Spain, were not uncommon.

Here is an authentic Spanish recipe, dated 1885, for the production of, and the author does at least describe it honestly, 'Artificial Port Wine':

Good red wine	50	litres
Sweet walnut dye	0.75	litre
Almond dye	1.50	litres
Alcohol	1.50	litres

Mix them all together well and leave them to rest for some days, at the end of which transfer to sulphured receptacles, fining the wine if necessary. To sweeten, take two kilos of grape syrup, or, failing that, two kilos of sugar previously made into syrup with a litre of water.

During times of peace, another useful source for Port was the then capital of wine manufactory, Cette (modern-day Sète), on the Mediterranean coast of France. There were many merchants there capable of producing a full range of 'Ports' to the customer's specification, without requiring any ingredients from Portugal itself.

For colouring material, as has already been seen, elderberries appear to have been the major source. Here, there appears to have been some confusion over the years with the Portuguese word *geropiga*. For many years this term was used to describe in the words of Oswald Crawfurd, the British Consul to Oporto, who prepared a report on wine-trade practices in the city in February 1867, 'the article being made with treacle, unfermented grape-juice, elderberry and brandy'. He said that true *geropiga* 'what is called a *vinho mudo*; that it must be checked at the height of the saccharine fermentation by the admixture of about 32 per cent of proof spirit . . . It is to be observed that there are two varieties of *geropiga*, —one the liquid I have described, and the other *geropiga tinta*, or coloured *geropiga*; that is, darkened with elderberry, and is, I believe, seldom used to colour wines in this country. The true *geropiga* is added to wines requiring sweetness without loss of strength.'

It would seem that the word now is taken to mean what Crawfurd describes as the true *geropiga*. George Robertson in his book, *Port*, says: 'When a very sweet port or *geropiga* is made, the fermentation is arrested at the earliest opportunity and the *aguardente* would then be increased to 135 litres (per Douro pipe of 550 litres), while a dry port would take less than the (normal) 110 litres.'

Certainly, one has to be very careful when talking to Port producers, when one uses the word *geropiga*, as to whether you are both talking about the same thing. I can remember one conversation that I had, when I took it to mean a mixture including elderberry juice, and the shipper, as it turned out subsequently, was talking about a natural, hyper-sweet wine. Fortunately, in the end, we managed to agree on terms of reference.

Whilst Mr Crawfurd may have felt that elderberries were no longer used in the production of Port in his time, it would appear that he was being either protective of the local merchants or totally naïve. It must have been a year of busy diplomatic activity in the Port trade, for on 6 July, the Honourable Robert Lytton, Her Majesty's Secretary of Legation at Lisbon, and who was later to become, as Lord Lytton, Viceroy of India, sent a detailed report on the trade to the Foreign Office. This can scarcely have been welcome to the trade. 'My own belief is,' he wrote, 'that no pure Port wine . . . has ever reached the English market . . . It is also my belief that the peculiar colour of nearly all Port wines hitherto drunk in England, (a colour which is strikingly different from all those drunk in Portugal, — by the Portuguese themselves at least,) can only be produced by artificial means, and is effected by an infusion of elderberry juice. The Paiz de Vinhateiro abounds in eldertrees, the berries of which are dried in the sun or in kilns. The wine is then thrown on them, and trodden till it is thoroughly imbued with their colouring matter . . . Mr. Johnstone, of the London custom-house, whose keen intelligence is exercised upon unequalled practical experience of this subject, has estimated the average quantity of elderberry matter in every 115 gallon pipe of Port wine entered at the Port of London to be as much as five gallons.'

It seems strange that two official reports within the same year should be so much at variance, but it seems, on the evidence, that more credence should be given to that of Lytton. It is not as though elderberries were the only colouring matter to be used in Oporto and London. We have already seen a mention of German bilberries, but it seems as though even more exotic substances were widely used. Morewood says: 'To heighten the colour of Port, the Portuguese infuse the juice of the berries of the phytolacca, an ingredient much more pernicious than elderberries, formerly used for the same purpose; these berries yield a spirit of a harsh and unwholesome character.'

Other substances were recommended; amongst these 'for the acquisition of a pleasant roughness peculiar to Port, the Juice of Sloes will accomplish it, when judiciously incorporated in the wine', was the advice of *Palmer's Publican's Directory*. Not to be outdone in happy hints for the trade, *The Vintners' and Licensed Victuallers' Guide*, suggested 'raspings of sanders', or sandalwood. There must have been broad recognition by the public of the adulterations that were taking place, for the *Oxford English Dictionary* says, under the heading 'logwood', 'The alleged use of logwood in colouring spurious or adulterated port wines was at one time a frequent subject of jocular allusion'. Local black-cherries were apparently also used as late as the 1920s, if one is to believe P. Morton-Shand.

A final alternative was the powder cudbear, which was developed as a purple dye from lichens, by a certain Dr Cuthbert Gordon, who then named it after the Gaelic form of his Christian name.

It is interesting to note that there were other defenders of the purity of the colour of Port, apart from Mr Crawfurd. Amongst these was Dr J.L.W. Thudichum, who was another controversial writer on wine in Victorian times. Obviously the whole problem must have concerned him considerably, for he spent an important part of the chapter devoted to the wines of Portugal in his *Treatise on Wines*, on the question of 'elderberry and logwood'.

'It is said that port wine is coloured with elderberries and other dyes, sweetened with jeropiga and treacle, besides being dosed with brandy; but I have been unable to find any evidence of this, at least as regards Alto Douro wines. Elder trees are very rare in the Alto Douro, and I can in this respect fully confirm the statement of Mr. Consul Crawfurd. Moreover, the Alto Douro wine of a good year at least, is so deeply coloured, in fact, so excessively loaded with colouring matter, that it cannot by any means require any addition of colour; the elderberries exported from Oporto are really used for colouring other wines than port wines, particularly the Spanish ports, Mountain ports, Cape ports, and Sicilian red wines that are carried to England, and thence exported to countries where people buy wine rather by the name it bears than by any quality it possesses. It is also not rarely stated, upon the evidence of Mr. Cyrus Field, in the report of the Parliamentary Committee of 1852, that port wine is now and then coloured red by means of Brasilwood, commonly called logwood; but this is a great error, as it is quite impossible to dye wine of any kind with logwood — for the colour of logwood is purple only in alkaline solution, and not in acid, in which it is only tawny. Moreover it is very astringent, a quality which almost all port wine possesses in excess. Logwood is never used in trade for dyeing anything purple, and the large quantities of logwood shipped to Europe are nearly entirely consumed in the production, by means of iron mordants, of firm black colours on many kinds of tissues; and, although it may occur that particular artists in mixing and counterfeiting, dye some pipes of white wine with elderberries, and give them astringency with logwood, nevertheless I believe that such products would not pay the cost and trouble of their production, and are, at all events, only an exceedingly small fraction of the wines which constitute the bulk of the exports from Oporto. I am, therefore, of the opinion that the sooner we dismiss these prejudices and errors regarding elderberry and logwood in port wine, the better.'

Whilst I am prepared to accept that Dr Thudichum has made out some sort of case for the protection of the reputation of logwood,

I feel that his defence of elderberry lacks something in logic. There are not many eldertrees in the Alto Douro, but there are a lot of elderberries available for export from Oporto, which are used to colour wines, which are competing with and often passing-off as Port. As late as 1929 one writer claims that approximately one per cent of all wine shipped was coloured with elderberries.

In conjunction with the widespread criticism of the artificial colouring agents used in the production of Port, there was also general discontent with the fortification of the wine. There were those who would have liked a totally natural wine, but there were many more who were prepared to accept a certain amount of spirit in it. It must not be forgotten that the practice of brandying wines was fairly widespread. Even many of the best wines of Bordeaux were regularly 'improved' by the addition of a gallon or two of brandy to each cask. What was more criticised was the excessive fortification of the wines and also the quality of the spirit that was often used.

One of the reasons for the Marquess of Pombal to take the distillation of spirit into the sole hands of the Oporto Wine Company was to guarantee the quality. There is no doubt that in the years to follow, the wine-makers and the merchants were often quite happy to use the cheapest spirit available, and, on occasions, that did not necessarily come from the grape. Whether grape spirit is essential to make the best Port is a question that I am not qualified to answer; however, if Port is to be considered a wine and not, perhaps, a grape-based liqueur, there is no doubt that the spirit should come from the grape.

Cyrus Redding was especially critical of not just the quantity of brandy that was used, but also of its quality and source. 'The quality of Portuguese brandy is for the most part execrable. It is frequently distilled from figs and raisins, of which no other use can be made. They even once tried to make it from locust pods, but that scheme failed, and they were obliged to resort to importation for the extra quantity they wanted. That the wines will keep and bear a sea-voyage without the addition of brandy to such an extravagant excess, there can be no doubt. A couple of bottles of good brandy to a pipe when put on board ship, would, if such an assertion were true, answer every purpose of preservation.'

What was the 'extravagant excess' of which he talks? If one is to believe Mr Johnstone, the London customs officer already mentioned in the report of Robert Lytton, as much as 34 gallons of brandy was added to the average pipe of port that was sold in Britain, 25 at the time of fermentation, six together with the elderberry infusion, two at the time of racking and a final one at the moment of embarkation. Even now, brandy appears to represent approximately a fifth of the ultimate product, though I am not certain whether the spirit used today is at the same strength as it was a century or more ago.

Whilst there appears to have been widespread criticism of Port in the trade in Britain, the merchants in Oporto were happy to continue in their cosmetic and profitable ways. There appears to have been little criticism on the Portuguese front, until the arrival of a young twenty-two-year-old to join his uncle's company, Offley Forrester, in 1831. This was Joseph James Forrester. He could almost have come from the pages of a Victorian uplifting novel. He took an interest in everything; he was a brilliant artist, linguist and sports-man. He played a gallant role in protecting the company properties during the siege of Oporto, which started the year after his arrival in Portugal. He charted the river Douro and the Port wine vineyards, he made friends with everybody and came to be created a Baron by the Portuguese government. However, he did not like everything he saw, and in 1844, he published anonymously, *A Word or Two on Port Wine, shewing how and why it is adulterated and affording some means of checking its adulterations.* Whilst it appeared with no author's name on the title-page, Forrester had made no secret of his feelings and soon came to accept paternity of this child which had all the local trade up in arms against him. This is scarcely surprising, for he did not mince his words. Here is his description of 'How Port Wine is Made':

> To produce *black*, *strong*, and *sweet* wine, the following are the expedients resorted to: The grapes being flung into the open vat indiscriminately on the stalks, sound or unsound, are trodden by men till they are completely mashed, and there left to ferment. When the wine is about half-fermented, it is transferred from the vats to tonels, and brandy, (several degrees above proof) is thrown in, in the proportion of twelve to twenty-four gallons to the pipe of must, by which the fermentation is greatly checked. About two months afterwards this mixture is coloured thus: a quantity of dried elderberries is put into coarse bags; these are placed in vats, and a part of the wine to be coloured being thrown over them, they are trodden by men until the whole of the colouring-matter is expressed, when the husks are thrown away. The dye thus formed is applied according to the fancy of the owner, —from twenty-eight to fifty-six pounds of the dried elderberry being used to the pipe of wine. Another addition of brandy, of from four to six gallons per pipe, is made to the mixture, which is then allowed to rest for about two months. At the end of this time it is, if sold (which it is tolerable sure to be after such *judicious* treatment,) transferred to Oporto, where it is racked two or three times, and receives two gallons more of brandy per pipe, and then it is considered fit to be shipped to England, it being about nine months old: and, at the time of shipment, one gallon more brandy is usually added to each pipe. This wine having thus received, at least, twenty-six gallons of brandy per pipe, is considered by the

merchant to be *sufficiently strong*, — an opinion which the writer, at least, is not prepared to dispute.

Port he described as being 'a nauseous, fiery compound of sweets, colours and alcohol'.

The trade in Oporto split, scarcely down the middle. There were 22 companies on the one side; Offley Forrester on the other. Generally speaking, he was supported by the Portuguese and even the local Cardinal preached against the 'intemperate opposition'. Over the years Forrester himself adopted a more diplomatic line and in the 'Oliveira Prize Essay of Portugal', which appeared in 1853, he seems much milder, though he does still have the occasional barb. 'For some time past the clamour of our interested competitors has "lulled", and although we have been silent, we have not been idle . . . We are determined that there shall be pure wine not only for the rich man, but also for the poor; not solely for the healthy, but likewise for the sick but it does not follow that, on this account, Brandy should be made to pass off as wine.'

Forrester became less of a crusader as he grew older and he regained the affection and respect of his British competitors in Oporto. Sadly he died in his early fifties when a boat, on which he was taking a pleasure trip, overturned in a Douro swollen by several days' rains. He was struck on the head by the mast and weighed down by a heavy money-belt about his waist, and so was drowned. The women of the party were saved, when the crinolines they were wearing served as inflatable lifebelts and they reached the shore in safety.

Though the brandy that is used to fortify wine should by law be made in Portugal, there are a number of occasions over the years when it has not been made from grapes — and it did not come from Portugal. We have seen that it might be made from raisins or figs, but even they did not provide enough raw material for distillation on some occasions. James Denman quotes the figure of 30,000 pipes of wine being distilled each year in Portugal, but by a decree in September 1858, for example, the importation of foreign spirits was permitted for the fortification of Port. Coincidentally, it just happened that the 1859 vintage wines required, according to a consular official, 'a more than average proportion of alcohol'. Given the strength of the wines and of the spirits involved, it is difficult to see how the extra quantity involved could be more than marginal. Nevertheless the British distillers took full advantage of the situation and Dr Druitt, in *Report on the Cheap Wines*, quotes some interesting statistics from the trade magazine, *Ridley's Monthly Circular*, of March 1865. Apparently during the previous year, Britain had imported from Portugal 3,344,871 gallons of Port — during the same period Portugal imported from Britain 1,630,304 gallons of spirit for fortification purposes. Whatever the spirit was made of, it certainly was not grapes.

105

Britain was not the only source of supply for alcohol for fortification purposes. Whilst Dr Thudichum was not unhappy about believing stories about logwood and elderberries, he did have certain doubts about the spirits used. He recounts that each spring 'the wine-merchants from Oporto then send up their wine-casks, some filled with brandy (I have seen many casks of Berlin shape, with Berlin brands in the adegas of the Alto Douro, and therefore believe that much Berlin spirit is put into port-wine)'. Not so long ago there was the slogan 'Port comes from Portugal'. In Victorian times it is true to say that much Port did not come from Portugal, and of that which was shipped from that country, a major proportion was made with, at least partly, foreign ingredients.

During the second half of the eighteenth century the sales of Port in Britain declined rapidly, partly as a result of the unfavourable exposure the production techniques received in the press. In medical circles, particularly, its excessive alcohol content was roundly condemned and it became totally unfashionable in certain circles to drink it. As Dr J.L.W. Thudichum FRCP wrote, and he was a lover of wine, 'Much has been written and said regarding the injurious character of strongly-brandied port wine, and in consequence the more polite classes of society have almost entirely turned from port wine, and do not drink it any longer. I have been present at dinners to which ten or twelve gentlemen sat down, and not one took port when it was brought round. An Oporto merchant in London gave a dinner party to twenty gentlemen, and not one of these was found to drink even a single glass of the merchant's own best vintage wine. If this antipathy should continue, it might, perhaps, aid in the reduction of the brandy in port wine to below *delirium tremens* point.' Whatever the 'more polite classes of society' might have done, port drinking was kept alive, for 50 years or more, by the less polite classes enjoying their port and lemon.

During this century, Port seems to have been a less-controversial, and a less-drunk wine. On more than one occasion, however, there has been doubt expressed as to what has actually gone into the final product. German scientists carrying out research in 1975 into the claimed ages of certain ports that were available on the market, discovered that whatever spirit was used for fortification, it was not based on the grape, as laid down by law. Certain of the Oporto shippers were implicated in the affair, but it seemed to blow over without any dramatic revelations. It is interesting that George Robertson, himself a respected member of the Port trade, in his book *Port*, is loath to criticise. On the contrary, he tells of the 1904 vintage, when there was a shortage of grape spirit in Portugal, and the shippers appear to have used almost anything that came to hand, brandy from the Azores (presumably distilled from sugar cane), grain and potato spirit from Germany, and even possibly grain spirit from

Scotland. 'Strange again,' muses Mr Robinson, 'that the year 1904 was a great year, and those lucky enough to have drunk the famous vintage port of that year will remember the beauty of that wine.'

In Portugal, this story of the strange spirit used for fortification has come to be known as the C14 Affair, after the testing process which discovered the scandal in the first place. Apparently, it appears that the Portuguese government considered that it had a surplus of grape spirit, so it sold the excess quantity to Yugoslavia. Soon, however, they found that there was, in fact, a shortage of spirit for fortification purposes, so they asked the Yugoslavs if they could buy the brandy back. The latter agreed and the spirit was loaded on a boat bound for Portugal. For some reason, and here the details are rather hazy, the ship put into Marseilles and the brandy was pumped off. It was then supposed to be reloaded and continue on its way to Portugal.

Subsequent analysis shows that the spirit which had returned from Yugoslavia and which was used for the fortification of Port was neutral industrial alcohol of a type only produced in France and Britain. No one will admit to having made the substitution. Did it take place in Yugoslavia, in France or in Portugal? The country to make the biggest fuss about the 'adulterated' wine afterwards, was France, but this is hardly surprising as they were the biggest customers for Port. In the event diplomacy appears to have triumphed and nothing much more was heard about the problem. It is even possible that the fine old Port that you are drinking at the moment was fortified with something other than grape spirit, for the wine was not withdrawn. No one seems to have suffered, but someone has profited financially from the switch. Could it possibly be that for a time some of us thought that we were drinking French Grape Brandy, which was, in fact, a spirit that had been distilled in Portugal and had been to Yugoslavia and back? One has heard stories of French Brandy coming from even less likely sources! The moral of the story must be that it does not really matter what you put into a wine, as long as it tastes all right in the end.

There is, finally, one aspect of the legislation on Port about which I am uncomfortable. Particularly on the continent, there is a vogue for old tawny Ports, with an age on the label. Thus, for example, if you see a bottle of Port, and it will not be a cheap one, with Thirty Years Old on the label, you might justifiably expect that the wine in the bottle is at least 30 years old. Not at all. What the law lays down, is that the wine, must 'have the characteristics of a thirty year old wine, and that the shipper must be able to show that he has in his cellar stocks of thirty year old wine, sufficient to cover the shipment'.

In effect, this is a similar arrangement to the 'Tunnel System' in Burgundy and the 'Bordeaux Agreement'. The difference is that, in theory at least, the French arrangements, which were never official, no longer exist, whilst the Port system is enshrined in the official legislation.

I am sure that it will be argued, and it probably has been, that in the Port lodges it is difficult to separate all the different wines by age, and that many of them have been refreshed. This might be true, but the argument falls down on the fact that the shipper has to show that he has wine of that age in his cellar. If he can show that, surely it must be simple to insist that that is the wine that he sells under the label. One must assume that a wine that is 30 years old, has the 30-year-old characteristics—or could it be that the benchmark against which the wines are judged bears little relationship to reality? It certainly would make life easier if the standard could be achieved by blending together a number of younger components. According to the law, that is quite permissible, if the taste matches the criteria. If one were to carry this through to its logical extreme, it would appear financially worthwhile for the shipper to maintain a stock of otherwise unsaleable wine as his age guarantees. He then blends what is needed from younger wines, at much lower cost.

One must feel happy that there is an apparent resurgence in the market for fine Ports. There is more than just national pride involved. One has come to accept the, however unpalatable, fact that the French may drink more Port than the British. The shippers have once again learnt how to adapt the style of the wine to the demands of their customers. Whilst *le petit verre de porto* that one is offered as an apéritif in France may be some way from a glass of Port as the British know it, it has enabled the Port Wine Trade to survive. Thus the considerable consumption by the French of what traditionalists would consider to be inferior wine kept the Port companies alive over a very difficult period.

To celebrate the three hundredth anniversary of their foundation, Croft Port commissioned a short book on their company. Its title is *Croft, A Journey of Confidence*. Sadly, the history of Port over the same three hundred years has not always been one of confidence for its consumers.

The Sherry family — and changelings

If Port bears the title of the Englishman's wine, Sherry must be the next in line for the throne. Indeed the history of Sherry drinking in Britain goes back to at least Elizabethan times, as is witnessed by the eulogies put in Falstaff's mouth by Shakespeare and by the inventory of the stock of the Mouth Tavern at Bishopsgate Without in London in 1612. Amongst the list of items is: 'One ranlett of Sherry Sacke, contayning sixteen gallande . . . £1 12s 0d.' It is also apparent that even in those times, efforts were being made to guarantee the authenticity of the wines that were on sale, for Markham, in the *English House-Wife*, says, 'Your best Sacks are of Jerez in Spain' and 'Sack, if it be Jerez — (as it should be) you shall know by the mark of a cork burned on one side of the bung'.

However, Sherry came to suffer much the same fate as Port in that it came to design itself to the demands of the British market and those demands were similar; wines that were high in alcohol and often masked by sweetness. Not only was the quality brought down, thus harming the image of Sherry, but also it left the door wide open for widespread copying, not only from within Spain itself, but, in due course, from France and ultimately from Hamburg and even Britain. All these products came to be called Sherry and it was not until February 1967, as a result of a case brought by the Sherry Shippers Association against the makers of 'British Sherry', Vine Products Ltd., that the name was finally protected. The Spaniards have claimed that the case was a victory for them as the ruling of the court was that the word Sherry by itself meant a wine produced in the Jerez district of Spain, but that such expressions as British Sherry, South African Sherry and Cyprus Sherry, were acceptable. Even more surprisingly, the continuance of the use of some of these terms is still permitted since the arrival of Spain in the Common Market. The fault for this situation must be laid firmly at the door of the Spanish producers, who over the centuries did little to attempt to protect their own interests. No one would dispute the fact that the word Sherry is a corruption of the name of the town Jerez, in Andalucía, where it was, and is, produced. Such other names as Champagne, Cognac and Sauternes have, for the most part, been dragged back from the public to the private domain. Sherry has largely failed.

Surprisingly, perhaps, the Sherry producers took steps to try to prevent Sainsbury's, the supermarket chain in Britain, from describing the real thing as Spanish Sherry, presumably on the basis that it might suggest that there are other sherries than those coming from Spain. On the other hand, it could be argued that it strengthens the image by making it clear that it comes from Spain. In the event, Sainsbury's resisted the pressure and the wine is still so labelled on their shelves.

The lack of efforts to protect the use of the name and the passe-partout quality of much of the wine led to widespread abuse. As the Victorian wine-merchant and writer, James Denman, said: 'The pure it is difficult, nay, *impossible to successfully imitate*: whereas the Ports and Sherries of commerce, being themselves mixtures, are peculiarly adapted for fraudulent imitation.'

Perhaps strangely, an early reference to the passing-off of other wines as Sherry concerns wines produced from vineyards within the area that now are permitted to call their wine Sherry, and indeed make wines that have a high reputation, the Manzanilla region around the town of Sanlúcar de Barrameda. In 1793, D. M'Bride dedicated a book on wine to the Prince of Wales. Whilst this was entitled *General Instruction for the Choice of Wines and Spirituous Liquors*, it was largely no more than a puff for a Spanish Tokay, of which only Mr M'Bride knew the source and which had remarkable medicinal properties. Despite his particular interest in one Spanish wine, he seems to have had a broad knowledge of the wines of the country and about Sherry, says, 'Xerez, or Sherry, a good dry white wine, in general use in Britain, and much admired. San Lucar, also, is another white wine of the same district, reckoned not so good as the Sherry: but, whether this is owing to the nature of the vine, the soil, or the manner of the making of the wine, is a matter I have not yet been able to ascertain; however, there is yearly much more of the San Lucar made than of the Sherry, and being cheaper is mixed with the Sherry; but whether mixed or separate, a moderate use of them at table is not unwholesome.'

Forty years later, James Busby, on his voyage of study through the vineyards of Europe, on behalf of the settlers in New South Wales, also noted that quantities of wine were brought into Jerez from other regions for subsequent sale as Sherry. Málaga is cited by him as a source for much of this external wine. By then, however, San Lucar was considered to be a genuine source of Sherry, though of the cheapest quality.

Perhaps surprisingly 'outside' wine still plays a part in the production of Sherry. As not enough Pedro Ximinez, or sweetening wine, is produced in the Sherry district, quantities of it are brought in each year from regions like Málaga and Montilla. Indeed, the whole economy of these two vineyard areas is supported by this trade. The rivalry between particularly the wines of Montilla and Sherry is considerable, but one has to rely upon the other.

What happened to the wines in Spain seems to have had little significance to what were regular, or more correctly, irregular practices in England, to create a wine that appealed to the consumer at the right price. Even in the eighteenth century, the wine that was appreciated in Spain itself was much lighter and drier than that consumed in Britain—the same is true today. However, even in Spain, Sherry must have been of variable quality, for a Victorian traveller in the country describes the wine he was offered at the Fonda de Londres in Seville as 'a miraculous compound of fire and water'. The Fonda de Jerez, in the same town, produced 'a yet more deadly draught', though there could be found in Jerez itself 'Sherry that makes a man smack his lips and wink joyfully'.

I have already given the ingredients for making Port, as suggested by the author of *Wine and Spirit Adulterators Unmasked*. He gives just as alarming a list of ingredients for a recipe for Pale Sherry. He suggests that the primary object is to produce a wine that is pleasing to the eye, and that for the fraudster, little is easier. Dependent on the degree of honesty of the alchemist, the base wine might be cheap brown Sherry. This can be substituted by, or increased in volume with, Cape wine. To lessen the colour, at no cost, add Brandy Cowe or groggings from an empty brandy cask. To give a nutty flavour use extract of almond-cake (though an alternative could be a mixture of sweet and bitter almonds and powdered oyster shells—one must imagine that oysters were considerably cheaper then). To make a softer, rounder taste, a small quantity of cherry-laurel water. Gum benzoin is yet one more useful flavouring additive, and, to reduce the colour to that necessary for Pale Sherry, three pints of lamb's blood should be mixed in with every hundred gallons of the blend. According to accompanying tables provided by the author the price of genuine Pale Sherry ranged from £65 per butt of the lowest quality to £105 per butt of the finest, and Brown Sherry from £58 to £110. With his formulae, either could be produced at a maximum price of £48 per butt.

Another, and rather later, anonymous writer says: 'Burnt sugar colouring, bitter almonds, peach kernels, oil of almonds, cherry-laurel leaves, sulphates of potash and soda, and a host of other adulterations, have led to the greatest confusion in the sherry business, so that sherry . . . seems to be declining in the public esteem.'

These blends made in Britain also had to compete with 'Sherries' made on the Continent. The Hambro' Sherry has already been described. Whatever the ingredients might have been, there appears to have been no shortage of customers for it. If the recipe above, which was based on at least some wine from Jerez in the mixture, could be produced for £48 per butt, the Hambro' wine was on sale at £11 to £14 the butt in London. The downfall of the 'wine' in the end was the fact that it was too high in alcohol. This attracted the attention of the Customs and Excise and in the Report of the Commissioners in 1863, sentence was passed. 'The importation of spurious wines into this country, principally from Hamburg, is a subject that has much engaged our attention during the past year. The practice which of late years has extensively prevailed of importing, under the guise and denomination of wine, an article containing a large percentage of spirit, but only a sufficient quantity, if any, of the known constituents of genuine wine to disguise the compound by the imitation of colour and flavour, is one which imposes a duty of great responsibility and difficulty on our officers, and is at the same time prejudicial to the interests both of the fair trader and the revenue.' As a result duty began to be levied on these mixtures, as though they were compounded spirits rather than the wines they claimed to be.

This campaign by the authorities must have met with success, for, in the following year, a war of words broke out in the trade. Representing the interests of the Hamburg camp were companies like Southard and Co. and Edward Chaplin. As the former said in a circular, 'Dealers have been subjected to much annoyance by the Customs authorities, who have stopped nearly all the recent arrivals and prohibited their admission for duty as wine, pronouncing by the opinion of their officers that they are only flavoured spirits and water, and consequently only admissable under the spirits duty. This step would be reasonable enough in cases when attempts are made to smuggle in spirits as wine; but to stop these parcels, which are indubitably wine, and can be proved to be so, is both arbitrary and unjust. It should be borne in mind that, next to London, Hamburg is the largest importer, and most extensive depot for foreign wines in Europe; and nearly all the shipments made from there are wines in the same sense and reality as the shipments from Portugal and

Spain, manipulated and fortified in precisely the same manner, and almost in every case their analysis would produce the same result.'

Edward Chaplin continued the same theme. 'Port is a mixture of different wines with brandy, so also is sherry, so also is Hambro' wine; the only difference in the latter being that it is a blend of wines of different countries, whilst the two former are, or should be, merely mixtures of wines from Portugal and Spain respectively . . . The business in wines from Hamburg has hitherto been almost confined to the lower qualities, chiefly because the trade has not yet taken a sufficiently firm footing to warrant the merchant here in keeping stocks of old wines . . . I can state most distinctly that my shipments consist solely of genuine wines fortified with the finest spirit, and it cannot be too distinctly remembered that the bulk of Hambro' wines are like sherry, port, &c., genuine wines simply blended with more or less skill.'

However Mr Chaplin might vaunt the purity and honest sources of his own wine, the trade magazine *Ridley's* had another description for Hambro' Sherries: 'In our opinion such liquids have no pretension to vinous attributes, being apparently compounded of spirit, *aqua pura*, capillaire and flavouring ethers, which, after amalgamation, may perhaps be allowed to feed on layers of raisins in the large vats at Hambro.' The writer also suspected that the spirit used was potato spirit and the water was drawn from the Elbe which ran conveniently in front of many of the wine factories.

As Dr Druitt wrote with feeling: 'Let us hope that some friends of humanity will interfere to protect helpless women and children, at Christmas and juvenile parties, from cheap Hambro' port and sherry.'

Hamburg was not without rivals in the production of so-called sherries, but it had the big advantage of being close to London for shipping purposes. There would be little point in shipping Elbe water too far. More distant, but more experienced in the world of wine production, was the French Mediterranean port of Cette, or Sète as it is now called. Even Thomas Jefferson, a lover of fine wine, had noticed the fraudulent practices when he visited the town in 1787. Fifty years later, Stendhal, too, noted with interest: 'Today I performed what might be described as some tourist chores. I saw a soap factory and a *chai*, or wine factory. Out of wine, sugar, iron filings and some flower essences, they made the wines of every country. A personage wrapped up in dignity assured me that neither litharge not any injurious substances were used in the factory. I took that with a grain of salt.'

The merchants of Cette were swift to profit from the discomfiture of their rival upstarts from Germany, for a copy of the *Moniteur Industriel*, from September 1866, reports: 'Among the white French wines imported into England are included imitations of Sherry and

Madeira proceeding from Cette and Marseilles, where the 'real nutty flavour' is skilfully imparted by the aid of chemical compounds. Probably Picardan wines find a certain sale in the English market, to be doctored into Sherry.'

The reputation of the wines called Picardan had been already established for many years. Jullien speaks of its being particularly useful as a replacement for Spanish wines in time of maritime blockade. Whilst he does not specifically mention it as being passed-off as Sherry, he does say: 'These grapes are also used in the preparation of fortified wines which bear some resemblance to those of Alicante, Rota and Malaga and of many other foreign vineyards. They are sold as coming from these places, but at much lower prices than those that are imported directly. These wines are not unhealthy; but they have neither the full tonic qualities of those that they replace, nor their aromatic flavour which they have not yet succeeded in imitating.'

For a time, too, Corsica seems to have been in on the Sherry producing act, with wine from the Cap Corse region being widely sold in Germany as Xérès. On the British and Italian markets, however, rather more discretion was used and it was simply sold as 'Spanish ' wine.

At least it can be said that the wine-makers of Cette were using wines as the base of their products, despite the fact that they might have to be 'arranged' with a variety of artificial flavourings and chemicals. The production of British Sherry, however, has little to do with wine as it is generally understood, though it must be accepted that grapes are used. According to Mr R.W.M. Keeling, who is quoted at length by Manuel M. Gonzalez Gordon in his book *Sherry*, there had been a long tradition, especially in the North of England, of selling a product called British Sherry, which was often considered, erroneously, to be non-alcoholic, and thus appreciated by abstainers, and which might be made from raisins or, just as likely, from rhubarb. *Law's Grocers' Manual*, a reference book, at the turn of the century states categorically: 'Some of the low-priced makes are nothing more than coloured water and sugar mixed, with just sufficient of the refuse of the distillery oil to keep it from turning sour.'

At about this time the production of British Sherry was established on a commercial scale by a Greek imigrant called Mr Mitsotakis who conceived the idea of concentrating unfermented grape-must from his native Greece, which then could be shipped to England at a low price, where water, yeast and sugar could be added. Fermentation would then get under way and quite drinkable 'wines' could be made and sold under widely recognised names like Port and Sherry. In addition to the low production costs, further financial incentives were given in the form of the preferential rate of duty that was levied on what came to be known legally as 'sweets'. Here, for a certain class of society, was the long-awaited alcoholic replacement for the now heavily taxed gin as a source of consolation. Whatever one may think of the merits of the product, it must be said that it has been able to masquerade for so long under the name of British Sherry. Its method of production bears not the slightest resemblance to the wine from Spain whose name it has adopted.

There is one stage in the production of Sherry which dates back to the earliest time, but which caused great controversy in Britain during the last century. This is the custom of plastering, or adding gypsum to the grapes before fermentation. What is strange is that no one really knows why this habit has been carried out for several centuries. The habit was recommended by classical writers such as Columella, because they thought, wrongly, that the wine fell bright or cleared more quickly. Later writers held that it lowered the acidity in the wine. The truth is that it increases the acidity and thus gives wines that ferment in a more balanced way and which are capable of lasting longer. It is probable that the habit first occurred naturally, from dust on the grapes. The wine-makers saw that better wines were the result and thus began to add further quantities.

As has already been shown, in Victorian times a broad range of noxious liquids were being sold on the British market under the name of Sherry. Many of these came from Spain itself and there developed a strong movement for 'pure' wines. This movement was strengthened by a report in 1865 on the Sherry trade, carried out by the British consul, A. Graham-Dunlop.

It is perhaps sad that the main attack on Sherry was led by the Dr Thudichum we have already met in the chapter on Port, who had come to London from Germany. Amongst the research that he carried out was a means of producing amontillado by chemical means, which was a failure. He then launched an attack on the habit of plastering wines, particularly Sherry, in a letter to the editor of *The Times*. Whilst there is no doubt that he had some justification in writing what he did, his case was not helped by the fact that he greatly exaggerated the figure for the amount of gypsum that he said was added to the must, nor by the nature, and failure, of the experiments that he had carried out in Jerez. Certainly many of the phrases from his letter were unlikely to make friends for him in the trade. 'Now it must be observed, that what has been described is the process of making "sherry", and not a process of adulterating it. It may be a question whether this process leaves much room for adulteration, or whether it is not itself adulteration; in other words, whether all sherry whatsoever is, or is not adulterated. To help your readers towards a solution, I remind them that medical authorities have long since pronounced the brandied and plastered sherries to be unwholesome. But the vendors of such sherries are not troubled by the administrators of the Acts of Parliament relating to adulteration . . . Sherries contain from

1.5 to 8 grammes of sulphuric acid as potash salt per litre, and the more the older and better they are; most "soleras" are near the higher figure.'

Not content with this salvo, he brought further guns to bear in a lecture delivered at the Society of Arts: 'I am quite open to instruction on the use of plastering, but have sought it in vain of some large producers or importers of Sherry. No doubt the 20 per cent of alcohol in Sherry is a frequent cause of kidney affection; but the cause is at least doubled by the potassium salt. I vote for Sherry without plaster acid, and less than 16 per cent of alcohol; such Sherry will require neither camomile nor nitric ether for a flavour. I vote for not changing ripe must into unripe by removing wine acid, and leaving sour apple acid. I delight in a glass of Amontillado, or even cheap "Vino de Arenas"; but I gladly leave the drink of Glauber's salts to the old gentlemen who, as the phrase goes "cannot get anything dry enough".'

Perhaps surprisingly, as *Vinum Xericum* is the only wine thought worthy of a position in the British Pharmacopoeia, Dr Thudichum received strong support from the medical profession in the persons of Dr Dupré, a lecturer and Professor of Chemistry at the Westminster Hospital (and a co-author of *A Treatise on the Origin, Nature and Varieties of Wine, being a complete manual of Viticulture and Oenology*, with Dr Thudicum), Dr Robert Druitt MRCP and John Postgate FRCS, Examiner and Professor of Medical Jurisprudence, Queen's College, Birmingham. Within the trade, the attack on 'impure' Sherries was led by James Denman who was also a writer. (Presumably he could find adequate sources of unadulterated Sherry, for his list offered a range with Sherry Arragonese starting at 18s the dozen and Ditto, Cadiz at 24s. As an alternative could be recommended from Greece, St. Elie, a dry wine, acquiring with age a fine Amontillado flavour and character; *incomparable at the price* 24s per dozen.)

The waters were muddied further by the ingenious invention of a certain Dr Hassall. His process was designed to remove all traces of gypsum from Sherry, thus making it softer, more palatable and greatly enhancing its flavour and value. The advertisement of Dr Hassall and his colleague, an analytical chemist called Otto Hehner, ran:

WINE—Deplastering and Improvement—Sherry is always subjected to the operation of plastering, whereby the wholesome tartaric acid is removed, and the aperient sulphate of potass substituted. The advertisers have secured a patent for the restoration of the original tartaric acid, and the removal of the sulphate of potass by a simple process, and are prepared to treat for the sale of the PATENT or for royalties. Wine thus treated is greatly improved.—Address, Medicus, St. Catherine's House, Ventnor.

Sadly the process of removing the gypsum involved the delicate use of a poison, salts of baryta. Not unnaturally, the concept received a poor press, and a writer in the *Sanitary Record* took a characteristic view. 'The invention is ingenious, but it appears to us the ingenuity is misplaced. The proposition to remove a non-poisonous salt by a poisonous barium compound, is certainly a novelty in the treatment of Sherry. It is hard to say what amount of doctoring this wine has already undergone in Spain and England before it reaches the consumers. The plastering, sulphuring, flavouring, colouring, and fortifying with alcohol, are accepted stages of manufacture to which the discontented Briton must resign himself. To add to these numerous processes another for "deplastering", as it is termed, by the addition of a poisonous salt, is carrying matters beyond all reasonable bounds.'

Despite the strength of the team for the prosecution, the defence mustered together some worthy protagonists, though the trade itself, through the columns of *Ridley's Wine and Spirit Trade Circular*, does not seem to have helped its case if the following extract from an article is a typical example. 'Our wine merchants are mainly responsible for any excess of added spirit to the higher class sherries. Over and over again we were told that they positively demand it of the shipper, who if left to himself and not made responsible, as he most absurdly is, for the condition of the wine for two years after it leaves his possession, would send it over containing several degrees less of spirit. It is excess of added spirit, and not gypsum or sulphur, which is the real bane of sherry.'

Better aimed were the attacks of Henry Vizetelly, a man of many parts, who had made a reputation for himself as a journalistic illustrator and publisher of illustrated newspapers. He determined to go to Jerez and learn the truth for himself. He had no compunction in attacking Thudichum's qualifications in a forthright manner: 'Everyone will remember the late outcry raised against sherry, chiefly on the part of testimonial-purveying M.D.'s always ready to court publicity by rushing into print under the pretence of enlightening an unintelligent public. Among other highly-coloured statements was one, made with an air of authority, to the effect that the grapes for each butt of sherry invariably had from 30 to 40 lbs. of gypsum thrown over them prior to being trodden and pressed, the main effects of which was to transform the tartar of the must into sulphate of potash, an aperient salt, 3 to 14 lbs of which were stated to be contained in every butt of this popular wine.'

'In common candour the author of this incredible misrepresentation ought not to have withheld from the public his qualifications to speak so confidently on the subject. He should have told them that he visited Jerez under the auspices of certain shipping houses to whom he offered, if not to repeat the miracle of Cana, at any rate to produce amontillado by purely chemical agency — that he was provided with considerable funds for the purchase of scientific instruments which he was incompetent to use, and that he resided in Jerez in style for a period of three months at the expense of his principal patron, during which time he lost him half his vineyard's produce through the so-called amontillado which he professed to fabricate turning out such vile stuff that it could only be employed for rinsing casks with, while a further experiment which he made in the bodega of a second shipper resulted in transforming the wine into vinegar.'

Having reduced the credibility of the leader of the opposition, he then flatly disputed the figures that Thudichum had given for the addition of gypsum. Rather than the 30–40 lbs per butt quoted, often it was not used at all and, at the most only a few pounds per butt might be used. Perhaps realising that medical, and chemical, arguments were of little interest to his readers, Vizetelly decided to bring matters closer to home and to appeal to national pride. 'The detractors of sherry can scarcely be aware that the superiority of Burton bitter beer is owing to the large amount of gypsum contained in the waters of the Trent and that quite as much of this innocuous substance enters into a pint and a half of that excellent beverage as into any bottle of sherry in existence.' Once the whole question was related to a bottle of Bass, the English consuming public had the whole picture in perspective.

Despite the force of reason behind much of the arguing on both sides, there appears to have been no general consensus as to the relative virtues, or vices, of Sherry. Perhaps the whole situation was clouded by the amount of spurious wine that was on offer on the British market. Nevertheless, it seems that the medical profession demanded clear guidelines and in 1898 their well-respected magazine, *The Lancet*, sent an Analytical Commission to Jerez to study production on the spot. Their findings make interesting reading: 'There are two facts in connexion with the production of sherry which are open to be construed as adulteration. The first is the addition of sulphate of lime to the crushed grapes before fermentation and the second the addition of a small proportion of spirit to wine intended for export. Against the former we do not think that a rational objection can be raised so long as the treatment is kept within limits, and this is invariably so. It may be called an artificial recourse, but so is also the adding of sugar-candy to champagne to make it sparkling or of gelatine, clay, and so on for the purpose of refining wine, beer etc.. We have explained how the same thing may be to some extent naturally effected by the simple occurrence of an unusual proportion of vineyard dust adhering to the grapes prior to pressing. We venture to suggest that this has been the origin of the so-called "plastering process". The sulphate of lime employed is a natural constituent of the soil contiguous to the vineyards. The question is, can this be regarded in the light of adulteration or fraud, since it does not add in any way to the bulk of the wine nor does it make it poisonous? On the contrary, it refines the wine and increases its power to develop those fragrant ethers which give to the wine its peculiarly pleasant characters in regard to bouquet, flavour, and agreeable stimulating qualities. Whatever character a sherry may possess this is due entirely to the product of the grape and to no foreign addition . . .'

'Then, with regard to the addition of spirit. This is in the majority of cases small although some account must be taken of the normal increase which takes place in alcoholic strength with keeping. It is a curious fact that sherry in keeping develops a slight increase in alcohol as the time advances. All spirit added to sherry, however, is obtained from wine itself, corn spirit in Spain being quite a superfluity, since wine spirit can be produced so cheaply and in unlimited quantity. Moreover, the importation of German spirit into Spain is made practically impossible by a prohibitive duty. Good brandy— that is, a genuine wine-distilled spirit—is being produced in Spain in commercial quantities which it is hoped will successfully compete with the stuff erroneously called brandy, not to say Cognac, but of which not a drop has been derived from the grape.'

'It follows as the outcome of enquiry that it cannot be correctly said that sherry in any particular contains a single ingredient foreign to its composition. We again lay stress on the fact that in coming to these conclusions we are speaking of vinum Xericum, the vin de Jerez, or the wine produced in Spain generally known as sherry, and not of those fictitious wines which are produced, or rather concocted, only too frequently elsewhere. Indeed, it is true to assert that Spain could not profitably produce fictitious wines, so essentially and peculiarly it is a country where the grape grows luxuriantly and abundantly.'

Plastering having now received a clean bill of health from the medical profession, or, at least, having been dismissed as no more than a benign tumour, one would think that the question had now been buried once and for all. However, even with my very limited experience of Sherry, I have been the victim of plastering on one occasion. Some years ago I submitted some samples to one of the Provincial Liquor Boards in Canada, only to have them rejected, not because of any low quality or high price, both proved highly acceptable, but because their chemists found that they contained traces of gypsum. What has been general practice in Spain for 2,000 years, was rejected out of hand in a Toronto laboratory.

One cannot help but feel that many of the problems that have come about in the world of Sherry abuse, have been the result of lack of interest in the product by those companies that produced it. Too late

119

did they try to stop the name being used by any and every region that produces wine (not to mention many that did not). No attempt was made to see that the wine, and the value of the name, was not debased particularly in Britain. More recently there have been moves to impose minimum quality standards in Spain, and Sherry now represents good value in a competitive world. After a stormy history, the present appears calm.

Vintage vagaries

Basically, any wine label will give you two facts; first, what the wine is and secondly either who has made the wine, or bottled it, or is selling it. Thus, the most basic wine may have a brand name and that of the supplier. A wine that is of higher classification may give in addition the actual source of the wine, be it a region, like Bordeaux, a village, like Saint Julien, or a vineyard, like Château Beychevelle. There will also be other information on the label. For ordinary table wines, it will be the strength, and for the better wines it will often be the vintage, or the year in which the wine was made. Depending on the country, or the region, the importance of the vintage date to the consumer will vary. As a general rule of thumb, the cooler the climate of the region, the more important the vintage date becomes. Thus, for example, in Burgundy, where there can be major variations in the quality of the wine from year to year, it is important to know in which year the wine was made. On the other hand, in the Valencia region, in Spain, the climate is such that one can rely on making wine of a similar quality each year.

The situation is especially important in those regions which are able to sell their finest vintage wines at a premium. Typical examples of these, in addition to Burgundy, are Bordeaux, Champagne and the Port-producing vineyards of the Douro Valley in Portugal. These regions can be split into two distinct groups; those that sell wines with a vintage on the label in only the truly exceptional years, such as Port and Champagne, and those that make vintage wines every year, but of potentially widely varying quality, such as Bordeaux, Burgundy and Germany. In the first case, the wine immediately gains cachet, and a premium price, because a vintage has been declared. In the second case, the wine-lover has to be aware of the climatic differences that may have given great wine in one year and poor wine in the next.

In Portugal, for example, Vintage Port represents no more than two per cent of the total amount sold, yet whatever quality image Port might have is dependent largely on that small proportion. To be classified as a Vintage, a Port must be 'of one harvest, produced in a year of recognised quality, with exceptional organoleptic characteristics, dark and full-bodied, with very fine aroma and palate, and which is recognised by the Instituto do Vinho do Porto as having the right to the description "vintage" and corresponding date'. It also must fulfil certain supplementary qualifications such as being bottled at a certain time and with certain labelling. Samples have to be lodged with the Instituto.

Given these regulations, one would imagine that there would be general agreement as to which years are capable of producing 'vintage' wines. In effect, there is a broad measure of accord, though one occasionally comes across rather strange exceptions. In the 1970s for example, the years 1970, 1975 and 1977 were generally considered to be outstanding and worthy to be bottled as 'vintage' wines. Most companies bottled all three years, whilst almost all the others bottled at least two of them; those which they considered to be the most suitable. Just one company, however, not only bottled all three vintages, but also the 1972 wine. Why it was that only Dow, Silva and Cosens decided on the merits of that year is not recorded. They decided that 1972 was 'a year of recognised quality' and their judgement of the situation was accepted by the Instituto.

A vintage Champagne, too, must comply with certain legislation that does not pertain to other wines from the region. Naturally it is produced only in the finest years, and each vintage will have its own particular style. As far as the legislation is concerned it must be 100 per cent wine of the vintage on the label, it must be of a minimum of 11 per cent alcohol, as opposed to the nine per cent of a non-vintage Champagne. The wine may not be sold until it is at least three years old, as opposed to the bare twelve months of other wines of the area. Also the vintage must appear on the cork as well as the label. Whilst Champagne can be made in any year, the authorities have taken protective steps to see that non-vintage wine is not solely made of wine from the poorest years. When a producer decides to make a vintage wine, he is permitted to use no more than 80 per cent of the wine that he has in stock of that vintage. Thus, some wine of the best years is always carried forward to be used in the non-vintage blends.

There are some who will say that in Champagne a non-vintage

wine can be better than a vintage one. No year is total perfection and any weaknesses can be remedied by blending in the wine of another year. Thus, there are some who will say that the Grande Cuvée, of Krug, for example, is the ideal Champagne, yet it is a wine without a vintage on the label. A vintage wine, however, will have its own personality that will change from vintage to vintage.

It can be seen that in the production of vintage Ports and Champagnes, there is strict legislation to protect the quality image that the word vintage conjures up. Elsewhere, however, there can be much more laxity in the way the word vintage is used. In many regions it is permitted to blend in a percentage of wine from one or more other years and still have vintage on the label. The thinking behind this is that as outlined for non-vintage Champagne—any slight holes that there might be in the quality can be filled in. Of course, once any wine of another year is permitted under a vintage label the door is wide open to abuse. Fashionable vintages can be stretched and there is the danger of all credibility being lost. It can become a very dangerous situation if it is not rigidly controlled.

In some regions, on the other hand, we have almost a mirror image. There have been efforts to promote non-vintage wines under the name VSR, which in French stands for *Vin Supérieur Recommandé*, or in English, Very Specially Recommended. The philosophy behind this is outlined in *The Wines of Burgundy*, by Pierre Poupon and Pierre Forgeot: 'Vintage years were sometimes a trap into which the consumer fell, so the Burgundian merchant adopted the custom as practised in Champagne by offering to his client *non-vintage wines*, in addition to wines of a specific vintage.'

'These non-vintage wines are, generally speaking, a careful selection from vintages not enjoying a high reputation. They can also be a harmonious blend of "Growths" of identical origin but of different years, giving well-balanced wines of regular and continuous quality.'

'The *Comité professional du Bourgogne* has created the abbreviation VSR and merchants in our region can offer their wines under this banner.'

'A large number of merchants and even vinegrowers, in the rest of France (especially in Bordeaux), have asked for permission to use this title. It is freely granted on the condition that the quality of the wine is worthy of it.'

It is in these last words that the potential weakness of the non-vintage, or VSR, system lies. Too often it is a convenient way of disguising blends of unsatisfactory wines from those vintages that would have difficulty in selling themselves. Whilst a good non-vintage blend can be better than the best of single vintages, the worst can be a great deal worse than one might be led to expect by what Poupon and Forgeot just said. Sadly, there is little or no control as to what goes into a non-vintage blend. Once again the answer lies in the probity of the supplier. If he has a good reputation that he wishes to maintain, he will see that any wine that appears under his label is worthy of that reputation. Unfortunately, there are many companies, often those that are selling wine as a commodity, either under someone else's label or under one of many names and labels that they have in their own portfolio, who concern themselves little with quality.

There is one other disadvantage that applies even to the best of non-vintage wines. As there is no vintage on the label, it is often impossible to have any very clear idea as to how old the wine is; as to whether it is ready for drinking; or has passed its peak. The idea of a 'best before' date on a wine-label is one that most producers fight shy of, because they are worried about the amount of wine that might be returned to them when it might still be in perfect condition. Whilst many non-vintage wines are sold ready for drinking, their life is finite and if there has not been stock rotation in the restaurant or at the wine-merchant, you might find yourself buying a bottle that is far too old. There is no way of telling. Whilst it would complicate life for the producer, surely it is not too much to ask that, on the label of non-vintages, there might be some indication of when the wine was bottled, or, alternatively, when it should be drunk. Even with non-vintage Champagne, this is a potential problem.

Vintages are as open to fraud as any other aspect of the wine-trade. In Burgundy, for example, the 1968 vintage was widely considered to be a disaster. On the other hand, that of 1969 was very successful, showing all the qualities that were lacking in the wines of the previous year. It does not need a very fertile imagination to think of the possibility that some of the older wine was used to stretch some of the younger, which would sell for a much higher price. That is just a theoretical example. Perhaps it is fairer to give two specific years that are widely abused in special cases.

Perhaps the most famous vintage of history is that of 1811, the original 'year of the comet'. Château Lafite of that year is supposed to have been one of the greatest wines ever made, or, at least so it was rated by Maurice Healey who tasted it in 1926, when 'it still drank graciously, with not more than a suspicion of fading'. H. Warner Allen called it the 'proverbial Comet year which, men said, presaged the fall of Napoleon and which was the greatest of all vintage years known up to that time'.

Even though, at the beginning of the nineteenth century, the whole question of vintages was not treated as seriously as it is nowadays, there is no doubt that the wines of 1811 caught the imagination of the public and, as a result, many of the less scrupulous members of the trade sought to profit from it. This is what an anonymous writer had to say about it, in 1829: 'The celebrated Comet Wines, as they are termed, were the produce of the vintage of the year 1811, when the great comet appeared. During the chief part of that year, the weather was remarkable for its excessive heat, and the Wines which were made at the same period would, it is supposed, in point of quality, surpass all that have since been procured. This circumstance of their having been of so superior a quality, connected with the fact that the produce was comparatively small, (as generally proves to be the case in very fine vintages), occasioned them to be quickly bought up by persons, who were no means likely to re-dispose of them; and it admits of a doubt whether even in the cellars of the richest individuals, any quantity to speak of now remains of the Wine, so aptly distinguished by the appellation of 'Vin de Comet'. One or two comets, however, have, I believe, made their appearance in the south of France, within the last three or four years, although *too small to be seen by the naked eye*; in this instance, therefore, we must not too readily impeach the veracity of the advertising gentlemen, as probably they may not mean to refer to a comet of so distant a date as that of 1811.' It seems a pity that a writer with such a sharp turn of sarcasm should remain unknown to us. He describes himself just as 'One of the Old School'. His opinion of much of the wine-trade of his time is certainly not very high.

The other example of the systematic stretching of a vintage is much more recent and might, for all I know, be still continuing to this day. The year is 1970, and the area Rioja. In Spain, there has traditionally been considerable flexibility as to the labelling of wine. Indeed, in many regions, largely because there is regular quality from year to year, the wine is not sold by the vintage, but by when it was bottled, in the first year, the third year, or whatever. Similarly, expressions like Viña Such and Such may not mean an actual vineyard, as it would suggest, but rather a specific style of wine. In Rioja, the longstanding way of producing wines, both red and white, has been to leave them in oak cask, or vat, for many years and bottle them shortly before consumption. Not surprisingly, this has meant that, over the years, the casks have been topped up with younger wine. The final result has been that the label on the bottle would bear the date of the original year of the wine, whilst a considerable proportion of it would come from succeeding years.

With the general acceptance of Spanish wines in the broader markets of Europe and the United States in the early 1970s there was a call for tightening up of controls so that the label should be a totally correct description of what was in the bottle. At the same time, there came about a rapid expansion in investment in the region, not only in the creation of new companies, but also in revivifying those that had been quiescent for generations. Much of the new money in Rioja came from enormous investment groups, like Rumasa. This particular group had expanded in a remarkable fashion since its foundation in 1961. I have in front of me a book produced for their fifteenth birthday, which lists 228 companies within the group, including 14 banks and 27 wine companies. Within the wine-trade, their initial expansion had been in Jerez, where they had rapidly absorbed a number of slumbering giants. Their second attack came in Rioja where they rapidly expanded the facilities of those companies that they purchased. As Jancis Robinson pointed out in an article in *Wine and Spirit* magazine, one of their bodegas was capable of stocking more than the total production of the region.

Whilst Rioja might produce the prestige red wine of Spain, in international terms it was a wine that represented very good value for money, particularly if one took into consideration the vintages that were appearing on the label. As José Peñin, in his *Manual de los Vinos de Rioja*, says: 'Many producers have told me that to make a reasonable profit on these older wines they would have to sell them at three times the price, and that, in Spain, there was not even a minority prepared to pay such a price, even to obtain something that was genuine.'

Where Rumasa led, there were others to follow, and it was only possible for them to generate a return on their considerable investments if the flexible traditions of Rioja vintages, and the admission of wines from elsewhere into the region, were allowed to continue.

According to Señor Peñin, the root of this philosophy lies in the fact that when the renaissance of the wines of Rioja took place at the end of the last century, it was at the hands of the merchants who had come from Bordeaux. It was they who lacked the concept of individuality between the vintages and of originality of source. If it had been the growers who had left Bordeaux, the situation in Rioja would have been considerably different.

The fact that it was the 1970 vintage that had such a great reputation, and apparently infinite sources, is due to a combination of reasons. Certainly, it was an excellent vintage and some great wines were made then, but they can only represent a small proportion of the total that have been sold as being from that year. First, 1970 was the year in which some of the 'new-wave' Rioja houses were founded and it was useful to have a famous vintage as the year of your establishment. It also made a useful *reserva* vintage for those companies which, after their takeover, had expanded very quickly. This also coincided with a sudden interest in Spain for the better things of life, such as fine food and fine wine. The final years of Franco, and the restoration of the monarchy, coincided with a resurgence of pride in the gastronomy of the country. The country's finest red wine had naturally an important role to play; the flag that it waved was the 1970 vintage.

What was the result of all this? It certainly does not appear to have been any lessening of confidence in the vintage within Spain itself. Presumably, however, the abuses must have become totally apparent to the authorities, for they banned the export of 1970 vintage-labelled Riojas to a number of markets; one of those is Britain.

In the longer term what has this led to? First, within Rioja itself, there has been a movement, led notably by Enrique Forner, of Bodegas Marqués de Cáceras, towards tighter controls in the production of, and thus more credibility for, Rioja. Now some twelve bodegas have joined together under the acronym ARBOR to form a group with just such objects in mind. With the entrance of Spain into the Common Market, there has had to be a rapid movement towards the acceptance of Community regulations in such matters as vintages. Some companies have welcomed such a move; others have protested strongly about it. What is true to say, however, is that the last year or two has seen rapid rises in the price of Riojas, partly due to three small vintages in succession, partly due to increasing demand from around the world, but also partly due to the fact that truth in labelling is now becoming a matter of course in the region.

Perhaps I should leave the final word on the subject to José Peñin, though I must admit that he was writing in 1982, before many of the recent changes had taken place. 'What value does a Spanish vintage chart have? Practically, none whatsoever. All the vintage charts for the wines of Rioja are generally based on the quality of the musts that have recently fermented. Such personalities with authority as Antonio Larrea and Manuel Ruiz Hernández rate the vintages on controls carried out by the Oenological Research Station at Haro. On the other hand, no authority has classed those wines that have been made and dispatched in bottle after having been mixed with other vintages.'

There are other reasons why a date might appear on a label without its meaning the year. Perhaps the simplest of these is the date of foundation of the firm, though I would think that there is little room for confusion on this score. More frequent, and this is particularly the case with the wines of Madeira and Sherry, is the date of the solera. The solera system was first devised in Jerez as a means of giving continuity of style to their products. Julian Jeffs describes it as 'fractional blending'. In effect it works in the following way: the shipper has in his cellar tiers of casks. When he requires some wine for his customers, he draws it from the bottom casks in the tier. This wine he replaces from the casks in the row above, and so on. When a wine is stated to be Solera 1832, for example, this means that the solera was first established in that date and that, theoretically, there has been an ever decreasing fraction of wine of that date in the blend that has finally come to be sold. Naturally the amount of this original wine must depend on the size of the original solera and how much of it is sold. I have never heard of any controls on the solera dating on labels and once again its relevance depends largely on the integrity of the shipper.

As far as Sherry is concerned wines bearing a vintage date are virtually unknown, though there are a very few specialist wines so labelled. Even a solera date is becoming much rarer. On the other hand with the wines of Madeira, the situation is somewhat different, for both the solera system and vintage dating system work hand in hand so there is a real possibility of confusion. A leaflet from The Madeira Wine Company, a consortium of producers on the island says: 'Dated Madeiras are a selection of the best wines from an exceptionally good year and are not blended with wines from any other year. These wines are matured in cask for *at least* 10 years in our lodges and then bottled. Madeira has the most extraordinary longevity, for a wine which was originally firm and sound can still be drinkable after a century and a half.' This would suggest that all Madeira with a date on the label are pure vintage wines. This is not true, as one can often come across solera dated wines and it is important to make the distinction, as the value of a vintage wine will be naturally much higher than that of a solera wine of the same date.

The first wines to be considered in this chapter were vintage Ports. Perhaps I should finish by pointing out that there are a number of other Ports, which are not *vintage* Ports, but might give the unwary consumer the appearance of being so. In Britain, perhaps the most common of these is what is known as Late Bottled Vintage Port, or LBV. By law, instead of being bottled when it is two years old, as in the case with Vintage Port, it must be bottled between four and six years old. Despite the fact that there is a stated year and the word 'vintage' on the label, the style of the wine is totally different. It tends to lack the intensity of flavour and colour that one would expect from a Vintage Port, and will mature much more quickly.

During 1987, there was much correspondence in the columns of *Decanter* magazine as to whether there was likely to be any confusion in the mind of the consumer between Vintage and Late Bottled Vintage Ports. The situation has been further complicated by a change in circumstances. Until recently, the Port houses have not offered LBV wines from the same years that they have offered Vintage Ports, thus they could claim with some justification that total confusion was impossible. That situation has now changed, for Taylor's, who were one of the houses to offer a 1980 vintage wine, have now put on the market a 1980 Late Bottled Vintage Port. In answer to criticism that there is likely to be confusion, Alistair Robertson, of Taylor, Fladgate & Yeatman, wrote in *Decanter*: 'If you visualize two bottles, side by side (or on a price-list)—one vintage 1983 and one L.B.V. 1983—the contrast in price, and the completely individual style of packaging and presentation underline their fundamental distinction. You cannot have two bottles of the same year with a different description, without automatically differentiating between them . . . Our L.B.V.—and I am sure those of other companies involved in this category—are made from our best wines *excluding those selected for Vintage Port.*' (The italics are mine.)

One cannot but agree with Mr Robertson in what he says. The simple fact, however, is that for most consumers the likelihood of seeing the two wines together, either on a wine-list, or in the flesh, is small. Far too often, they will be met at second hand in a restaurant, where, perhaps unknowingly, an LBV wine might well be offered simply as Taylor's 1983, which it is, but at the same time is not.

The situation is further complicated by Ports calling themselves Vintage Character when they would be of a similar style to a vintage wine but not bear a date on the label or simply bear a year, without its being a Vintage Port or a Late Bottled Vintage Port. The fact is that the legislation permits a broad variety of wines to be sold with a vintage year on the label. To know the difference, you really have to have a detailed knowledge of the Port wine-trade and the laws that govern it. As has already been said, Vintage Ports and LBV Ports have to be bottled at specific times, but dated Ports can, by law, be bottled at any age, as long as the label, or back-label, states when it was bottled. Thus there can be a broad range of wines including a Crusted Port, which in some ways resembles a very old Vintage Port, Fine Old Tawnies, so beloved by the French, and Garrafeira wines, as drunk in Portugal, which are dated wines, bottled many years before they are drunk. If you know the law, and you can see the bottle, you might have a very good idea as to what to expect from the wine. If, for one reason or another, you cannot see the bottle, you might be in for a considerable surprise. This is not to say that any of these wines are not excellent wines. The fact is that their styles vary considerably, as do their costs of production and their values.

To give a clear idea of what can happen in the confused world of Port dating is not easy, but this sad letter in *Decanter*, from a Mr Alrick L. Smith, of Berg in Switzerland, offers some insight: 'For me as a Port lover, having once been served a glass of L.B.V. as "authentic" vintage port in a top Indian restaurant is something that can, perhaps, be excused. This, however, happened to me subsequently in April of this year, in one of the top hotels in Porto. Even worse, on that visit to Porto I bought a bottle of 1955 vintage port from the Royal Oporto lodges which, on opening today, turns out to be (1955 perhaps) wood-aged tawny. I feel obliged to protest against a possibly unwitting, but nevertheless growing, element of fraud regarding port wine which is certainly being nurtured by its intricacies of designation.'

'I have had the following unpleasant experiences. A 1977 vintage Hutcheson's purchased in Luxembourg, turned out to be a 1978 L.B.V.; of 12 bottles of Barros 1970 vintage port purchased in Zurich,

6 turned out to be 1975. The bottles and corks to substantiate these claims are still in my possession.'

'Two British shippers sold me bottles of 1970 vintage port in Porto recently, without the Instituto de Vinho do Porto (I.V.P.) seal—contrary to I.V.P.regulations. 1970 vintage wine supplied to me by a Portuguese shipper (name withheld, but relevant documentation is in my possession) was, as I subsequently discovered, falsely declared to the I.V.P. as 1975 vintage port, so as to obtain permission for export.'

'It is bad enough for the consumer to have to struggle with the nuances of single quinta, vintage and crusted ports. It is worse for the shippers to now be promoting L.B.V. (a poor alternative to a twenty-year-old tawny and no comparison with vintage) on the back of true vintage port. But the situation is becoming serious. Increasing unscrupulousness will kill the trade. Draconian measures with regard to port wine classification are now needed to ensure that Portugal's entry into the E.E.C. will guarantee the rightful place of its King of wines in the cellars of future generations of winelovers.'

If one is to believe Mr Smith, and I for one do not doubt a single word of what he says, it would seem that there is a very cavalier attitude within certain parts of the trade in Portugal to the laws controlling the production and sale of Port. That this is nothing new is something that we have already seen, but it is sad that it is apparently continuing to such an extent. One of the basic problems is that Port wine is one thing to an Englishman, another thing to a Portuguese and a third thing to a Frenchman. Each of them would like a vintage date on the label, but they all want it for different reasons.

In many ways, a wrong vintage is the easiest thing to put on a wine-label. It is a simple fraud, but one that people are often too lazy to criticise. At its simplest, it comes when one is offered a different vintage wine from the one mentioned on the wine-list. It cannot always be a coincidence that the year you are given is rarely of higher standing than the one on the list. How widely a wine's vintage is not what it is claimed to be, we shall never know. It may be, that with wine-making techniques improving rapidly, there will be little appreciable difference between the vintages. When that happens it will be a sad day. If, on the other hand, the value of vintages is being devalued by continuing fraud in their use, perhaps it would be just as well if it were to happen.

Permitted additives?

I suppose that in an ideal world, wine would be made from organic-ally grown grapes and from nothing else. The grapes would be picked and crushed, with the natural yeasts on the skin setting off the fermentation process. At the end of it all, there would be perfect wine. Sadly, life is not as simple as that. Over the centuries, treat-ments for both the fermenting must and the wine itself have been developed — some of these are acceptable to the consumer (if he gets to hear of them) and the lawmaker; others are not.

If one thinks about it, it is scarcely surprising that the early wine-makers, with their primitive knowledge of oenology, had to seek recourse to a host of materials to make wines that were any way acceptable to the drinkers. Then, wines, for the most part, were drunk in the year following the vintage and towards the end of the summer following many of the old wines must have been in poor condition. The arrival of the new vintage was awaited with much more genuine relief and excitement than any Beaujolais Nouveau in our present day. To see that there was wine fit to drink throughout the year, in an age when bottles either did not exist, or were very rare, was the permanent concern of the vintner.

His role was outlined in a paper presented to the Royal Society 'assembled at Gresham College' in 1692, and subsequently published under the title of *The Mystery of Vintners: or, a Brief Discourse concerning the various Sicknesses of Wines, and their respective*

Remedies, at this day commonly Used. The anonymous author divides his role into four parts:

> The first is, the Natural Purification or Clarification of Wines, whereby of themselves they pass from the state of Crudity and Turbulency, to that of Maturity: by degrees growing clear, fine and potable.
> The Second, the unseasonable Workings, Frettings and other Sicknesses, to which, from either internal or external Accidents, they are afterward subject.
> The Third, their state of Declination, or decay, wherein they degenerate from their Goodness and Pleasantness, becoming Pall'd, or turning into Vinegar.
> The Last, the several Artifices used to them, in each of these States or Conditions.

In many ways, the situation has little changed. The major role of the wine-maker is to see that the wine, or wines, for which he is responsible, are pleasant to the palate, the eye and to the nose. He still has to see that the wine is bright when it is bottled, first of all by fining, or clarification, and later by filtration. In certain markets, notably the United States and Japan, it is essential that the wine stays star-bright, that it does not throw, for example, a tartrate deposit in cold weather, as it would do naturally. Such a deposit does not affect the quality or the taste of the wine, but, to certain eyes, it is unsightly, so it must be prevented.

He must see that the wine is stable when it is bottled, so that it does not begin to referment. He must see that it has a good colour and a good bouquet. All these are obtainable naturally, under ideal circumstances, but the regulations permit the use of certain treatments and additives. If one has a flexible mind, some of these treatments might be considered natural. For example, almost all white wines are now chilled before they are bottled so that they throw the tartar that is in suspension then, rather than later. This is a treatment that occurred naturally to wines in cellars during the winter. Similarly, milk has long been recognised as a useful agent for clarifying wine. Now, one of its derivatives, caseine, is more commonly used.

Most countries have specific lists of what is permitted, and what is not, and this list varies quite considerably from country to country. For example, within the Common Market, there are groups of permitted additives under the headings acidifying and de-acidifying agents, clarifying agents, stabilising agents, preservatives and anti-oxidants, yeast and yeast nutrients and the all-embracing 'others'.

Under these headings there are many things which would appear to cause no concern. For example it is now widely accepted as a healthy practice to sanitise the grapes by killing any wild yeasts that there might be upon them before taking them to the press-house. Thus premature and uncontrolled fermentation can be avoided. Selected yeasts are then added after pressing. This would seem to be sensible. Likewise there might be something to be said for the permitted addition of tannin to must or wine. Not only can it help with clarification, but it can also replace deficient body and keeping qualities. Tannin is naturally present in grapes and their stalks and it often naturally increases by ageing the wine in oak casks. It does seem sad to me, however, that the tannin that is used by the wine-maker does not come naturally from the vine or its products but from chestnuts or the galls formed on oak trees. I suppose that it is just as natural to use oak gall as oak casks.

For clarifying the wine a number of traditional methods are used such as isinglass, egg-whites, milk and gelatine, even dried, powdered blood. Ox-blood was for a long time the traditional fining agent for certain sherries. Now, more commonly used are clays like bentonite and kaolin, which carry the finest particles in suspension down to the bottom of the cask or vat. I am not sure that I am at all worried as to what is used for fining, for by its nature, it does not remain in the wine.

Of more concern are some of the stabilising agents used. The one that worries me most is what is sometimes called 'blue finings' or potassium ferrocyanide, which is used to remove traces of iron or copper from wine. I read in the booklet of the English Vineyards Association that it 'must be used only under the supervision of an oenologist or technician' and that 'Potassium Ferrocyanide is not the same substance as, and does not have the same toxic properties as, Potassium Cyanide'. This comes as some consolation, but, personally, I would prefer not to have any compound of cyanide near any wine that I might be drinking, at any stage in its production.

As a treatment, this is most commonly practised in Germany; there is, however, one other cyanic product permitted 'in those Member States where it is traditional'. In this case the tradition lingers on of keeping wine in vats away from contact with the air by covering the wine with paraffin discs impregnated with allyl isothiocyanate, which is a derivative of mustard-seed oil. Whilst I am one for preserving traditions in wine-making, here is one that I feel could be abandoned without too much discomfort to any wine-maker and with more peace of mind for any drinker of Italian wines that might just discover that such a product might have come into contact with his wine. In both cases alternative treatments are available.

As has been mentioned in the opening chapter of this book, from classical times it was common for wine to be mixed with other substances. In many cases this was simply a question of making the wine palatable. It is probable that the Greek wine Retsina is a direct descendant of this tradition. I am sure that many of the base wines that are used would be at best unpalatable if resin from the Aleppo pine was not added to them. Whilst Retsina might be an acquired taste, bad wine rarely is.

Another modern wine which benefits from this tradition at least in part is vermouth. This came about for two reasons; it was found that herbs often stabilised a wine when added to it and also, for medicinal purposes, the goodness of the herb, or of a selection of herbs, could be concentrated when wine was used as a base. In medieval times the Church was the centre not only of wine production, but also of medicine. It is in vermouth that these two strengths come together.

Whilst the Common Market has its list of permitted additives, so does the United States, and the two lists differ in a number of ways. Apparently in the United States the list of permitted additives runs to 74 different products or chemicals, starting in alphabetical order with acetic acid (I find it hard to believe that vinegar can improve a wine) and running through such mouthfuls as diethylpyrocarbonate, for slaying microbes, and polyvinylpolypyrrolidone, an aid to clarification, to Yeastex 61, which can only be a fermentation booster.

There has been a certain backlash in America against many of the ingredients that are used in wine-making. One of the leaders of the movement was the maverick New York wine-grower Walter Taylor, who sought to expose many of the practices of the major wine companies in the state, where the regulations permitted the addition not only of all these chemicals but also of water and a significant proportion of wine from outside the state, and even the country. To promote the 'cleanliness' of his own wines, Mr Taylor has not hesitated to promote the 'negative' in other people's wines. 'To reduce the sediment in wine, there are two practiced methods; one using sodium chloride, the other using hydrochloric acid. The Bully Hill Wine Company uses neither of these methods, thus there is the possibility of sediment in the wines. What this means is that our wines are made with a very low salt content, something significant for people on a low-salt diet.'

To the best of my knowledge, no one has ever suggested that wine should not be drunk by those on a low-salt diet—apart from Walter Taylor. Similarly, whatever one may think about hydrochloric acid, it is not generally used for fining wines. If it is permitted in the United States, and I have no reason to disbelieve Mr. Taylor on this point, it is not widely used for such a purpose, there are so many alternative ways of brightening a wine which are totally effective.

A by-product of Walter Taylor's campaign is that for the labelling of ingredients on wine-bottles. This suggestion surfaces regularly both in the United States and in Brussels. In America, it might be of interest to know if there are any 'foreign' wines in a blend. In the Common Market this is less of a problem because wines from outside the EEC cannot be brought in for blending purposes, and if the wine is a blend from different countries within the Common Market, the label must state so. Though it need not say from which countries, and in which proportions, those wines come.

If it is a question of actually listing the chemical ingredients, the whole situation becomes farcical, given that most wines as they appear on the market are a blend of wines from a number of different sources. In Burgundy, for example, these may be neighbouring growers, but for a French table wine, the ingredients may come from a number of different regions of France. In 1975, the Californian Wine Institute claimed that it would cost the producers of Californian wines a total of 100 million dollars a year to carry out a programme of ingredient labelling. This figure sounds as though it was conveniently plucked out of the sky, by the Institute's then President Harry G. Sterlis, but he then went on to make a more important point. Whatever such a law might cost the producer, would, in the end, have to be passed on to the consumer. Would *he* be prepared to pay the extra for such information? Walter Taylor would say yes; I, and I feel many more people, would say no.

On a similar track is the question of organic wine. Here, logic seems to play a more important role. If the consumer wishes to buy organic food, or wine, he realises that he must be prepared to pay extra for the way in which it is produced. I have every respect for such a person. I am not sure that the wine, or the food, is going to taste any better, but the fact that it is produced *naturally* does have some appeal. Here, however, one comes up against a question of semantics. It appears that the makers of organic wine are permitted to use sulphur, as that is a product which occurs in nature. (I might add that many of the nastier things that have been put into wine also appear in nature. I hope that they are not permitted by the organic authorities.) Now sulphur has long been used as an antiseptic in wine-making, but it is one product that is frequently used with a heavy hand, making wines unpalatable. My experience of organic wines is limited, but I have been told that many of them suffer from having been over-sulphured. It is possible that, because the number of permitted treatments is limited, excessive compensation in the form of those that are permitted may result in some problems.

If, from the earliest times, it was the tradition to give wines a more agreeable taste by perhaps adding some honey, or hanging a *bouquet garni* in the cask, there grew up a regular code of treatments for wine during the seventeenth and eighteenth centuries. Often these were written down and, as well as forming specialist books, they also played a regular part in the household encyclopaedias that were so popular in Britain during the eighteenth century and which had titles such as *Valuable Secrets in Arts and Trades*, *The Laboratory, or School of Arts* and *Arcana Curiosa: or Modern Curiosities of Art and Nature*. In such books, one could learn how to make fireworks, catch fish, cure your dog of distemper, or yourself of the pox, make Lombardy sausages, as well as how to treat a wine that is going off. It would be interesting to compile a complete list of cellar-work from such books, but I have selected just a variety of the ingredients that have been used, or recommended, from the seventeenth century until the present day. Some of these are mentioned in specific cases elsewhere in this book; for others, it will be their only brief appearance.

For these substances to have been selected for their various purposes, almost everything that is animal, vegetable or mineral must have been tried and one can only imagine, in a number of cases, that the recipes ever succeeded. Indeed, on occasion the cure must have literally been more deadly than the original problem. Here, then, is a brief selection as to what you might have found in your wine.

Arsenic In the eighteenth century, arsenical sulphur, or hepar, was used to remove lead from wine. As one French writer of the time said: 'This last method of treatment . . . demands a lot of attention.'

Bacon-fat 'Take the fat of bacon melted, pour it into the hole of the vessel, so it may only touch the superficies of the wine, and it will never grow eager.' Presumably the fat congealed on top of the wine and stopped its coming into contact with the air.

Beech-shavings These were generally used for clarifying wines. Some writers said that oak shavings could also be used.

Beetroot Widely used, particularly in England, for colouring cheaper wines, especially Port.

Bilberries Berry-dye was extracted from German bilberries and was a regular ingredient in Victorian England of domestically blended Ports.

Brandy In many North European countries, natural wines were not sufficiently warming, so fortified wines, such as Port, Sherry, Madeira and Marsala became popular. It has always been accepted that they should be fortified with brandy. However, in the eighteenth century, it became common to add brandy to almost all the wines that were shipped to Britain, including Bordeaux and Burgundy. As Cyrus Redding wrote 150 years ago: 'Brandied and adulterated wines are the bane of Britain.' During the second half of the last century there was a movement against such wines and merchants began to advertise their products as 'free from heat'. What may be less generally realised is that, until recent times, it was perfectly legal to add a proportion of brandy to Burgundies if they were being shipped to the British or Scandinavian markets. The French verb for such a practice is *viner*, which must be a euphemism, if ever there was one. Rather than *wining* a wine, one is *brandying* it.

Briony This would seem to be the answer for so many of those vineyard regions which recently have had the wrong balance between the production of red and white wine. Burgundy, Australia and California could all learn something from these instructions:

> 'To make White-wine Red and Red White.
> Take ashes of white Briony to make Red-wine White;
> and, on the contrary, ashes of Black Briony to make
> White Red. *Probatum.*'

I have certain reservations about this cure-all as, apparently, briony roots were regularly hawked about as being those of the mandrake, with its magical properties. To me, deception in one field might lead to deception in another.

Bugloss This used to be grown in the South of France for its roots, which when infused in brandy give a bright red colour. This was used for giving additional colour to cheap wine and also for staining the ends of Port corks, to give them an air of authenticity that they probably did not deserve.

Cider This was regularly used to stretch Bordeaux wine. A centre of this adulteration for many years was the island of Guernsey. Wine would be shipped there from France, 'treated', and then passed on to England.

Cochineal Again used for colouring wine.

Diethylene-glycol Used in Austria and elsewhere as a means to the artificial sweetening of wines. More details can be found in Chapter 7 on Austria.

Eels This might well be the least likely additive to wine, but in a strange way it may be one of the few recipes of the time likely to achieve exactly what it sets out to do. Whilst this is taken from a late eighteenth-century book, it was widely recommended at least 200 years earlier:

> 'To cure those who are too much addicted to drink Wine.
>
>   Put, in a sufficient quantity of wine, three or four large eels, which leave there till quite dead. Give that wine to drink to the person that you want to reform, and he or she will be so much

disgusted of wine, that though they formerly made much use of it, they will now have an aversion to it.'

Elder Of all the trees of Europe, there can be none which was of greater use to the wine-maker. The flowers were infused in white wines to make them more fragrant. The berries were widely used for colouring wine. Indeed, the abuse was so widespread in Portugal that the Marquess of Pombal ordered that all the trees in the Douro Valley should be destroyed. As for the bark, this, too, had its uses:

'To preserve wine good to the last.

Take a pint of the best spirit of wine, and put in it the bulk of your two fists of the second peel of the elder-tree, which is green. After it has infused three days, or thereabouts, strain the liquor through a cloth, and pour it into a hogshead of wine. That wine will keep good for ten years, if you want it.'

Fuschine According to George Ordish, in his history of phylloxera and its effects, the *Great Wine Blight*, this was an aniline dye that was used in the Midi for colouring the artificial raisin wines that were made in the absence of sufficient grapes. The more common name of the dye is Magenta, so called after the victory of the French over the Austrians in 1859. A patent was taken out under this name in London the following year.

The main danger of the product was that arsenic was one of its constituents. To be over the safe limit, fuschine would have to contain over four per cent arsenic, if used in the recommended proportions of one litre to 40,000 litres of wine. The French newspaper, *Le Temps*, stated that between ten and twelve tons were being used annually in the production of wine. If being used as stated on the packet, this would suggest that it coloured an approximate equivalent of something over 500,000,000 bottles of wine each year.

Gooseberries The main ingredient of artificial champagnes made and sold in Britain during Victorian times.

Gypsum Widely used in Mediterranean countries. It was originally thought that its addition to fermenting must would reduce the acidity and improve the colour of the wine. In fact, it increases the acidity in musts which otherwise might lack them and gives the wine more balance. Discussed more fully in Chapter 9 on Sherry.

Herring roes were used to preserve stum wine. This was wine that was kept to start up secondary fermentation in other wines. In other words it was a wine whose own fermentation had not terminated and could help other wines finish theirs.

Horseradish By infusing bags of wild horseradish cut into pieces for two days, and repeating the dose until the required effect was acquired, wine could be cured of 'a bad taste and sourness'.

Lead Straight lead, melted, 'and thrown into water' and put in a cask of wine was said to prevent it from turning. More common, and more dangerous, however, was:

Litharge or lead oxide. Nowadays this is apparently used in the production of paint and car batteries, but in the world of the vintner in the seventeenth and eighteenth centuries it was considered to have almost magical properties and was known as the Water of Saturn. It was used variously for settling troubled wine and also for enhancing its colour.

That it was dangerous was realised early on, for its use was banned in France in 1696, when a number of people died of lead poisoning, as a result of drinking wine treated with litharge.

Whatever the law might have been, it was widely abused, as this story, by a contemporary French writer, bears witness: 'About 1750, the authorities were surprised by the vast quantities of spoilt wine that was coming into Paris, theoretically for the production of vinegar. As a result they launched enquiries and discovered that there was indeed a considerable increase in this business. In each of the three years up to their beginning the enquiry, almost thirty thousand tuns of spoilt wine had come into the city, whilst in 1710, 1711 and the following years, the figure had been between a thousand and twelve hundred tuns. Their research bore fruit. They discovered that a number of wine-merchants borrowed the title of Master Vinegar Maker in order to bring in spoilt and bitter wines. When these wines arrived in Paris, as was the custom, they spent three days at the Hotel de Bretonvilliers, where six pints of good vinegar was added to each tun. Notwithstanding all this, the merchants found the means of destroying the acidity in these wines and making them drinkable.'

'The Magistrates have on a number of occasions pursued many merchants who have adulterated wine. They have even punished some who have created wine without a single grape, and others who sold cider or perry as wine, after having coloured it red.'

'The use of litharge was the secret of the wine merchants who made drinkable the spoilt and bitter wines which they had brought in under their title of Master Vinegar Makers.'

'This dangerous prodecure, despite the attention of the Police, is still far too frequently followed, not only for spoilt and bitter wines and those of mediocre quality, but also to give wines a sweet taste.

Such adulterated wines change those that drink them, so that they drink more and more. This causes them, as we have already said, damage, which can prove to be mortal.'

The point of bringing the wine in as vinegar, was so that the merchants would not have to pay any taxes on it.

The authorities must have been successful in eradicating the practice, for Cyrus Redding, in 1833, wrote: 'In France, it does not appear that lead in any form has been employed in making or altering their wines, though in Germany, a century ago, it it said to have been detected. On the thirteenth of March, 1824, a member of the Chamber of Deputies moved a law to punish the practice. The motion was rejected, and very properly, because neither litharge, nor any other preparation of lead, was shown to have been used, nor was any instance cited in which it had been discovered, though an ordinance was made against its use in 1696. Wines seized in France as bad, by the council of health, and analyzed, never showed the presence of lead. From 1770 down to 1825, not one instance had occurred in the analysis of the wines, which were brought to Paris, of this dangerous intermixture, upon the authority of M. Cadet Gassicourt, whose duty it was to examine them.'

Somehow Mister Redding seems to have missed what had been a common practice in Paris during the first half of the previous century. It may have been stamped out there, but the use of litharge was still an everyday affair in the London wine-trade. Indeed, trade manuals recommended its use and attempted to minimise its dangers. 'The size of a Walnut of Sugar of Lead, with a table spoonful of Sal-Enixum, is put to forty gallons of muddy Wine, to clear it; and hence, as the Sugar of Lead is decomposed, and changed into an insoluble sulphate of Lead, which falls to the bottom the practice is not quite so dangerous as it has been represented', prattled *The Vintners' and Licensed Victuallers' Guide*.

A more realistic position was taken in Accum's Culinary Poisons. 'The most dangerous adulteration of Wine, is by some preparations of Lead, which possesses the property of stopping the progression of ascescence of Wine, and also of rendering White Wine, when muddy, transparent; I have good reason to state that Lead is certainly employed for this purpose; the effect is very rapid, and there appears to be no other method known of rapidly recovering ropy Wines. Lead, in whatever state it is taken into the stomach, occasions terrible diseases; and Wine adulterated with the minutest quantity of it, becomes a slow poison.'

Logwood The dye obtained from this Central American tree was widely considered as being used for colouring Port. Whether this is true or not is hard to say though Henry Vizetelly, in his *Facts About Port*, seems to doubt it, when he writes: 'It has often been asserted that logwood has been used to impart colouring matter to Port wine; and the authors of a bulky Treatise upon Wine endorsed this preposterous assertion with their authority.'

Magui This berry from a Chilean shrub served as an alternative to elderberries, particularly in the difficult times after phylloxera. According to George Ordish, imports into Europe rose from 26 tons in 1884 to 431 tons just three years later. Of this quantity, almost three-quarters went to France, presumably to colour the raisin wines that were then growing in popularity.

Medlars   'To take away the Mustiness of Wine
Take Medlars, cut them in Four Pieces, hang them so in
  the vessel
as they touch not the wine.'

Methanol is the highly poisonous wood-alcohol which has commercial uses as a solvent, fuel and constituent of anti-freeze. It has occasionally been used to 'soup up' wines and was responsible for the more than 20 deaths in the recent Italian wine-scandal.

Mugwort Professor Saintsbury, in his *Notes on a Cellar Book*, says that one of his friends claimed that Manzanilla received its distinctive taste as a result of having mugwort infused in it. Strangely, this is a story that is repeated nowhere else that I can see, and appears to be totally without foundation, though it might account for the story that Frank Hedges Butler tells about an Earl of Derby, 'who was great sufferer from gout. His physician recommended him to get some Manzanilla from his wine merchant. The Earl did so and, having tasted it, returned it with his compliments, saying that of the two he preferred the gout.'

Mustard-seed A somewhat unlikely ingredient for making wine sweet. Half a pound in the bottom of a barrel was guaranteed to make a '*vin-doux*'.

Oyster-shells Were ground up having been put in a fire until they were red-hot. The resultant powder was added to manufactured Sherry, often mixed with chalk, to 'bind and concentrate the whole'.

Parsley   'To correct a bad Flavour in Wine.
Put in a bag a handful of garden parsley, and
let it hang by the bung-hole in the cask, for
one week at least. Then, take it out.'

Raspberry brandy was recommended from as early as the seventeenth century. One author suggested putting a drop in the bottom of the bottle when you fill it from the cask for immediate drinking. Two centuries later, it was used in London to try to give some finesse to the heavy wines that were currently imported as Claret.

Red Sanders was a dye extracted from the Red Sandalwood tree, which grows in the East Indies. It was widely used for colouring sweets, but also was called upon in the preparation, in Britain, of Ports and Clarets.

Salt was widely used in the treatment of wines and, as we have seen, it still used for clarifying purposes in the United States. From classical times it has been thought that the addition of a handful of sea-salt to each cask of wine has improved it. Indeed the French oenologist Puvis writing 140 years ago was led to believe that there must be some merit in the practice, because it had been followed so religiously for so long. His own experience gave him no real reason for such a belief. The addition of salt to wine has been forbidden in France for a century or so.

Sloes To colour Claret, it was suggested that a syrup should be made from sloes and sugar. This could be added in the proportion of one pint to each hogshead. The trade manual that offered this useful tip also suggested that much Port might benefit from it.

Soot When added to Malmsey and Bastard, it would help keep them fresh.

Swallows' beaks
   'To prevent one from getting intoxicated with drinking.
   Take some swallows beaks, and burn them in a crucible. When perfectly calcined, grind them on a stone, and put some of that powder in a glass of wine, and drink it. Whatever wine you may drink to excess afterwards, it will have no effect upon you.
   The whole body of the swallow prepared in the same way will have the same effect.'

Turnsole is a purple colouring agent that was formerly widely used for colouring wine, and also foods and materials. There seems to be some confusion as to what it was made from and the word was also used, and the French equivalent *tournesol*, for a broad range of flowers whose heads turned to follow the sun, such as the giant sunflower. Some authorities say the dye was made from the *heliotropium*, but in fact it came from *Crozophora tinctoria*, the small turnsole, which was cultivated in the South of France. It also came to be made from lichens.

Vinegar

To sweeten a tart wine. Put in a hogshead of such a wine, a quarter of a pint of good wine vinegar saturated with litherage: and it will soon lose its tartness.'

Zedoary This root could be added to a cask 'to help stinking wines'.

As can be seen, the list of ingredients that can be used in the production of wine is large. No one would dispute that many of them are, in themselves, perfectly harmless. Some of them do not come into contact with the wine itself or are taken away with any deposit, but some of them are dangerous and many of them are, or more properly were, used specifically to deceive the consumer. Cyrus Redding must have felt strongly when he said: 'Vegetation has been exhausted, and the bowels of the earth ransacked, to supply trash for this quackery.' Wine that is totally natural, and in which nothing other than the grape has intervened, may not always be the best wine. It is not easy to draw the boundary between what is acceptable and what is not. On the other hand, it is not difficult to see that much of what we have been offered as wine has come from way beyond that boundary.

↬12↫

Take one pound of bananas . . .

From the earliest times there has been a tradition that if you cannot find the wine that you want, you make it for yourself. Those that had the highest reputations during classical times were widely copied and there were even books which told you how you might most success-fully achieve this. The reasons for copying through the centuries have been numerous. For example, when one was at war with France, it was not easy to buy French wines, though they do seem to have been available, either from smugglers or from trading ships that might have been captured on the high seas. Similarly, for commercial reasons, there might be punitive duties on the wine from a particular country.

The fact that Britain was primarily a maritime nation meant that certain wines historically were of importance on the market in that country. Originally, the favourites were those that could easily be imported from the Continent; Claret from Bordeaux, Rhine wines from Amsterdam and wines from Auxerre from Rouen. Later, in times of war, it was wines from islands such as Madeira, the Canaries, the Azores and Sicily which became popular, perhaps out of all measure to their relative importance. Because of their access from the sea they could be supplied readily with goods from the powerful British merchant marine, who would take wines not just for the ever eager British merchant market, but also for such places as the Cape, the West Indies and even Iceland.

Duties, too, in early times, were liable to vary depending on the port through which the wine was imported. An example of this is the

144

town of Chepstow in Monmouthshire. Towards the middle of the sixteenth century, a certain Thomas Pope shipped 90 tuns of wine into that port and then redistributed it in smaller vessels about the West Country. John White, the king's representative in his role as Deputy Butler, claimed prisage (the right to a certain number of casks of any wine from any shipment) on that which had been sent to the Somerset port of Bridgwater. Pope disputed this by claiming that 'all customs and duties in the port of Chepstow belong to the Earl of Worcester, as Lord Marcher there. He and his ancestors and all others, whose estate he has in Chepstow, have always had all manner of customs of wines and other wares coming from the seas by way of merchandise in that port.' A few years later Queen Elizabeth sent a messenger to the same town to find out why duty had not been paid to her on some casks of Gascon wine which had been brought in. After being roughly handled, he was brought before the Steward of Chepstow, who threatened to nail the messenger in the pillory by the ears and then throw him into prison. He was only set free and sent on his way after much discussion.

Duties played an important role in encouraging the making of wines at home and even the beginning of Gladstone's planned reform of wine-duties in 1859, when there was a common duty of 3/- per gallon on all wines, did not lessen the traffic of fraudulent wine, though it may have stopped some of the home wine-making. One immediate result was that vast quantities of out of condition wine which had been lying on the quay at the Port of London, with the duties unpaid, because there was no way in which the merchant could make a profit on them if he were to pay the duty, suddenly had a low potential cost price, even after the paying of the duty. There was no shortage of merchants happy to now buy them and use them as raw material for conversion into fancifully named Ports and Sherries.

In the following year Gladstone created a separate duty for high strength wines and this encouraged the practice, which has continued to this day, of merchants importing wines at two different strengths and then blending them to try to avoid having to import all the wine under the higher rate of duty. Any form of taxation which encourages blending in Britain is a form of taxation which leads to fraudulent habits.

It is hard to say that there is any more deceit in the wine-trade than in any other, but there have always been those who have been happy to exploit any lack of knowledge on the part of the consumer. Certain wine regions have relied for much of their trade in the past on the fact that an important proportion of what they have produced has been of a style that has enabled it to be passed-off as something else. Tarragona made wine similar in style to Port; much of it came to be sold as such. On occasion it would be a town that relied for its existence on fabricating wines. As we have seen Hamburg and Sète were two such examples. The fact that both were sea-ports enabled them to bring in the necessary raw materials from wherever they wanted and to ship the finished products out to those customers who were eager to purchase them. They had no shame in what they were doing and their recipes could be had by those who were interested enough to ask for them.

It is easy to try to equate the production of Sète and Hamburg, but, in fact, the production of the two towns was distinctly different. At Sète, wine, and often old wine, was the base ingredient for all the compounds. Indeed, the wines of Sète must have had their admirers and defenders. In my copy of *Wine and Wine Countries*, by Charles Tovey, which was published in 1877, in one place, where the author is talking about blending, there is an indignant contemporary hand-written footnote, 'Again, why condemn Cette? This book constantly mentions the blending of the produce of various vineyards in Port, Sherry, etc.' Perhaps that writer was unaware of the other ingredients, apart from wine, which went into the mixtures for which that town was noted!

Indeed, there is some admiration for the Hambro' wines in the report by a Mr Prestwich on the wines exhibited at the International Exhibition of 1862. This report was subsequently published by the Society of Arts. In speaking of the 'wines' of Northern Germany, the report says:'They show a marked improvement in applied chemistry, but are not encouraging as showing an improved taste in this country. These northern makers seem to exhibit in the manufacture both of wines and brandies a knowledge of the subject, and of the use, probably, of those curious new flavouring ethyl ethers which threaten a strong competition with our own makers and distillers, and even with the commoner foreign white wines, notwithstanding transport and duties.'

It was apparent that, in a fit of national pride, there were those who were happy to snatch the crust from the Hamburg wine-makers and produce similar commodities in Britain. Shortage of ready money appears to have been the only problem of the advertiser in *The Times* of 15 October 1864:

TO WINE MERCHANTS, — Wanted, by a gentleman of exper-ience in making up the Hambro' sherries &c., and having the required plant for the purpose, the SUM of 1000L. Address, R.S., care of Mr. W. Abbott, 7, Little Tower Street, E.C.

It is difficult to know how to regard the question of home-made wines. Particularly in Britain, the tradition of making them has been long, for they were drunk not just for pleasure, but also for medicinal purposes. Recipes for drinks played a major role in one of England's earliest cookery books, *The Closet of the Eminently Learned Sir*

Kenelm Digby Kt. Opened, which was published in 1669. Sir Kenelm Digby, himself, had led a curious career. His father had been executed for his part in the Gunpowder Plot. He married the mistress of Sir Edward Sackville, later Earl of Dorset, and became a crypto-pirate preying on French and Flemish shipping in the Mediterranean. During the Civil War, he appears to have been some sort of double-agent, but was welcomed back at Court after the Restoration. He also seems to have desired the reputation of a medical, rather than culinary, man, though his remedy for curing gangrene, with a Sympathetic Powder that was capable of operating at a distance of several miles, appears to have met with a certain lack of credibility. He, nevertheless, was one of the Founder Members of the Royal Society and gathered together quite a coterie. His steward, George Hartman, wrote *The Family Physitian* and in the portion entitled 'The true English Wine Cellar', included a recipe for artificial Champagne, which was 'comparable with the best of that which is made in the province'. It was two of Sir Kenelm's followers also who patented, in 1662, a process for making glass bottles, that was to revolutionise the wine-trade.

A rival book, *the Queen-like Closet*, appeared shortly afterwards under the name of Hannah Wolley, and this, too, included a number of recipes for fruit wines, including one for a Cordial Cherry Water, 'for fainting fits, or a woman in travail, or for anyone who is not well'. An anonymous French writer in *Les Délices de la Campagne* of 1654 says that Hypocras can be made 'in an instant, with cinnamon essence, wine and sugar; you can also add any flavouring that you find agreeable such as aniseed, fennel, cinnamon, cloves and suchlike'.

As we have seen, it did not take long in Britain for the names of genuine wines to become attached to those which were made from anything other than the grape. Within the home-made wine fraternity there has been mixed opinion as to whether you should, for example, call something that is made from cowslips and sugar and yeast, cowslip wine or sherry. The latter habit was encouraged, until very recently, by there being readily available on the market kits for the production of 'Beaujolais type', 'Sherry type', and 'Hock type' 'wines'. These have now disappeared, but their literature still carries on.

I would like to quote from a current best-seller on the subject of home-made wines. In the first chapter of *Making Wines Like Those You Buy*, by Bryan Acton and Peter Duncan, the authors say: 'It is a curious fact that home-made cakes are valued as being much better than bought cakes while the reverse is the case when wines are considered.' They then suggest that modern science has enabled this thought to be reversed. What they fail to say, of course, is that home-made cakes are largely made from natural ingredients, as are

147

commercial wines, whilst factory produced cakes must rely on modern 'science' for their production. I pose this, I hope, rhetorical question: 'Should one prefer a Chablis made in the Yonne *département* from the Chardonnay grape, or that suggested by Messrs Acton and Duncan, from green gooseberries, white grape concentrate, elderflowers, water, sugar, pectinol, nutrients and Chablis yeast starter?' What they recommend may taste very pleasant, but whatever it is it is not Chablis. Do you want cherries, raisins, bananas and red grape conc. in your Chianti? Sadly, some of those ingredients are too close to some that have been used in Italian wine scandals for comfort.

'How good are those wines going to be?' they ask. 'An honest answer to this question is that if you pay attention to everything in this book, about 80% of the wines you produce will be as good as the wines you buy in the cheaper ranges of commercial wines and about 10% will be of such excellent quality that they will not be disgraced in the company of more expensive commercial wines. About 10% may be disappointing and we can afford to carry that amount of failures. We do not claim that with the ingredients we use or in the smaller quantities we make we can match the best of commercial wines. Such wines as Chambertin in the Burgundies, Vintage Port, Château d'Yquem in the Sauternes, Château Latour in the clarets and the best Hocks and Moselles stand in a class of their own and always will.' It is a relief that the Marquis de Lur-Saluces, of Yquem, can sleep untroubled!

The very use of wine names for these home-made products is a fraud, particularly when the names have specific geographical connotations. I am sure that comparison can be made; one product may be preferred by some people, the other, by others, but by no stretch of the imagination can such products be allowed the names that they are given in this book.

Compare what they have said, with the words of Moritz Jagendorf in his book on a similar subject, *Folk Wines, Cordials and Brandies*: 'Thus, out of the fruits of the earth, out of the leaves of the trees, out of the wind and weather, you create a drink famous in history, famous in lore, and often famous in taste. You create a drink that gives inspiration for song, laughter, poetry and great art. You have an undisputed opportunity to exercise your will in the choice of the medium, the color, taste, fragrance, bouquet. It is a hobby in which you are lord.'

'If your wine making is confined to a city apartment, you will have nearly all the same pleasures if you work with your mind and imagination even as you work with your hands.'

'Add to this a generous list of new gustatory experiences. I will never forget the sensation when I tasted for the first time the opulent, brown, Malaga-like elderberry wine. It made me think of wealthy olden Johnsonian merchants or gentlemen sitting around a table toasting lustily in loud voices. There is a Persian-perfumed feeling in rose-petal or rose-geranium wine. And with the first glass of parsley wine there was the surprising exotic adventure of having come into a new world of taste.'

Mr Jagendorf does not hold back from using bananas in his wine— but he calls it banana wine; he does not hesitate to compare his elderberry wine to Málaga—but he does not call it Málaga. Whether his recipes produce better wines, I do not know, but I certainly prefer reading them.

Here then is a series of recipes, over the last three centuries, which have sought to pass under the colours of something that they are not. The list is not definitive, but it is representative, for it includes 'wines' that should be made at home, and it includes 'wines' that only can be made on an industrial scale. They are grouped by their titles, which I feel in many cases must be fanciful. What else could this first one be?

A secret for making artificial wine

Take a loaf as it comes out of the oven, steep it in strong vinegar, then lay it by and keep it; to make wine immediately you need only steep a piece of this bread in a glass of water, and it will give the colour and taste of wine.

Arcana Curiosa (1711)

How to make Rhenish wine

Take one handful of dried limon peels and put them into 10 or 12 gallons of white wine, and put in one pint of damask-rosewater; then rowl it up and down, and lay it upright, and open the bung of it, and take a little branch of clary, and let it steep 24 hours; and take it out, and it will taste very well.

The Art and Mystery of Vintners and Wine Coopers (1692)

How to make Rhine wine

Take a cask of 252 pints of white Rochelle wine, or Cognac wine, or Nantes wine; rack it off and put it into a freshly scented cask; fine it with the correct mixture for white wine, of which we have already talked, that is to say with isinglass; put in it 25 or 30 pounds of skimmed honey and 4 pounds of moist brown sugar, beat them all together and give the mixture enough time to fall bright. To give it a bouquet add a decoction of poppy seeds, which will give it the real taste of a Rhine wine.

Le Parfait Vigneron (1783)

British Rhenish

To every gallon of fresh apple-juice, add two pounds of loaf-sugar. Boil and skim this till quite limpid. Strain it. Ferment it as other wines; and when the head flattens, rack it off clear and tun it. Next season, rack it off again; add a pint of brandy to every three gallons. *Obs.* This is a highly reputed wine, but we have no actual experience of its qualities.

Cook and Housewife's Manual (1829)

An artificial Claret

The juice of clary, or the water of clary distilled in a cold still, one part; Red-streak, or pippin cider, half a part; Malaga raisins beat in a mortar, six pounds; the fat Mother of Claret, one pound; of the chrystals of tartar half a pound; and being close covered, let it ferment the space of fifteen days, then draw off the liquor clear into a barrel; to every gallon thereof add half a pint of the juice of black-berries or gooseberries and a pint of spirit of clary to the whole; then take three spoonfuls of flour, the white of two new laid eggs, a dram of isinglass, being all beat together, add it into the barrel with two pounds of the syrup of clary, and it will refine down and become wonderful rich.

English Wines (1691)

English Claret

An admirable wine, very like claret, and even surpassing common claret in strength, may be prepared by the following process—take any quantity of Malaga raisins, chop them very small, put to every pound of them a quart of water, and let them stand in an open vessel having a cloth thrown over it for a week or nine days, stirring them well daily. Then, drawing off as much of the liquid as will run, and straining out the rest from the raisins by pressure, tun up the whole in a seasoned barrel; and, to every gallon of the liquid, add a pint of the cold juice of ripe elder berries, which has been previously boiled and scummed. Let it stand, closely stopped, about six weeks; then draw it off, as far as is tolerably fine, into another vessel; add half a pound of moist sugar to every gallon of liquor; and when it gets perfectly fine, draw it into bottles.

The Family Receipt Book; or, Universal Repository (c. 1817)

English Champagne

To three gallons of water put nine pounds of Lisbon sugar, and boil the water and sugar half an hour, observing to skim it well. Then take a gallon of currants picked, but not bruised, and pour the liquor boiling hot over them. When it be nearly cold, put into it come barm, keep working it for two days, and then strain it through a flannel or sieve. Put it into a barrel that will just hold it, with half an ounce of isinglass well bruised. When it be done working, stop it close for a month, then bottle it, and in every bottle put a very small lump of double-refined sugar. This is excellent wine, and has a beautiful colour.

John Farley: *The London Art of Cookery* (1784)

Best white Gooseberry Champagne

To every Scotch pint of ripe white gooseberries mashed, add a quart and a half of milk-warm water and twelve ounces of good loaf-sugar bruised and dissolved. Stir the whole well in the tub or vat, and throw a blanket over the vessel, which is proper in making all wines, unless you wish to slacken the process of fermentation. Stir the ingredients occasionally, and in three days strain off the liquor into a cask. Keep the cask full, and when the spiritous fermentation has ceased, add for every gallon of wine a half-pint of brandy or good whisky, and the same quantity of sherry or Madeira. Bung up the cask very closely, covering the bung with clay; and when fined, which will be in from three to six months, rack it carefully off, and rack it again if not quite bright.

N.B.—The fruit here should be rather over-ripe. A very excellent white-currant wine may be made by this receipt, or a wine of white gooseberries and white currants mixed.

Cook and Housewife's Manual (1829)

Artificial Champagne

To imitate these wines, we need to choose top-quality base wine, which must be perfectly bright and with a pleasant agreeable taste. Such wines can be treated in two ways; for the first which is now going to be described, we must obtain a mineral water machine, like that in figure no. 15 on the plate, for example, in which the wine is put in the gasometer so it can be saturated, and as soon as the pressure reaches 7 or 8 atmospheres, the wine should be bottled into bottles strong enough to resist the pressure of the carbonic acid gas, with the corks fixed tightly, with string first and with wire after.

The wire should be heated, so that it will be flexible afterwards and can be easily removed.

Preparation

White wine	100 litres
Loaf sugar	5 kilos
Vanilla extract	8 grammes
Lemon extract (peel)	8 grammes

The sugar should first of all be turned into syrup.

Miguel V. Rodriguez: *La Perla del Viticultor y Licorista* 1885

To make as good wine as Spanish wine

1. Take one hundred pounds weight of dry raisins, from which pick off the stems, and open the fruit with a knife. Put these in a large wooden tub, very clean. Boil fifteen gallons of rain-water, purified by straining through the filtering paper. Pour it over the raisins, and cover it to preserve the heat of the water. Twenty-four hours after, take off the raisins, which will be swelled, and pound them in a large marble mortar, then put them again in the tub. Heat fifteen gallons more of water, which pour over the other with the raisins, and throw in twenty-five pounds of coarse sugar. Stir all well and cover the tub over with two blankets. Three days after, by a cock placed at the bottom of the tub, draw out all the liquor, and cask it, adding six quarts of brandy to it. Press the ground with an apothecary's press, and put the juice in the cask, with two pounds of white tartar pounded into a subtile powder, in order to promote the fermentation, and five or six ounces of polychrest salt, and a knot of garden cress seed, of about sixteen or eighteen ounces weight, and another knot of seven pugils of alder flowers. These knots are to be suspended by a thread in a cask.

2. If the wine look too yellow, you must strain it though a jelly bag, in which you shall put one pound of sweet almonds, pounded with milk. The older the wine so much the better it is.

3. To make it red, dissolve some cochineal pounded in a certain quantity of brandy, along with a little alum powder, in order to draw the better the dye of the cochineal, which put to digest on a sand bath. Till the brandy has assumed the proper degree of colour, give it to your wine in a sufficient degree.

4. It is preferable to clarify the sugar well, and to put it in the cask instead of the tub.

Valuable Secrets in Arts and Trades (c. 1795)

Art of making Austrian wine in all countries

The following curious receipt is literally translated from a celebrated German oeconomical writer—Pick red or purple grapes from their stalks, into a pail; then put them in a vat, strewed over with white mustard seed in the proportion of about half a pint to ten gallons. The vat, after bruising the grapes with a wooden masher, must be well covered, and the mash every day thoroughly stirred. In eight or ten days it is to be pressed, and have the expressed mash or must passed with the liquor into the barrel, the height of a hand being left unfilled. It must now be very often stirred, both day and night, with a proper stick, to prevent it's farther fermentation. When it becomes quiet, and settled, the barrel is to be filled up with more must; but not with old wine, as the mustard meal is necessary. When a large quantity of this wine is to be made, there should be several vats, in none of which the mash ought ever to be more than two feet deep. The German receipt gives no farther directions; but the barrel, of course, is to be closed, and the liquor drawn off and bottled in due time, after the usual method.

The Family Receipt Book; or, Universal Repository (c. 1817)

Constantia

To make 100 litres:

Very old Banyuls wine	88	litres
Infusion of orris root	1	litre
Spirit of raspberries	2.25	litres
Spirit of tar	15	grammes
Grape syrup 35 degrees	5	litres
Alcohol 85 degrees	4	litres

Mix together carefully and leave to rest for two months, then fine with gelatine (15 grammes dissolved in half a litre of water) and rack after a week on the finings.

Note: All wines benefit from aging, especially dessert wines: they should only be released for consumption after you are certain that they leave nothing to be desired. Absolute brightness is also an essential condition.

A Cette recipe quoted by Bertall: *La Vigne* (1878)

(He also gives similar recipes, with variations in the ingredients, for a range of sweet wines including Tokay, Port, Sherry, Madeira and Malaga.)

White elder wine, very much like Frontiniac

Boil eighteen pounds of white powder sugar, with six gallons of water, and two whites of egg well beaten: then skim it and put in a quarter of a peck of elderberries from the tree that bears *white* berries: don't keep them on the fire. When near cold, stir it, and put in six spoonfuls of lemon juice, four or five of yeast, and beat well into the liquor; stir it every day; put six pounds of the best raisins, stoned, into the cask, and tun the wine. Stop it close, and bottle in six months. When well kept, this wine will pass for Frontiniac.

Mrs Rundell: *Domestic Cookery for the Use of Private Families* (c. 1894)

To imitate Malvoisie

Take of the best galangal, cloves and ginger, each one drachm. Bruise them coarsely, and infuse for twenty-four hours, with brandy, in a well closed vessel. Then take these drugs out, and having tied them in a linen bag, let them hang in the cask by the bung-hole. Three or four days after, your wine will taste as good and as strong as natural Malvoisie.

G. Smith: *The Laboratory, or School of Arts* (1799)

Two ways of making or dividing Malmsey

If you have three butts of Malmsey you may make four if you please: if you have two you may make three; if one butt, you may make one and a half thereof, with such laggs as you have of White, Claret, and Canary that are old, with two gallons of cutt to every butt, so that it be Spanish cutt. That way you may rid your laggs and old Canary away. The Art followeth.

Take to every butt six eggs both yelks and whites, and a handful of bay-salt, beat them well together, mixing therewith a pint of old Sack, and put it into the butt; then beat the butt well; and if it want a colour, take two gallons of Red-wine, and a quarter of a pound of coriander seed well beaten small; mix them together, and put them into the butt; then give it six or eight stroaks more, then stop it three or four days; broach it after at your will.

The Art and Mystery of Vintners and Wine Coopers (1692)

English Sherry

To every pound of good, moist sugar, put one quart of water. Boil it till it is clear; when cool (as near as possible to cold without being so) work it with new yeast, and add of strong beer in the height of working, the proportion of one quart in a gallon. Cover it up, and let it work the same as beer; when the fermentation begins to subside, tun it; and when it has been in the cask a fortnight or three weeks, add raisins, half a pound to a gallon, sugar candy and bitter almonds of each half an ounce to the gallon, and to nine gallons of wine half a pint of the best brandy. Paste a stiff brown paper over the bung-hole and if necessary renew it . For all British wines, brown paper thus pasted on is preferable to a bung. This wine will be fit to bottle after remaining one year in the cask; but if left longer will be improved. If suffered to remain three years in the cask and one in bottles, it can scarcely be distinguished from good foreign wines, and for almost every purpose answers exactly as well.

The New London Cookery (c. 1827)

Artificial Dry Sherry

When the class of sherry that you have to make is common or ordinary, it is useful to make it by the following formula, which has the advantage of giving excellent results at a cost fifty per cent lower than others.

It is prepared with

White wine	50 litres
Almond dye	1.5 litres
Brandy	2 litres
Alcohol	1.5 litres

Mix them all well, leaving it to rest for six or eight days, fine and rack off into clean, sulphured vessels.

If you want a sweet sherry add two litres of grape syrup or if you do not have any, 2 kilos of sugar which has previously turned into syrup with one litre of water.

Miguel V. Rodriguez: *La Perla del Viticultor y Liquorista* (1885)

It was, however, with Port that the imagination of the *chefs de cuisine* really ran riot.

Russian port

Cider	3 Kilos
Brandy	1 Kilo
Gum Arabic	0.008 Kilos

D. Nicolas de Bustamente: *Arte de Hacer los Vinos* (1875)

To make British Port

To six gallons of water, put six quarts of elderberries, when quite ripe, and three quarts of blackberries, and six quarts of damsons; boil them all together for three-quarters of an hour; then strain it through a hair sieve, and put to it twelve pounds of loaf sugar, and still it till the sugar is dissolved; when the liquor is near cold, add some new yeast, and let it stand till the next day; then tun it into the vessel, with fifteen pounds of raisins chopped small, and one gallon of sloes, baked; stop it close, and let is stand in the barrel twelve months, then bottle it.

N.B. The longer it is kept, the better it will prove.

Addison Ashburn (1807)

An excellent recipe to make neat Port

Let the hogshead be matched, then fill as follows:

12 gallons of strong Port
6 gallons of Rectified Spirits
3 gallons of Cognac Brandy
42 gallons of Fine Rough Cyder

Cost about 18s. per dozen

Palmer's Publican's Directory (c. 1825)

Imitation Port Wine

Good Cyder, forty-five gallons; Brandy, six gallons; good Port wine, eight gallons; ripe sloes, two gallons; stew them in two gallons of Water, press off the liquor and add to the rest; if the colour is not strong enough, add Tincture of Red Sanders or Cudbear. In a few days, this Wine may be bottled; add to each bottle, a tea-spoonfull of the powder of catechu, mixing it well; it will very soon produce a fine crusted appearance, the bottles being packed on their sides as usual: soak the ends of the corks in a strong decoction of Brazil Wood, with a little Alum, which, along with the crust, gives an appearance of age.

The Vintners' and Licensed Victuallers' Guide (c. 1825)

And finally one of my favourites.

Lord Pembroke's artificial red Port Wine

Mix well together forty-eight gallons of turnip juice, or strong rough cyder; eight gallons of malt spirit or brandy; and eight gallons of real port wine: adding a sufficient quantity of elder berry juice to colour it: add some of the young branches of the elder tree to give it a proper roughness. Keep it, in cask and bottle, about two years before drinking it. This is Lord Pembroke's receipt; which perhaps, may be improved, with regard to roughness, by the juice or wine of sloes; and, in colour, make to any required tint, by cochineal, logwood, or Brazil wood. French brandy will certainly be better than malt spirit; and, perhaps, either a good bodied raisin wine, or even a raisin cyder, may sometimes, according as excellence or cheapness is the object, be advantageously adopted instead of rough cyder or the juice of turnips.

The Family Receipt Book; or, Universal Repository (c. 1817)

Whilst the compiler of this last recipe book may have had some doubts about the ingredients of the Port, the originator of the recipe had none whatsoever. Lord Pembroke, who was the grandfather of Lord Palmerston, is reported as having made a habit of saying to his guests at dinner: 'I cannot answer for my champagne and claret, as I only have the word of my wine-merchant that it is good, but I can answer for my port-wine. I made it myself.'

As can be seen from the small selection of wine recipes that I have quoted, their aim and, one assumes, their ultimate quality, vary considerably. Some are there specifically to defraud the consumer, others are more for home consumption. Of the fraudulent propositions, it seems sad that some should be specifically aimed at the trade, in trade publications. In other words, magazine editors were deliberately inciting their readers to deceive the public, even to the extent of staining the corks to give an impression of age. It is doubtful whether in any country such practices could happen today, but it is as well that we should be aware of the past and hope that such happenings as the Italian banana boat scandal, when 'wines' were created from ingredients no more far-fetched than those in some of these recipes, are just isolated happenings. Indeed with the production of wine now being so much in surplus around the world, it is no longer worthwhile, with a few exceptions, as in the Austrian case, to make totally artificial wine. What is more probable is the rebaptising of wine, and that does not preclude having water poured on its head.

The Spanish technical wine writer Nicolas de Bustamente, in his book *Arte de Hacer los Vinos*, considers in some depth the falsification of wine, and the many recipes for it that were current in Spain during the last quarter of the nineteenth century. For him a totally natural wine is best, but he then goes on to give a form of classification of other ingredients used in descending order of acceptability. To him, something can be said for any grape product, water, pure sugar, and to a lesser extent, alcohol, for they all form part of wine in any case. Less acceptable are fruit juices and cider, for whilst they might be natural products, they are not normal constituents of wine. Whilst not dangerous, 'they are difficult to digest, rise quickly to the head, and immediately intoxicate'. Lower still are colouring additives such as elderberries, cherries, blackberries and logwood, for they tend to alter the taste of the wine and make it bitter. It would be better to have a lighter coloured wine that was natural. Worst of all are chemical additives like litharge; they should be avoided at all cost.

It is easy to criticise the wine-makers of the past centuries. They were working under totally different circumstances from those of today. Controls were less evident and wine names had not acquired the exclusive element that they now have. Nevertheless, one has the impression that lack of control was deliberately abused by many. Those that knew how to were happy to take advantage of ignorant palates. The same too often happens even today.

How? and why? and how? and how? again

If one begins to look into the question of fraudulent wines, one soon becomes aware that it is a broader and deeper subject than one might ever have imagined. Since beginning this book, I have begun to wonder whether I have opened some Pandora's box. Have I let loose upon the world a host of worries for the consumer about the evils of the wine-trade? Is there left at the end of it all the hope that there might be some answer to stop it all? I hope that the answer to the first question is a qualified 'No', but I cannot be optimistic enough to hope that there is anything more than hope, and perhaps not very much of that, as far as the second question is concerned. I feel that now there are four questions that should be asked, and an answer to each of them found. Firstly, 'How much fraudulent wine is there?' and associated with that, 'Why is there so much?' Thirdly, one can ask how it might be reduced. Finally, and perhaps most important of all, 'How can the consumer recognise a fraudulent wine when he meets it?'

Just before I started writing this last chapter, I had a drink with the head of the wine department of a major supermarket chain. When I told him what I was doing, he first expressed concern that the credibility of the wine-trade might suffer, and then began to ask me whether I had mentioned such a case and such a case. As he jogged my memory, it soon became apparent that in this book I have only mentioned a fraction of the total number of cases of wine-fraud *that have come to light*. I have used italics here because, by the very nature of the subject, no one hears about the successful cases of fraud, but only those that are discovered. It is impossible, therefore, to quantify the amount of fraud that there is in the wine-trade. The figure might seem high, but this is simply because of the fact that, because the growers have wanted to create quality images for their products, they have chosen to tighten the controls on production. Far too often, these controls do nothing to improve the quality of the wine, but much to improve its price. There are more frauds now because there are more regulations.

The tendency towards fraud must also increase because, with the expanding market for wine world-wide, a demand has been created that is often impossible to meet—legally. One answer, of course, is to increase the area under vines. There is now ten times as much Chablis produced as there was 35 years ago. Whilst much of this is due to the fact that viticultural techniques have improved, much is also due to the fact that permitted areas for planting have been considerably extended. Thus vines that might have been producing fraudulent Chablis 35 years ago, are now producing the real thing. In that particular case the growers are lucky, for there was room for expansion. In most cases, on the other hand, increased production, as far as the laws are concerned, must have come about by better house- or vine-keeping.

Wine-fraud appears to take place at two levels. First at the very top end of the price-scale, because the margins are there, and at the very bottom end, because the quantities are there. Naturally, the latter end amounts to a much larger percentage of wine consumption and thus abuse at this level is met with by more drinkers, though it is probable that these drinkers are not worried about the source of the wine as long as it is drinkable—and enjoyable. One has only to look at the scale of fraudulent practice in Austria, for example, to be aware that nearly everybody who drank wine in that country must regularly have drunk illegal wine. As has already been explained, whilst it may have been the diethylene-glycolised wines which caught the interest of the press around the world, they represented no more than a small proportion of the trafficked Austrian wines that were in circulation. It is perhaps sad that journalists played up the potential dangers of these wines to an extent that was out of all proportion to the minimal medical damage that they could cause, whilst they ignored the festering state of a significant part of the wine-trade in Austria. In the country fraud seemed to be endemic, yet attention was drawn to one specific case. Whilst the whole body was gangrenous, the specialists paid all their attention to the foot, whilst largely ignoring problems that were at the heart. That Otto Nadrasky was probably responsible for the production of much more wine that had no connection with the grape at all, than of wine that was artificially sweetened, is a matter of some importance; yet, he will probably be remembered as the man who added anti-freeze to wine—which is factually incorrect.

The scale of fraud at the cheaper level of wines in Germany, too, has been on a monumental scale. The invert sugar scandal was followed by what might be described as the immigrant wine baptism scandal. In both cases, the authorities admitted that millions of bottles of wine were involved, and it is likely that the authorities only know about a small proportion of the wines that were fraudulently sold, yet the British press has shown minimal interest on either occasion. Perhaps surprisingly, the largest fall in consumption of German wine occurred when some German companies were shown to have sold wine with diethylene-glycol in it. It seems that there are two standards in the minds of the consumer, and the journalist; one for the wines of Austria and another for the wines of Germany. It is true that the Austrian public relations in the matter were disastrous, whilst the Germans appear to handle their affairs, in two senses of the word, rather better.

Here, then, is another matter that must be taken into consideration when the scale of wine-fraud is considered. We only know what we are told. It may be that there are many major cases of fraud which are never drawn to our attention. I have the feeling that the French are much more adroit at handling the public relations in such matters. When I worked in France, I regularly heard that there was a major scandal in such or such a region, but no matter how much one searched in the newspapers, it was only occasionally that the matter came to the surface.

In other countries, such as the United States, where there has been much less in the way of restrictions as to how wines are made, and more freedom as to how wines can be labelled, there has quite naturally been less illegal wine on the market. Nevertheless, there have been occasions when major companies have abused even that liberal legislation. This has particularly been the case with varietal wines. With the ever increasing demand for Cabernet Sauvignon and Chardonnay, on more than one occasion a wine so labelled has been found to contain less than the minimum percentage required of the named grape variety. It is interesting to see that many growers in California, and elsewhere, are insisting on regional appellations, often of quite a small size to personalise their wines. A natural result of this is the introduction of more laws; laws which might be abused.

Both Spain and Portugal appear to have had a pragmatic approach towards the labelling of wine. For them, this has had to change with their entry into the Common Market. Not only will the application of appellations and vintages have to meet the standards demanded by the other countries, but also, the quality levels will have to be clarified to conform to the taxation levels and pricing polices that are laid down within the Common Market. There is no doubt that there is a groundswell of feeling amongst many of the more outward looking producers that tighter controls can only help in the long run.

In Britain, it is true that the move towards the importation of more wine in bottle is also a move towards less fraud. As we have seen, there is still the possibility of changing labels, but for this to be carried out satisfactorily, it can only be done on a small scale without there being major problems — such as the replacement of cartons. It is not so long ago that there was a number of soup-kitchen bottling companies in the British trade that were capable of creating wines to the customers' orders, and arranging the paperwork to deceive the authorities. Fortunately, their deception appears to have been inadequate, for they now seem to have disappeared, sometimes after being prosecuted.

Also the number of those who would like to call themselves wine-trade traditionalists is on the decline. Whilst I have nothing against, and am indeed proud of, many of the traditions of the wine-trade, such companies seemed to be much keener on the preservation of those aspects of the wine-trade that made life easier. I have in mind, particularly, the non-acceptance of *appellation contrôlée*. It is surprising how many people in the trade in Britain resented the introduction of guarantees as to the source of a wine. Whilst they would be very unhappy if they were offered a spurious Cartier watch or Parker fountain-pen, they considered that there was nothing wrong in describing wine as a Nuits Saint Georges, when they knew perfectly well that it did not come from there. These 'traditionalists' seem to have had a peculiar set of double standards.

How much fraudulent wine is there? To start with, of chemically arranged wine, there is probably a significant amount, but this is a question of degree. I am certain that there are many wines which have been over-chaptalised, or over-sulphured, or even might have had an illegal, but harmless substance (water, for example) added to them. Technically these are illegal wines and I wish that they did not exist. However, the opportunites for minor breaches of wine-law, which varies so much from country to country, are legion and one would be naïve if one thought that both the growers and the merchants did not profit from them.

On the other hand, I do not feel that there is widespread and systematic abuse of specific aspects of the wine-laws, like the invert sugar story of Germany, or the diethylene-glycol scandal of Austria. The responsible government departments in the various wine-producing, and wine-importing, countries are now much more aware of what they should seek. Whilst, in the past, some producing countries might have been prepared to turn a blind eye to some of the practices in the field of additives, they have learnt a salutary lesson from the Austrian, and similar, stories. Export markets, and the hard currency that they bring in, can be lost overnight. To re-establish a presence, in the face of the ever-increasing opposition, may cost much money and take a great deal of time. Sadly, as far as much of the Austrian wine-trade was concerned, there was little pressure on them for the two years after the diethylene-glycol scandal, for there were two small vintages, and no surplus wine to export. It is only now that it is having to wake up to reality and to go out to court customers that they abused and then ignored for two years.

Whilst I say that the authorities now have a better idea of what they have to look for, it must also be borne in mind that they can only work within the limits of their own experience. I am certain that there is someone, at this moment, who is seeking out the perfect additive that will enable better wine to be made more cheaply from inferior raw materials. This additive will be unknown to the authorities, so they will not test for it until another scandal breaks on the world. If the same thing were to happen with baked beans, it would be called food-technology. In the wine-trade, it is simply fraud.

As to the passing-off of wine, I have little doubt that this has been widely carried out in certain countries. I think that no one would dispute that the rapid increase in the popularity of the wines of Rioja, for example, led to certain companies in Spain bringing in wine from other regions to stretch the wine that they had purchased genuinely. Whilst I am not totally convinced that this particular problem has completely disappeared, I am sure that it is one of rapidly decreasing importance. The expansion was too rapid and undue pressure was put on the sources of supply. Now a finer balance has been achieved. Nevertheless, I must always have doubts of the total authenticity of any wine, where a source is guaranteed by the label, which suddenly undergoes a boom in sales. Given the fact that it takes three or four years from planting for a vineyard to come into reasonable production, individual regions cannot, on many occasions, adapt themselves quickly enough to the vagaries of the market. It is during that bridging period that the maximum pressure occurs.

Depite what I have said, not even the most pessimistic commentator would consider that anything more than a tiny minority of wine that is on sale is in any way not what it claims to be. It must be unsatisfactory, nevertheless, that there is even this small amount that creeps through the network of controls to arrive in front of the consumer. What can be done to stop it?

No matter how rigorous the wine-laws of any country might be, they only begin to be effective if they are applied. At the outset of the Austrian wine-scandal, the government of that country announced that it was going to introduce the severest wine-laws in Europe. To anyone who knew anything about the situation, the statement was little less than laughable. The wine-laws that the country already had were perfectly adequate. They may not have been the tightest in Europe, but if they had been applied effectively, there would have been no scandal at all. All the abuses that were prevalent in the country were forbidden by the existing laws. For political reasons, both at a national and a provincial level, the authorities decided to let matters ride. The scoundrels were known throughout the country long before there was any outcry. At the end of the day, the government should have been in the dock as much as the guilty wine-merchants.

Once again, in Germany, with the invert sugar scandal, it is documented that inspectors had provided sufficient evidence for senior trade figures to be prosecuted a long time before any action was taken. The authorities at first decided against taking action, for political reasons, and it was only when there was no alternative that they were forced to move. One might say that the 'Bordeaux Agreement' and the 'Tunnel System', as applied in Burgundy, were no more than tacit acceptance on the part of the authorities that illegal practices were taking place. Perhaps the officials accepted that it was impossible for them to control the system that had been created; the manpower that it would demand was far beyond their resources. Even now, the compulsory tasting of all *appellation contrôlée* wines in France only serves to eliminate bad wines, not wines that lack the character of what they claim to be. As much has been admitted to me by a French official during the past week. If one considers the implications of this, one soon realises that more controls can ultimately lead to less control.

As the demand for consumer protection increases, so will the demand for tighter or increased controls. The compulsory bottle-size of 75 centilitres is on its way. I totally agree with this because there has long been confusion in the mind of the wine-drinker as to how much he might expect in his bottle. This is not a new problem. In 1802, a Leith wine-merchant, James Walker, wrote *Hints to Consumers of Wine on the Abuses which Enhance the Price of that Article: Their Nature and Remedy*. Whilst much of his book is taken up with the plaintive plea that one can hardly expect a wine-merchant to tie up his capital in ageing wine for his customer, the one real abuse that he attacked was that of the variety of sizes of bottles that were prevalent at the time, without any information being given to the purchaser. Thus, the less scrupulous merchants would use smaller bottles and save not only on the cost of the wine, but also, and this is important in historically high duty countries like Britain, on the cost of the duties.

There are many bodies pressing for health warnings on bottles of wine; for ingredient listing; and, this I heard suggested for the first time just a week ago, for a nutrient statement. Now I can see merits in all three of these propositions, though, certainly as far as the last two are concerned, they would mean considerable extra ultimate costs to the consumer. Nevertheless, if these are to be applied, they have to be checked and I know of no country in the world which has a wine inspectorate that is capable of effectively carrying out the work that they have to do at present. To add to that load either means less effective general control, or a much greater investment in the control systems. My feeling is that we should improve what we have in applying current laws, before we extend the breadth of the laws themselves.

For laws to be effective, there must be the appropriate punishments to accompany them. In England, these have varied considerably over the ages. In 1364, John Penrose, a Vintner, was summoned before Adam de Bury, the Mayor of London. He was found guilty of selling bad wine and was 'ordered to drink a draught of the wine and the remainder poured over his head and he to forswear the calling of Vintner in the City for ever'. Whilst the first half of the sentence does not appear too severe, by today's standards the second is drastic. If all those who sold bad wine were to have their livelihoods taken away, there would be a very different wine-trade.

In 1426, Sir John Rainewell, who was then Mayor, 'having received information against the Lombard Merchants, that they were guilty of mal-practices in the adulteration of Wines, and finding, upon inquiry, that the charge was well founded, he ordered that the noxious compound, to the quantity of 150 butts, should be thrown into the kennel'. It seemed strange to me that the dogs should have to suffer inundations because of the poor quality of Italian wines, but some research has shown that a kennel in mediaeval times was the name of a street-drain, so the sufferers would appear to be rather the rats.

Over the years, there were regular controls of wine, but it would appear that whatever legislation was in force, it was widely abused. In order to reduce the problems, Charles II went to the other extreme and had passed an Act in Parliament which effectively forbade the mixing of one wine with anything else. Whilst this certainly prevented the adulteration of wine, it also stopped both blending and such harmless practices as fining. In any case, when one reads books on the treatment of wine from just years after his death, one imagines that it was not applied.

In the nineteenth century, there was a strong public outcry about the abuses in the trade led partly by members of the medical profession and partly by members of the trade itself. Nevertheless, there are few records of prosecutions being brought for wine-fraud in Victorian times, which is scarcely surprising as even trade handbooks were openly proposing recipes for making counterfeit Port, Sherry and Madeira. Interestingly a case came before the Court of the Exchequer in November 1826, in which a Mr Oldfield, trading as the Westminster Wine Company, was prosecuted for selling as Sherry a mixture of Sherry, Cape Wine, bitter and sweet almonds, powdered oyster shells and chalk. He was also charged with using fictitious permits, which enabled him to balance his books so as to account for these extra quantities of wine passing through them. The situation was further complicated by the fact that Mr Oldfield appeared, in evidence, to have given instructions for this illegal blending to be carried out whilst he was in the King's Bench prison. In the event, all charges, bar one of issuing a false permit, were dismissed. It is interesting to note that the maximum fine for the illegal blending of what were quite considerable quantities of wine was £300, whilst that for misuse of a permit was £500, for each occasion. It is also interesting that the case was brought as the result of information brought by a disgruntled employee, rather than on the initiative of the authorities.

As has been mentioned in Chapter 4 on Champagne, another merchant successfully sued for libel a newspaper which had accused him, with apparent justification, of passing-off as top quality Champagne, a wine of very doubtful origins. It seems that a further useful way of getting rid of spurious wines was to hold an auction as being 'wines from the cellar of a gentleman, lately deceased'. Through such outlets were passed vast quantities of 'Ports of 1820 and 1834, those inexhaustible vintages'.

If few prosecutions were carried out against fraudulent wines, the Customs and Excise made inroads on the importation of many such products from abroad, by imposing duties on them as though they were spirits rather than wines, thus effectively pricing them out of the market. Nevertheless, despite all the unfavourable publicity, and the efforts of the Customs, fraudulent wines were still accepted as a matter of course if one is to believe the evidence of *Law's Grocer's Manual*, which appeared at the turn of the century. Despite the fact that the introduction of the grocer's licence had been blamed by some for the increase in fraudulent wines, the anonymous author warns his readers severely to beware of being offered spurious wines under the guise of Claret, Port and Sherry. *German Champagne*, we are told, is 'merely a sweet port of sparkling beverage, manufactured out of American or French apples by an addition of water and with the help of certain chemicals'. Nowhere is there any suggestion that such a product might be illegal.

Whilst there has been a number of prosecutions in Britain over the past few years, the levels of fines imposed has generally been out of proportion to the profit that the fraudster might have gained. If one considers that by relabelling a case of French table wine as Chablis, there must be a potential net gain of approximately £2 per bottle, and even more when the Chablis prices boom, it does not take much imagination to calculate what the profits must have been for those companies which systematically either relabelled wine imported in bottle, or bottled it themselves under false labels, over a period of years. Often they are charged on a nominal basis, certain quantities representing far larger amounts that may have been fraudulently sold. It may have been that the judges have been deceived by the gentlemanly aspect of the man in the dock. Could he possibly be guilty of deliberate fraud? When an, albeit distant, cousin of the Queen is found to have sold false wines over a long term of years, is he nothing more than a victim of circumstance? The answer is, 'No—he has made his living knowingly in such a way for years.' The sooner that fines in wine-fraud cases reflect not just the profit that has been made, but also a punitive swingeing surplus, the healthier will be the wine-trade. As has been shown in Austria, large quantities of artificially cheap wine on the market can cause totally innocent people to suffer as a result of having to compete. They are the ones who are likely to go bankrupt, whilst even after he has paid his fine, the fraudster can afford to laugh.

Sadly, it is not just in Britain that malpractice escapes lightly. In Italy, the men charged with lacing their wines with methyl alcohol, and causing the subsequent death of more than twenty people, were released from custody because not enough evidence was forthcoming to enable them to be held. It may be that they are innocent of the charges; it may be that they will be taken into custody again, but it appears strange to me that they were initially held in prison if it was not considered that there was enough evidence on which to base charges.

In the Winegate scandal in Bordeaux, the architect of the whole fraud, Pierre Bert, made a mockery of authority and turned his experience into a profitable best-seller. It would appear that in the field of wine, it can be shown that, only too often, crime does pay.

At the end of it all, how can the consumer avoid buying any wine that is fraudulent? Unhappily, there is no simple answer to this question, but there are a number of steps that he can take to minimise the risk. First, if, for example, in a restaurant, the wine that you are brought is not exactly as described on the list, mention the fact to the wine-waiter. The difference might be in the source of the wine, the producer or the vintage. All three of them can give good reason for substantial variation in the quality of the wine. You should be shown the bottle before it is opened and the cork before you taste it. If, as sadly occasionally happens, the wine-waiter adopts a superior attitude, suggesting that he is the man that knows all and you know little, do not hesitate to say, if it is true, that he has produced a wine that is not the one he offered to sell you—and he said nothing about it. Also point out that it is you that has to pay for the wine.

The relationship with the wine-waiter should not be an unhappy one. He is there to help you, not to deceive you. The quality of knowledge of those serving wine is improving rapidly, but unfortunately, there is still a small minority capable of ruining a meal. I came across a sommelier from that school in a Michelin rosetted restaurant in Burgundy. He offered an expensive bottle of wine, already opened, without showing a cork, and without a label on the bottle. He was dismissive when the origins of the wine were questioned. That is one restaurant which will see me no more. On the other hand, do not hesitate to ask the advice of the wine-waiter when you are in doubt. He should know the wines that he is selling.

Similarly, ask your wine-merchant to help you, but complain to him if you think that you have been sold another wine than the one you were offered. There is nothing mystical about wine, but, far too often, people do not like to complain because they are afraid that they would then enter into a totally unknown world, where they might have to retreat before a barrage of superior knowledge. If you feel that you are unable to gain any satisfaction, in Britain, you then contact your local Trading Standards Officer. It is his responsibility to follow up your complaint. Whilst he might spend most of his time checking mileage readings on second-hand cars, he is also interested in the world of wine—as a number of telephone calls to me over the years have shown! Despite the big coverage that any wine-scandal might get in the press, it is surprising how few complaints are actually made to the authorities by private individuals.

How does one recognise a fraudulent wine? Very rarely by the label, it must be admitted. Certainly my suspicions were aroused by some Burgundies that were on sale, purporting to have been bottled in Beaune for the British market. One of the words appeared to have been written in Dutch, rather than English. It subsequently turned out that the wine was a French table wine that had been bottled in Holland—and it is sadly Holland that has taken over much of the nineteenth-century mantle of Hamburg and Sète. Whilst there are many totally reliable fine wine merchants in the country, there also appear to be a number of rogues. I think that I would personally prefer not to buy any wine bottled in Holland, unless the bottler's name was one that I recognised.

I would suggest that one must always beware of the unexpected bargain. Whilst there are always genuine offers, it is best to compare prices for a similar product from a number of sources. If one is much cheaper than all the rest, there has to be a very good reason for it. Yes, one can sometimes find bankrupt stock; yes, there may be wine sold off cheap because, for example, it has thrown a harmless deposit; but there is always the possibility that it is being sold cheaply because it is not the same wine in the bottle as is claimed on the label.

It is not always that the false wine is sold cheaply. One of the names that was mentioned in connection with German wine being tainted with diethylene-glycol was that of Pieroth, the enormous Swiss-owned company that makes a speciality of selling directly to the consumer. Whilst they might be cutting out the middleman, their prices are high. On more than one occasion in articles, I have drawn attention to some of their practices which I have considered to be questionable. They have never bothered to reply. The glycolised wine was not the first time that they have come to the attention of the courts. I would not buy their wine.

To give lists of respectable suppliers is not easy and I would in no way be capable of giving a comprehensive one, for my drinking experiences are limited. Nevertheless, each consumer should try to learn which growers and which merchants can be relied upon to supply good wine. Only experience can tell this. Notes, if only mental ones, should be made of the sources of good, and also bad, wines. As Cyrus Redding wrote: 'The best test against adulterated wine is a perfect acquaintance with that which is good.' Whatever I might have said, and written in this book, there is no doubt that there is very much more good wine about than bad., This is due to a number of reasons; the improvement in the methods of producing grapes and making wine, a new generation of wine-makers, who have been to wine-school and have not had to rely largely on tradition, more competition in the market-place. They have all had a role to play.

Since the sixth century BC, when the Carthaginian agricultural writer, Mago, gave detailed instructions on how to make fine wines, and instructions as to what additives should be used to disguise those of lesser quality, there has been, until this day, a triple bill in the world of wine. First come those wines that are totally genuine and natural; secondly are those which have been 'arranged' to improve them, and finally, there are those that are totally fraudulent in one or more ways. As has been shown, in certain regions, like Burgundy, it has been difficult to produce drinkable wines solely of the first category. One hopes that the proportion, nevertheless, is increasing and the reliance on the second group for a regular part of the 'Burgundy' wine trade is diminishing.

In an ideal world, there should be no need for wine-fraud, but it will continue just as long as substantial profit can be made from it; as long as the penalties inflicted on those discovered in fraudulent practices are not severe enough to serve as a disincentive; as long as certain authorities are prepared to turn a blind eye, probably thinking that foreign earnings are more important than national pride; and finally, as long as the consumer is happy not to query a wine about which he has doubts, either through ignorance or indolence. Wine-fraud is with us, but there are enough genuine, enjoyable bottles about for it not to worry me too much.

Bibliography

ACTON, Bryan and DUNCAN, Peter, *Making Wines Like Those You Buy*, 3rd edn (Argus Books, Hemel Hempstead, 1985)

AMERINE, M.A. and SINGLETON, V.L., *Wine, an Introduction for Americans* (University of California Press, Berkeley, 1965)

Arcana Curiosa: or Modern Curiosities of Art and Nature (J.N., London, n.d.)

ARLOTT, John, *Krug: House of Champagne* (Davis-Poynter, London 1976)

—— and FIELDEN, Christopher, *Burgundy Vines and Wines* (Davis-Poynter, London, 1976)

ARNOUX, *Dissertation sur la Situation de Bourgogne* (Samuel Jallasson, London, 1728)

ASHBURN, Addison (1807)

BÉGUILLET, *Nouveau Traité de la Vigne avec la Meilleure Méthode de la Cultiver*, 3rd edn (E. Bidault, Dijon and Dupleix et Laporte, Toulouse, 1773)

BELLOC, Hilaire, *Advice* (Harvill Press, London, 1960)

BERT, Pierre, *In Vino Veritas* (Paris, 1975)

BERTALL, *La Vigne, Voyage Autour les Vins de France* (E. Plon et Cie., Paris, 1878)

BESPALOFF, Alexis (ed.), *The Fireside Book of Wine* (Simon and Schuster Inc., New York, 1984)

BONAL, François, *Le Livre d'Or du Champagne* (Editions du Grand-Pont, Lausanne, 1984)

BOUILLE, Michel, *et al.*, *Le Minervois* (Editions Le Paysan du Midi, Maurin-Lattes, 1978)

British Pharmacopoeia (Spottiswoode and Co., London, 1864)

BUSBY, James, *Journal of a Tour Through Some of the Vineyards of Spain and France* (Stephens and Stokes, Sydney, 1833)

de BUSTAMENTE, D. Nicolas, *Arte de Hacer los Vinos* (Madrid, 1875)

CAMPBELL, Ian Maxwell, *Wayward Tendrils of the Vine* (Chapman and Hall, London, 1947)

CHAPTAL, Comte, *L'Art de Faire le Vin*, 2nd edn (Deterville, Paris, 1819)

CHAPUIS, Louis, *Vigneron en Bourgogne* (Robert Laffont, Paris, 1980)

CHARNY, Francois, *Le Sucre* (Presses Universitaires de France, Paris, 1950)

The Closet of the Eminently Learned Sir Kenelm Digby Kt. Opened (H. Brome, London, 1669)

COCKS, Ch. and FÉRET, Ed., *Bordeaux et ses Vins*, 9th edn (Féret et Fils, Bordeaux, 1922)

CROFT, John, *A Treatise on the Wine Trade*, rev. edn (Crask & Land, York, 1788)

DANGUY, R. and AUBERTIN, Ch., *Les Grands Vins de Bourgogne* (H. Armand, Dijon, 1892)

Les Délices de la Campagne (Pierre Des-Hayes, Paris, 1654)

DÉLISSEY, J. et PERRIAUX, L., *Les Couriers-Gourmets de la Ville de Beaune* (Centre d'Etudes Bouguignonnes, Dijon, n.d.)

DENMAN, James L., *The Vine and its Fruit*, 2nd edn (Longmans, Green and Co., London, 1875)

—— *Wine and its Counterfeits* (The Author, London, 1876)

DOUTRELANT, Pierre-Marie, *Les Bons Vins et Les Autres* (Editions du Seuil, Paris, 1976)

DRUITT, Dr Robert, *Report on Cheap Wines* (Henry Rensham, London, 1865)

DUIJKER, Hubrecht, *The Great Wines of Burgundy* (Mitchell Beazley, London, 1983)

—— *The Wines of the Loire, Alsace and Champagne* (Mitchell Beazley, London, 1983)

DUMAY, Raymond, *La Mort du Vin* (Stock, Paris, 1976)

EISENCHTETER, M., *Le Bourgogne au 18eme Siècle* (Bourgogne Geisweiler, 1983)

ENJALBERT, Henri, *Histoire de la Vigne et du Vin* (Bordas, Paris, 1975)

ETIENNE, Robert, *Bordeaux Antique* (Federation Historique de Sud-Ouest, Bordeaux, 1962)

FAITH, Nicholas, *The Winemasters* (Hamish Hamilton, London, 1978)

The Family Receipt Book; or, Universal Repository, 3rd edn (Oddy and Co., London, n.d.)

FARLEY, John, *The London Art of Cookery*, 2nd edn (J. Scatcherd, J. Whitaker, J. Fielding, London, 1784)

FÉRET, Edouard, *Bordeaux et ses Vins*, 13th edn (Féret et Fils, Bordeaux, 1982)

FLETCHER, Wyndham, *Port, an Introduction to its History and Delights* (Sotheby, Parke, Bernet, London, 1978)

FORRESTER, James Joseph, *Oliveira Prize Essay on Portugal* (S. Weale, London, 1853)

—— *A Word or Two on Port Wine, shewing how and why it is adulterated and affording some means of checking its adulterations* (J. Menzies, Edinburgh, 1844)

FRANCIS, A.D., *The Wine Trade* (Adam and Charles Black, London, 1972)

GALET, P., *Précis de l'Ampelographie Pratique*, 4th edn (Paul Déhan, Montpellier, 1976)

GENRET-PERROTTE, *Rapport sur la Culture de la Vigne et la Vinification dans la Côte d'Or* (Loireu-Feuchot, Dijon, 1854)

GEOFFROY, Etienne Louis, *Hygieine Sive Ars Sanitatem Conservandi* (Pierre-Guillaume Cavalier, Paris, 1771)

GEORGE, Rosemary, *The Wines of Chablis* (Sotheby Publications, London, 1984)

GINESTET, Bernard, *La Bouillie Bordelaise* (Flammarion, Paris, 1975)

GODINOT, Chanoine, *Maniere de Cultiver la Vigne et de Faire le Vin en Champagne* (Barthélémy Multeau, Reims, 1718)

GONZALEZ GORDON, Manuel M., *Sherry* (Cassell and Co. Ltd., London, 1972)

GRAND, Commandant G., *Histoire d'Arbois*, 4th edn (Editions Protet, Dole, 1974)

GRIVOT, Françoise, *Le Commerce des Vins de Bourgogne* (SABRI, Paris, 1964)

GUYOT, Dr Jules, *Sur la Viticulture du Centre-Nord de la France* (Imprimerie Impériale, Paris, 1866)

GWYNN, Stephen, *Burgundy* (Constable and Co. Ltd., London, 1934)

HALLGARTEN, S.F., *Rhineland Wineland*, 3rd edn (Elek Books, London, 1955)

_____ *Wine Scandal* (Weidenfeld and Nicolson, London, 1986)

HANSON, Anthony, *Burgundy* (Faber and Faber, London, 1982)

HARTMAN, George, *The Family Physitian* (Richard Wellington, London, 1696)

HEALEY, Maurice, *Stay Me With Flagons*, 2nd edn (Michael Joseph, London, 1950)

HEDGES BUTLER, Frank, *Wine and the Winelands of the World* (T. Fisher Unwin Ltd., London, 1926)

HENRIQUES, E. Frank, *The Signet Encyclopedia of Wine* (New American Library, New York, 1975)

JAGENDORF, M.A., *Folk Wines, Cordials and Brandies* (The Vanguard Press, New York, 1963)

JEFFS, Julian, *Sherry*, 2nd edn (Faber and Faber, London, 1970)

JOHNSON, Hugh, *The World Atlas of Wine*, 3rd edn (Mitchell Beazley, London, 1985)

JULLIEN, A., *Topographie de Tous les Vignobles Connus*, 2nd edn (Huzard et al., Paris, 1822)

KEHRIG, Henri, *Le Privilège des Vins à Bordeaux Jusqu'en 1789* (Masson, Paris, 1886)

KITCHINER, William, *The Art of Invigorating and Prolonging Life*, 6th edn (Geo. B. Whittaker, London, 1828)

KNOX, Oliver, *Croft, a Journey of Confidence* (Collins, London, 1978)

LAW, James, *Law's Grocer's Manual*, 2nd edn (Gilbert and Rivington Ltd., London, n.d.)

LEGLISE, Max, *Principes de Vinification* (C.I.B., Beaune, 1974)

LEGRAND, NAPOLEON E., *Champagne* (Malot-Braine, Reims, 1896)

LICHINE, Alexis, *Wines of France*, 3rd edn (Cassell and Co. Ltd., London, 1956)

LUCHET, Auguste, *La Côte d'Or à Vol d'Oiseau* (Michel Lévy Frères, Paris, 1858)

MACAULAY, Rose, *They Went to Portugal* (Jonathan Cape, London, 1946)

M'BRIDE, D., *General Instructions for the Choice of Wines and Spiritous Liquors* (Richardson, Debrett and Murray, London, 1793)

McNULTY, Henry, *Champagne* (Collins, London, 1987)

MANDEVILLE DE REGISMONT, Dr Léonce, *l'Algérie Viticole et la France*, 2nd edn (Les Frères Douladoure, Toulouse, 1929)

MARKHAM, Gervase, *The English Housewife* (London, 1675)

MARTIN, Germain, *Essai sur la Vente des Vins (Plus Particulièment des Vins de Bourgogne)* (Barbier-Marilier, Dijon, 1904)

MAUMÈNE, E.-J., *Traité théorique et pratique de travail des vins, leur fabrication, leurs maladies* (Fabrication des vins mousseux, Paris, 1873)

Maxims of Sir Morgan O'Doherty, Bart (William Blackwood and Sons, Edinburgh, 1849)

Le Médoc à Travers le Livre (Société de Bibliophiles de Guyenne, Bordeaux, 1978)

BIBLIOGRAPHY

MILLER, Philip, *The Gardener's Dictionary*, 2nd edn (C. Rivington, London, 1733)

MOREWOOD, Samuel, *A Philosophical and Statistical History of Inebriating Liquors*, 2nd edn (Wm. Curry Jun. and Wm. Carson, Dublin, 1838)

The Mystery of Vintners: or, a Brief Discourse concerning the various sicknesses of Wines, and their respective Remedies, at this day Commonly Used (W. Whitwood, London, 1692)

La Nouvelle Maison Rustique, 10th edn (Desaint, Paris, 1772)

ORDISH, George, *The Great Wine Blight* (J. M. Dent and Sons Ltd., London, 1972)

PARMENTIER, *Instruction sur les Sirops et les Conserves de Raisins, destinés a remplacer le Sucre dans les Principaux Usages de l'Economie Domestique* (Méquignon Ainé, Paris, 1809)

PEÑIN, José, *Manual de los Vinos de Rioja* (Penthalon, Madrid, n.d.)

PENNING-ROWSELL, Edmund, *The Wines of Bordeaux*, 2nd edn (The International Wine and Food Publishing Co., London, 1971)

PEPPERCORN, David, *Bordeaux* (Faber and Faber, London, 1982)

PITOIT, Sylvain et POUPON, PIERRE, *Atlas des Grands Vignobles de Bourgogne* (Jacques Legrand, Paris, 1985)

(PLAIGNE), *L'Art de Faire, d'Améliorer et de Conserver les Vins* (les Frères Reycends, Turin, 1783)

PLATTER, John, *John Platter's Book of South African Wines* (The Author, 1980)

POUPON, Pierre and FORGEOT, Pierre, *Les Vins de Bourgogne*, 10th edn (Presses Universitaires de France, Paris, 1985)

PRESTWICH (Society of Arts)

PUVIS M.-A., *De la Culture de la Vigne et de la Fabrication du Vin* (Librairie Agricole de Dusacq, Paris, 1848)

QUEYRAT, Enrique, *Los Buenos Vinos Argentinos*, 2nd edn (Hachette, Buenos Aires, 1974)

QUIMME, Peter, *The Signet Book of American Wine*, rev. edn (New American Library, New York, 1977)

RAY, Cyril, *Bollinger* (Peter Davies, London, 1971)

—— *Lafite*, rev. edn (Christie's Wine Publications, London, 1978)

REDDING, Cyrus, *A History and Description of Modern Wines* (Wittaker, Trencher and Arnot, London, 1833)

Regulations Governing the Descriptions of Special Types of Port Wine, 2nd edn (Instituto do Vinho Porto, Oporto, 1978)

Relacao dos Factos Practicados pela Commissao dos Commerciantes de Vinhos em Londres (Impressao Regia, Lisbon, 1813)

ROBERTSON, George, *Port* (Faber and Faber, London, 1978)

ROBINSON, Jancis, *The Great Wine Book* (Sidgwick and Jackson, London, 1982)

RODIER, Camille, *Le Vin de Bourgogne—la Côte d'Or* (L. Damidot, Dijon, 1920)

—— *Les Clos de Vougeot* (L. Venot, Dijon, 1949)

RODRIGUEZ, Miguel V., *La Perla del Viticultor y Liquorista* (Ramon Clemente Rubisco, Ciudad Real, 1885)

ROUGET, Charles, *Les Vignobles du Jura et de la Franche-Comté* (Auguste Côte, Lyon, 1897)

Rumasa XV Aniversario (Rumasa, Madrid, 1976)

RUNDELL, Mrs, *Domestic Cookery for the Use of Private Families* (Milner and Co., London, n.d.)

SAINTSBURY, George, *Notes on a Cellar Book* (Macmillan and Co. Ltd., London, 1920)

SHAND, P. Morton, *A Book of Other Wines — Than French* (Alfred A. Knopf, New York, 1929)

—— *A Book of French Wine*, 2nd edn (Jonathan Cape, London, 1960)

SHAW, T.G. *Wine, the Vine, and the Cellar*, 2nd edn (Longman, Green, Longman, Roberts and Green, London, 1864)

SIMON, André, *The Wine Trade of England Past and Present* (The Wine Trade Club, London, 1911)

—— *English Wines and Cordials* (Gramol Publications Ltd., London, 1946)

—— *The History of Champagne* (Ebury Press, London, 1962)

—— *Wine in Shakespeare's Days and Shakespeare's Plays* (Wine and Food Society, London, 1964)

SITTLER, Lucien, *La Viticulture et le Vin de Colmar à Travers les Siècles* (Editions Alsatia, Paris, 1956)

SMITH, G., *The Laboratory, or School of Arts*, 6th edn (C. Whittingham, London, 1799)

SPENCER, Edward, *The Flowing Bowl* (Grant Richards, London, 1903)

SPEECHLY, William, *A Treatise on the Culture of the Vine*, 3rd edn (Longman, Hurst, Rees, Orme and Brown, London, 1821)

SUTCLIFFE, Serena (ed.), *Great Vineyards and Winemakers* (Macdonald, London, 1981)

—— *The Wines of Burgundy* (Mitchell Beazley, London, 1986)

SWANSON, George, *Tastes in London History by a City Ale Conner* (London, 1953)

THEURIET, Charles, *Histoire de Nuits Sous Beaune* (Dijon, 1886)

THUDICHUM, Dr J.L.W., *A Treatise on Wines*, 2nd edn (George Bell and Sons, London, 1896)

—— and DUPRÉ, Dr A. *A Treatise on the Origin, Nature and Varieties of Wine, being a complete manual of Viticulture and Oenology* (Macmillan, London and New York, 1872)

TOVEY, Charles, *Wine and Wine Countries* (Whitaker and Co., London, 1877)

TOWER, Charles, *The Moselle* (Constable and Co. Ltd., London, 1913)

Valuable Secrets in Arts and Trades (J. Barker, London, n.d.)

VASSEROT FUENTES, Adolfo, *Málaga Wine* (Grupo de Ordenación Comercial Exterior, Málaga, 1978)

VERGNETTE-LAMOTTE, M. de, *Mémoires sur la Viticulture et L'Oenologie de la Côte D'Or* (Douillier, Dijon, 1846)

—— *Le Vin*, 2nd edn (Librairie Agricole de la Maison Rustique, Paris, 1868)

VIZETELLY, Henry, *Facts about Port and Madeira, with notices of the wines vintaged around Lisbon and the wines of Tenerife* (Ward, Lock, London, 1880)

—— *A History of Champagne with notes on the other sparkling wines of France* (Vizetelly & Co., London, 1882)

WALKER, James, *Hints to Consumers of Wine on the Abuses which Enhance the Price of that Article: Their Nature and Remedy* (Peter Hill, Edinburgh, 1802)

WARNER ALLEN, H., *The Wines of France* (T. Fisher Unwin Ltd., 1928)
—— *A History of Wine* (Faber and Faber, London, 1961)
WATERS, Ivor, *The Wine Trade of the Port of Chepstow* (The Chepstow Society, Chepstow, n.d.)
Wine and Spirit Adulterators Unmasked by One of the Old School, 3rd edn (J. Robins and Co., London, 1829)
WOLFF, Christian, *Riquewihr, Son Vignoble et ses Vins à Travers les Ages* (S.A.E.P., Ingersheim, 1967)
WOLLEY, Hannah, *The Queen-like Closet: A Rich Cabinet, stored with all manner of rare receipts* (1670)

Index